Great Scouts!
CyberGuides for Subject Searching on the Web

Great Scouts!
CyberGuides for Subject Searching on the Web

Nora Paul
and
Margot Williams

Paula J. Hane, Editor

CyberAge Books

Medford, New Jersey

Great Scouts!
CyberGuides for Subject Searching on the Web

Library of Congress Cataloging-in-Publication Data
Paul, Nora.
    Great scouts! cyberguides for subject searching on the Web / by Nora Paul & Margot Williams : edited by Paula J. Hane.
        p. cm.
    ISBN 0-910965-27-7 (pbk.)
    1. Internet searching.   I. Williams, Margot. II. Hane, Paula J. III. Title.
ZA4201.P38   1999
025.04--dc21   99-18356
                                                                                                                CIP

Printed and bound in the United States of America.

Publisher: Thomas H. Hogan, Sr.
Editor in Chief: John B. Bryans
Managing Editor: Janet Spavlik
Production Manager: M. Heide Dengler
Cover Design: Bette Tumasz
Book Design: Trejo Production, Princeton, NJ
Indexer: Sharon Hughes

Contents

Foreword

Will Rogers, this nation's first great stand-up comic, used to observe that he only knew what he read in the newspapers. Reality, when viewed by a logical mind, is the greatest stand-up comedy routine, even in Will's era. One often encounters near misses between logic and illogic in life. Recently *The New York Times* carried an article announcing a scientific study that had found evidence that removing healthy breasts along with cancerous ones reduced the risk of breast cancer by 90 percent. Logically, one might have surmised that amputation of an organ would block disease in it, but what seems illogical is how 10 percent of the subjects under study managed to get breast cancer without having breasts.

Of course, we get *The New York Times* from its Web site (www.nytimes. com) for logical reasons—one, it's free (which makes the ad for home delivery of print in the premier spot on their home page another amusing illogicality) and two, it's better. Better? Sure. You can read the paper hours and hours before home delivery, particularly if you live outside the Eastern Time zone, since the Web version goes online promptly at midnight ET. More important, the articles often contain links to the material the reporter used to produce the piece. Unfortunately, that breast cancer article didn't have the lucky links you can find so often in their Technology section. However, it did tell us who wrote the study, the official name for the procedure (bilateral pro- phylactic mastectomy), and the title of the medical journal publishing the piece. The lengthy article by *The Times* covered the details of the study as well as a variety of opinions as to its importance from experts across the country. It also covered warnings from a more negative expert against applying the study's apparent suggestions.

In the past—the ancient era of print-only or even the era of Early Online begun in the late 1960s—the labor, time, and expense involved in finding more information would have led almost everyone except experts in the field to stop right there. But now that we live in a Web world, it only took me three or four minutes to find and print out a press release from the medical research establishment that produced the study. The press release encom- passed a lengthy interview with the study's principal investigator. The inter- view included questions and answers that both recommended and warned about using the treatment. It also explained satisfactorily the apparent illogic of breast cancer in the breastless. In three or four more minutes, I jumped over to the Web site for the medical journal—trusting soul, aren't I?—where I found the article listed and available for a mere $10 ("Insert Visa numbers here"). The medical journal Web site did give away an editorial (subtitle, "The Price of Fear") that appeared in the same issue and, while praising the research, warned strongly against the procedure.

Now what on earth does this depressing topic have to do with this hand- some book? The world has changed forever. What I did in just eight minutes on the Web for this topic, an average educated layperson can do on any topic. The topic I just discussed could save a life, but the research techniques I used could just as easily have saved a fortune, saved a vacation, or saved a trip to the store. The Web awaits us all for whatever purposes we have in mind.

But the very prolific nature of the Web threatens users. With so much out there, how can one find what one needs quickly, effectively, and in a timely manner? How can one work Web resources into one's day, without risking the Web gobbling up hours out of the week? How can one develop the skills and resources to tame the Web into a reliable, informed, and obe- dient assistant?

You've already made the right move—you're reading this book. Among librarians and information professionals, there's a saying, "The only bad question is an unasked question and the only client we can't help is the one who doesn't ask for help." Odd to think of Marian/Marion the Librarian, the ones in sensible shoes, as hotshots in the New Information World Order, but it's true. Look at it this way. These guys could find information before there was any online. Then they made online pay when it cost an arm and a leg. The Web is their happy hunting ground.

Among librarians, newspaper librarians have a special status. They work the shortest deadlines (instant turnaround), over the largest expanse of subjects ("all the news that's fit to print"), and see their research published for all the world to see. They have to get it fast and get it right. Among newspaper librarians, Nora Paul of the Poynter Institute of Media Studies and Margot Williams of *The Washington Post* are the elite's elite. They serve as models for other newspaper librarians. The title of this book—*Great Scouts!*—is probably biographical.

Let me give you a tip as you go through this book. The book is set up to give you a lot of answers to questions you are likely to ask, but it can teach you a lot more. Watch how the authors think, how they question sources, how they approach them. In this era of information affluence, questions and the ability to ask the right ones have become almost more important than answers. These authors have spent their careers as generalists answering questions from specialists. Generalists telling specialists what they need to know—that's not something you see every day. Usually it works the other way around. They serve reporters and editors, a notoriously skeptical bunch. They have constructed styles and techniques that both find sources for a wide array of subjects and winnow out the best from the good and the right from the wrong.

When I looked at the subject areas covered in this book, it reminded me of something that I couldn't quite recall. Then I realized it covered all the sorts of topics you can find in a week's worth of a good national newspaper—the politics, crime, business news, international affairs, sports, entertainment that fill each daily, as well as the special coverage of science, religion, travel, and other mainstream topics of interest to a broad readership that appear weekly.

After I finish writing this foreword, I think I'll go to the book's Web site and use the help instructions on my browser. With a little talent and a little time, I should be able to create my own personal portal filled with links to all the lovely, content-jammed, reliable sites that intersect my interests with the distilled wisdom in this book. Why not? With the Great Scouts leading my fact-finding safari through the shortcuts and around the poisoned waterholes, I should have saved enough time. With the Great Scouts guiding us, we should reach the lead camp in time for a quick gin and tonic and a couple of hunting stories around the old campfire.

—Barbara Quint
Santa Monica, California

Barbara Quint is Editor in Chief of Searcher: The Magazine for Database Professionals *and online columnist for* Information Today, *both published by Information Today, Inc. With Paula J. Hane she writes the NewsBreak stories on the Information Today Web site (www.infotoday.com). She is a longtime online searcher and respected industry observer.*

Acknowledgments

Between us we have over forty years of online research experience (we started when we were very, very, very young!). In the past few years we've seen more and more newbies come out with THE guide to research online, and we were getting steamed. "What do they know, we've been doing this for decades!" Well, we finally goaded ourselves to put up or shut up—and we decided to do this book. Therefore, we'd like to acknowledge each other, for being so full of ourselves and our knowledge that we finally got riled up enough to collaborate. It's been fun.

We'd also like to acknowledge the untold thousands of journalists on whose research needs we honed our online skills, and we'd like to acknowledge the hundreds of unsung news research colleagues from whom we have learned so much.

I (Margot) would like to thank my sister Ann Wyrick for her support and Barbara Saffir and Arthur Smith for their help.

Most of all, I (Nora) would like to acknowledge my two unbeatable sons, Nathan and Spencer Paul, who encouraged me to stick with it, even if it meant pizza for the third night in a row. Thank you, dear boys.

About the GREAT SCOUTS! Web Page

At the Information Today Web site, you will find the *GREAT SCOUTS! Web Page*, featuring links to scout sites mentioned in this book. The authors will periodically update the page, removing dead links and adding additional sites that may be useful to readers.

The *GREAT SCOUTS! Web Page* is being made available as a bonus to readers of *GREAT SCOUTS! CyberGuides for Subject Searching on the Web*. To access the page, an Internet connection and Web browser are required. Go to:

www.infotoday.com/greatscouts!

DISCLAIMER: Neither publisher nor authors make any claim as to the results that may be obtained through the use of the *GREAT SCOUTS! Web Page* or of any of the Internet resources it references or links to. Neither publisher nor authors will be held liable for any results, or lack thereof, obtained by the use of this page or any of its links, for any third-party charges, or for any hardware, software, or other problems that may occur as a result of using it. *The GREAT SCOUTS! Web Page* is subject to change or discontinuation without notice at the discretion of the publisher and authors.

1

Beyond Search Engines: Subject-Specific Guides to the Internet

So, you've gotten your computer all set up. You've signed up with an Internet access service. Now you are happily out there in cyberspace, finding all that great information that the Information Age promises to deliver to your screen. Right?

OK, well, maybe you're not so happy. In fact, if you're like the majority of Web users, you've noticed that finding information on the World Wide Web can lead to frustration at not locating good resources or frustration at getting just too much stuff.

We get frustrated and we're "experts" in research online. We have been using computers and remote access to information since 1978. For the first fifteen years, however, we used the very well-organized databases of commercial archiving services like Dialog and Lexis-Nexis. In these information spheres it was easy to figure out where to go. There were directories of the databases, scope notes that told what was in each database, listings of the keywords and fields of information that could be searched when looking for an article. But with the advent of the wild, wooly information world of the World Wide Web, that sense of organized, knowable information resources rapidly disappeared.

The World Wide Web has been likened to the world's largest library but all the books are dumped in the middle of the floor and there is no card catalog to help you locate anything. As the Web grew and multiplied (there are current estimates that the Web contains 800 million pages of information), the ability to know where to go became harder and harder to maintain. Who was going to catalog the Web?

Along came Jerry Yang and David Filo, Ph.D. candidates in electrical engineering at Stanford. These early heroes of the World Wide Web, and now mega-success stories, created the first indexing attempt. In 1994, as the access to documents sitting on computers around the world in this new "HyperText Mark-up Language" (HTML) started to become available, Yang and Filo started keeping a list of the addresses of these new Web sites. Their list, first called "Jerry's Guide to the World Wide Web," became Yahoo!—the first categorized listing of Web sites.

Five years later, Yahoo! is still the number one source people go to for guidance about where to go on the Web for sites on particular topics. The organization scheme, with logical categories and sub-categories, was familiar and comfortable. The links you were sent to by the directory were reliable and useful. Yahoo! filled the need, the hunger for guidance on the Web to good, specific Web sites. We love Yahoo!, too. It is often the first place we go when we're looking for a specific site or for a list of some good resources in a particular category.

The trouble, though, with Yahoo! is that it is impossible for it to be doing a good categorization of every valuable resource on every topic that it is trying to cover. It doesn't particularly rate or rank the resources available there—all listings are equal in Yahoo's eyes. Also, its original mission, to be a selective directory of good resources, is becoming somewhat diluted in its very success as a commercial service—often sites of iffy quality will get into the Yahoo! directory in a prominent position on the list because they have paid an advertising/placement fee. But overall, of the directory listings of the Web created through human indexing of sites, Yahoo! continues to be the best.

However, as the scope and range and volume of material on every imaginable subject grows and grows on the Web, it is simply impossible for any one guide to look at carefully, organize logically, and make accessible the best resources on all these topics. That's why we wrote this book.

The need and desire for subject-based directories of Web resources has been recognized and met by thousands of entrepreneurial, knowledgeable, and kind-hearted people. Often taking the Yahoo! model of categories and sub-categories, they are scouring the Web, or taking submitted sites and putting them into subject-focused directories. We call these sites subject-specific search sites and the people who compile them are our *Great Scouts!*

Studies show that the major activity consumers spend their time on when using the World Wide Web is doing research (Price Waterhouse Consumer Technology Survey). We decided that the researchers of the Web needed a guide to those resources that could help them find subject-specific resources. This would be a book that went beyond the overall "research on the Internet" guides, a source that took them beyond Yahoo!, beyond the big search engines, such as Infoseek, AltaVista, and HotBot. We wanted to help people locate, understand, and evaluate these Great Scout sites. So we started to scour the Web for these subject-specific directories. This book details for you what we found.

Just as with the best of the Scout sites, we had certain criteria we looked at when deciding whether or not to include a site. For some of the subjects we cover in the book, there were a number of great Scout sites. We selected two for complete profiles and mentioned some of the others. For other categories, we located the best possible site, but they often didn't meet every criterion. In those cases we selected and profiled the ones that hit the most criteria categories and pointed out the areas where these Great Scout guides were lacking.

The criteria we used included:

Selection of Resources: The way sites to be linked to in the guide were evaluated. The best guides were selective, valuing quality of the links over quantity. The range went from:

- Researched links: People at the scout site were responsible for locating and evaluating Web sites on the topic.
- Combination of researched and submitted links: Some of the links on the scout site were researched, some were submitted by others but were checked and evaluated by people at the scout site.
- Self-submitted but evaluated links: All the links on the site were submitted by others, but link editors at the scout site evaluated them for relevancy and appropriate categorization.
- Totally self-submitted: Links were submitted and categories selected by those who submitted the sites, and automatically entered into the scout site directory.

We gave preference to those in the first two categories, but for some subjects we used scout sites that relied on self-submitted sites but provided some evaluation. Scout sites that relied totally on self-submitted links were not selected because the point of a Great Scout site is the evaluation and selection it provides. Without that you have essentially a catch-all service, no more helpful to locating good subject sites than a large search engine.

Stability of the Site: Just as Yahoo! started as the personal project of a couple of college students, many subject-specific sites began as someone's personal project. Many of these subject links listings were pet projects that eventually were dropped or neglected. When looking at and evaluating the subject scout sites to include in this book, we looked at who was sponsoring the site and their level of commitment to keeping the site going. Many of the scout sites in this book are backed by advertising or a Web design service. Others are part of a larger company. Some are sponsored and supported by a university or research center. Only those that indicate they are in this effort for the long run were selected for the book.

Currency of the Site: An immediate knock-out for a site was an indication that the page or listing of links had not been updated in the past three months. Only sites that are constantly refreshed, checked, and added to were selected.

Usability of the Site: When evaluating the scout sites to include, we looked at the usability of the site. Was it easy to figure out what the scout site was trying to accomplish? Could you find out how to use the site and the different functions easily? Was the organization of the site logical and easy to use? What immediately knocked a site out of the running for Great Scout listing were annoying graphics, intrusive sound files that start up when you get to the page (the ragtime piano playing at a forensic site, for example), or broken links within the guide Web site itself.

Now, a word about frames. Some of the scout sites we include did use frames when linking to the sites in the directory. We have a bias against scout sites that pull the sites they link to into the guide's frame. It makes sense, of course, for the scout site creator to keep users of the site in the site rather than being linked out. However, for the users of the directory, putting the site into the scout site's frame makes bookmarking good sites cumbersome and makes it difficult to tell where exactly you are and what you are looking at. So, while some of the scout sites we link to are using frames, we included them somewhat reluctantly.

Searchability of the Listings: We looked carefully at how users of the scout site could locate links in the directory. Many sites include both a browse function, getting a list of links alphabetically or by a category and sub-category, and a search function where the user can type in a word and locate any links that have that word in the title, address, or description of the site. We preferred those scout sites that allow both browse and targeted search of the links. However, some of the sites we selected had such good organization of the subject categories and logical organization of the links that those scout sites were selected even without the search function.

Metainformation: Information about the scout site itself was an important part of our selection. Many sites with good links listings had no information about why, how, when, and where they found the links they used. It is an important part of any selection of Web sites to evaluate the creators of the site. Metainformation about the Web site itself is an essential part of that evaluation. Scout sites that did not give any information and had no contact information about the person or organization that created the site are not included in this book. When the metainformation was not complete, we located the guide creator to interview him or her about various aspects of the guide. If we could not locate the creator of the guide, we did not include the site.

Listing Charge: The only scout sites we selected for this book were those that list links for free. Some subject-based link directories charge a fee to Web sites that want to be listed. We did not use those in this book.

Scout Site Usage Charge: All the scout sites in this book allow free use of the links directories available on the site. While some of the scout sites listed in this book might have additional services or functions that require a password/registration or usage fee, only those that allow free access to the links area of the site were selected.

Link Checking: Everyone knows the virtual impossibility of keeping lists of links totally up to date. Web site addresses change, Web sites disappear or move to different servers. However, one of the functions of a Great Scout site is keeping as current as possible. We checked each of the scout sites we were evaluating to see if it had a number of missing or broken links. If more than half of the randomly checked links were missing, we would not include that scout site. In our descriptions of the scout sites selected, we profile how and how often the links are checked. Link-checking software is available now, and used by most of the selected scout sites, which ensures a higher degree of valid links.

Link Description: There are literally dozens of scout sites and link listings on every subject you can imagine. What distinguishes a Great Scout site from a list of links is the annotation and description given of the sites to which they link. The best of the Great Scout sites evaluate and rate the sites. The scout sites we selected at least provide some description of what the site contains or where it comes from. Only those scout sites that at least edit the self-description of self-submitted sites were used in this book. Many scout sites that are listings of self-submitted sites have self-submitted site descriptions that are replete with misspellings and other editing errors. These sites are not used in this book.

Once we selected the Great Scout sites we wanted to profile for each subject, we went through and described them. Here's what the Great Scout profiles contain (Note: not all items appear in every site profile, and some profiles include additional information):

Site name, logo, and Web address: The official name of the Web site containing the subject-specific directory, its logo (if permission was granted to use it), and the Web address where it can be found.

Contact: The "off-line" contact information as well as an e-mail address to contact for information about the site.

Why we picked this site: A description of why this particular scout site deserved to be included as a Great Scout.

Created: Date the directory began; often this date pre-dates the World Wide Web because the directory creator had a bulletin board service or a Gopher document.

How many sites: This number indicates the number of sites to which this subject guide links. Often, this number was calculated from the total number currently in the directory and an estimate of the number of new links added each month.

Audience: The particular audience or user that the creator of the scout site has in mind when compiling the links. Most are for general interest users of the Web, but some have a specific audience in mind.

How sites are selected: Here is where we detail the methods by which sites the guide links to are selected, whether it is self-submissions or scout site editor selections. Notes about the scout site's criteria for selection are included.

How it's supported: Who sponsors the scout site, how it is funded, and groups it is affiliated with are noted in this area. This is often an indication of site stability and long-range commitment to the directory.

Topics covered: Although each of these scout sites is focused on a particular subject, the way it breaks that subject into smaller categories is helpful. In this portion of the profile we describe the topic areas the guide uses.

Searching: Details about how you can locate links listed in the directory are given here. Hints about searching, cautions about use of the search functions, and tips for how best to locate resources are given.

What you get: Information about the link description given when you've located one of the resources. Sometimes it is very elaborate information with instructive annotations and even ratings of the site, other times there appears simply the Web address. For the most part, we selected the scout sites that included the most information about the sites to which they were linking.

Design: A few details about the look and feel of the Web site. Our preference was for scout sites with clean and simple designs that made the content the star, not the fancy graphics that often slow down access to the site.

Other features: Other notable areas of the scout site, beyond the links directory, are given, especially if they aid the user in search of specific topic information.

We hope *Great Scouts!* gets you going on the trail of great information on whatever topic you are interested in pursuing. Remember that the thrill is in the hunt and, with these helpful guides along with you, you're sure to bag the information you need.

2

Omni Sites as Finding Tools

In our quest for the best topical scout sites, we tapped a multitude of major directories and general guides. These come in several flavors and it's best to be conscious of their differences. The omni sites try to do everything for everybody. Their popularity and longevity are proof of their success. The size and breadth of these omni sites, however, prevent them from keeping any subject—or your particular target subject—as a top priority in sharp focus. Use the omni sites as prospecting tools for locating the specific information lode that lies just below the general sources on the surface.

Yahoo! and Its Imitators

The search for subject-specific guides began with the mother of all Web directories—Yahoo! In the competition between machine-made indexes like AltaVista, HotBot, and Infoseek, and the human-made directories described below, Yahoo!'s useful topical arrangement, easy search function, and simple design sent it spiraling up to the top of the Web early in the Internet gold rush.

For users overwhelmed by the mind-boggling number of "hits" produced by simple searches in the 100-million-page indexes of the biggest search engines, Yahoo!'s helping human hand is blessed relief. It's not surprising that this innovative guide to the Web became the top site on the Web itself. Now Yahoo!'s imitators are legion, with even the busiest search engines rushing to add subject directories, topical "channels," and rated site reviews. They're all covering the same bases.

We are Yahoo!'s biggest fans and use it as familiarly as a TV remote control. When we remember the name, but not the address, or when we're looking for a broad topic or its major breakdowns, Yahoo!'s search or browsing arrangement can usually take us there, or at least somewhere nearby.

But sometimes Yahoo! drops us off in a crush of competing sites, or too far from the specific topic on our map. With more than a million sites divided into more than 25,000 categories, Yahoo! has grown so big that its sheer size is diluting its efficacy. The numbers of sites described under the "Business and Economy—Companies" category and the lengthening lists of scantily described sites within many categories are making our favorite Yahoo! clumsy.

Yahoo! is fat and we love it and use it. But when we need to get narrow, we aim for the specific. Here's how you can use Yahoo! and the other omni sites to help uncover the best topical guides and starting points for the topics of your choice.

In Yahoo!, start at the top level of a category—like Arts & Humanities— and look for the sub-categories "Indices" or "Directories." You may find the guides to the resources of the subject in either place. A Yahoo! review or spectacle icon frequently highlights specific sites. You still have to check out each one yourself, using the criteria we've suggested in Chapter 1.

If Yahoo! doesn't deliver a satisfactory guide for a topic, there are other omni guides you can turn to, or that you may prefer as starting points.

Competitors to Yahoo! are Snap (www.snap.com) and the directory features at Excite (www.excite.com), Infoseek (www.go.com), Lycos (www.lycos.com), and other search engines. All of these services are trying to become portals—a flashy combination of search engine, directory, news service, shopping center, chat room, mailbox, stock guide, and weatherman that does its best to keep you in one place rather than out on the Web.

Selected and Reviewed by Great Scouts

Another group of human-made general directories are more selective and evaluative than Yahoo!. Britannica (www.britannica.com) is a newcomer from the folks at the revered *Encyclopaedia Britannica*. The directory is topically arranged, like Yahoo!, and you can search it. What you get are evaluative reviews written by *Britannica* editors and rated to up to five stars. Britannica's contents are small; all sites are recommended in some way, so there are no losers here.

Magellan (www.mckinley.com/magellan) has been around for a while and is now a subsidiary of Excite. Magellan's 60,000 reviewed sites can be searched or browsed by category. A special feature of Magellan is that you may search for sites limited to those without mature content: These sites have a green light.

The selective directories try to cover every subject under the sun and thus do not go into much depth on any single topic.

A truly outstanding site is the Scout Report Signpost (www.signpost.org), from the editorial staff of the Internet Scout project at the University of Wisconsin-Madison and funded by the National Science Foundation. The Scout Report newsletters bring bi-weekly reviews of the newest and best sites discovered by Susan Calcari and the other Scouts. Signpost is a searchable directory of more than 5,000 Scout Report summaries from the newsletter, each one containing a brief review and link to the recommended sites. There is also a searchable, browsable directory of more than 2500 detailed reviews, organized by Library of Congress subject headings.

Guides to the Guides

Yet another type of helper is the "guide to the guides"—collections of annotated lists created by experts and academics. At the Argus Clearinghouse (www.clearinghouse.net), a highly selective collection of topical guides is offered for searching and for browsing. Only 5 to 10 percent of submissions are selected by the staff of librarians at the Clearinghouse, founded in 1993. The selected guides are rated with one to five checkmarks by criteria including resource description, quality evaluation, design, arrangement, and metainformation (information provided about the guide itself, like its purpose, standards for inclusion, etc.).

Each reviewed and rated guide included is a focused Web bibliography on a specific topic, ranging from the Mystical Side of the Web to Computational Fluid Dynamics. If a guide isn't updated in over a year, it will be removed.

The oldest catalog of the Web was created by the Web's founder, Tim Berners-Lee in 1993. The WWW Virtual Library is a distributed responsibility cataloging project with over 200 volunteer experts who maintain their specific sections under broad topical categories: society, science, regional studies, recreation, business and economics, law, information management, humanities, engineering, education, communications and media, agriculture, international affairs, and computer science.

The 275+ sections reside on various servers around the globe. Individual sections vary in quality and size. At the WWW Virtual Library home page (www.vlib.org), you can view the listing alphabetically, browse it by hierarchical category, or do a keyword search for the name of a list, its link, and the e-mail address of the maintainer, called the vlibrarian.

In the following pages, you will see more than a few of the WWW Virtual Library's guides as top picks or recommended sites. The spirit that keeps them going is the original Netizen ideal of distributed information, freely available to all.

Scholars' Choices

Many universities and colleges have developed guides to the Web for their students and opened them to the whole Web community. Be aware that often there are links to resources that are only available to students of the institution.

One of the best of the scholarly collections of Web resources is InfoMine at the University of California at Riverside (lib-www.ucr.edu) with more than 15,000 sites included in its catalog. Another great site is The Voice of the Shuttle (humanitas.ucsb.edu), a scholarly selective directory of sites relating to humanities research, including anthropology, area studies, cyberculture, literature, minority studies, philosophy, women's studies, and more. Each subject has a highlights section that offers new users a quick look at the best sites.

BUBL (originally the Bulletin Board for Libraries when it started up in the pre-Web days of 1990) is a United Kingdom government-funded information service that includes BUBL LINK (Libraries of Networked Knowledge). BUBL LINK (bubl.ac.uk/link) is a catalog of selected and recommended Internet resources covering academic subject areas from "Academic Libraries" to "Zoroastrianism." For each of 1200 subject areas, there are BUBL descriptions of at least five and no more than fifteen relevant resources. You may search or browse the catalog for items that include descriptions, locations, and live links that are checked monthly.

People's Choices

At About.com (www.about.com), formerly The Mining Co., "real people" experts and enthusiasts are your guides to more than 500 non-academic topics, from ballet to stock car racing and personal finance. It's a compilation of independently created guides that follow a basic template, with descriptions of each topic on the Web, links to resources, discussion groups, news, and personal help from the guide. The individual contributions vary in quality and comprehensiveness, so choose carefully from this extensive site. Our major complaint is that the frames keep you within the About.com window and you don't really know where you are unless you open the link in a separate browser window.

There are several other sites that compete with About.com's community-oriented approach to building a Web guide with volunteer guides as scouts. They include Suite101.com (www.suite101.com), a member-based community that also recruits "contributing editors" to create Web guides in their areas of expertise. These sites have frequent changes in voluntary contributors, so watch for varying quality and currency of information.

For something completely different, try WebRings, a concept that encourages like-minded Web sites and their owners to join together in rings with links from one to the next. WebRings are particularly useful for finding alternative or offbeat topics that won't turn up in commercial or scholarly directories, as well as Web communities that have developed just under the radar of the mainstream guides. The RingWorld Directory (www.webring.org) is the place to go to browse or search the listings of 40,000 WebRings, covering topics ranging from anime to home birth to Seinfeld.

Another collection of the best subject sites (ranked according to the votes of the visitors to the site) is TopTenLinks (www.toptenlinks.com). Site reviewers pick the top ten sites in each topic for content, speed, style, navigation, design, and permanency, and visitors get to vote. This is an interesting idea, but the site needs more traffic for the voting to be meaningful. You may pick up some sites on popular topics and lifestyles here that you won't find in the academic directories, however.

Keeping Up

Where do you go to find the latest and greatest Web sites in your area of interest? Here are some tips that we use:

- Visit the "What's New" sections of your favorite subject directories regularly. The experts who tend to these sites pick up the newest attractions quickly.
- Subscribe to discussion groups (or listservs) in your subject area. The members of the group will know about the latest sites and offer them in e-mail. To find a discussion group and instructions on how to join, go to the Liszt Web site (www.liszt.com).
- Subscribe to the Scout Report or one of its three subject-oriented announcement services for recommended sites in science and engineering, business and economics, and social sciences (www.scout.cs. wisc.edu/scout/report).
- Keep up with your reading in newspaper technology sections, computer magazines, and journals in your subject area.
- Keep in touch with "wired" friends and colleagues and talk to your librarian.

Part I

Life
&
Times

3

Education
on the Web

From readin' and 'riting and 'rithmatic, the old schoolhouse has gone to modem and monitor and click, click, click. Schools are getting wired. President Clinton's Educational Technology Initiative vows to bring technology to the classroom and make students ready for the 21st Century (www. ed.gov/Technology/). So far, so good. By February 1997, a year after the Telecommunications Act was signed, 65 percent of America's schools were connected to the Internet. The grants and funding available to schools wanting to improve their computer resources grow. Microsoft (no fools in the marketing department) is creating a new client base early by funding major purchases of computers by schools. The E-Rate, the educational rate for telecommunications, part of the Telecommunications Act of 1996, has helped with funding of access (for more information see the E-Rate Hotline: www.eratehotline.org/.

From pre-school through college, learning how to use the Web is becoming as basic as ABC. Any self-respecting school has a Web site, many supported by the Microsoft-funded Global SchoolNet Foundation (www. gsn.org). For a list of schools on the Web see the Hotlist of K–12 Schools on the Web at www.gsn.org/hotlist/ or Web66, with many international schools, at web66.umn.edu/schools.html.

More and more students have their own home pages (see Student Homepages at www.westegg.com/students/ for university and college students' home pages). Course syllabi and communications with the professor are happening online in higher education (see the World Lecture Hall at www.utexas.edu/world/lecture/). Kids in primary school can get help with their homework through the Web (check out Homework Central at www.homeworkheaven.com/). You don't even have to go to school to be in school anymore—school comes to you. Distance learning, Web-courses, and online learning is a growth industry. (See TeleCampus at database.telecampus.com/home/)

Educational resources on the Internet help students through the information and materials available for research. It even helps the, shall we say, lazy student with sites like Research Papers Online (www.ezwrite.com/) and Essayworld.com, which offer thousands of free or cheap research papers.

Educational resources on the Internet help teachers through the same information and materials in preparing courses. It even helps the, shall we say, uninspired teacher with sites like Homework Central's Teacher Resources, which has hundreds of lesson plans by grade and subject (www.homeworkcentral.com/indexhc.html).

Educational resources help students find the college they want to go to, help parents select the neighborhood schools that are doing the best job, and help educators get grants and funding. Let's give an apple to these scout sites for school and educational resources.

Great Scout Sites for Education

Education World
www.education-world.com/
Contact: jkoerber@education-world.com for content questions, kmickey@education-world.com for PR questions.

Why we picked this site: Education World's motto, "Where Educators Go to Learn," is most appropriate. Originally designed to be a directory of education-related Web sites, they have expanded their mission with lots of original content, such as articles, project ideas, and lesson plans, with the addition of editor-in-chief Gary Hopkins, who had previously been at the *Weekly Reader*. As Jon Koerber, director of development, said, "They come for the fish (the directory), but they stay for the service (all the great readings and material available)."

"We see ourselves as the *TV Guide* of the Internet for educators-not only do we show you where to go, but we have some articles thrown in." Looking through their massive site, it is clear their goal, "to create a home for educators on the Internet," has been smartly met.

Created: Spring 1996.

How many sites: 110,000 sites organized into 6,500 categories.

Audience: Originally, Education World's target audience was teachers, administrators, families, and students. As resources for families and students grew, it was clear that teachers still need a resource just for them. Education World's focus now is on K–12 school teachers.

How sites are selected: Sites are found by a combination of submissions by teachers and others who have created educational resources and of the culling through the Internet by Education World researchers. Submitted sites are checked by researchers who ensure they are valid, relevant, and that the description and keywords/categories used are appropriate. There are major monthly updates to the database supplemented with weekly updates of submissions from users. The database recently went through a complete check to see if links still linked and sites were still what they said they were. "You know how those big search engines give you bad hits all the time; the Education World database is now at least 90 percent clean," said Koerber. With the addition of software that automatically scans the database for bad links, that number should stay as high or increase.

How it's supported: Education World is seen as a marketing and branding tool for anyone interested in getting into or meeting with educators. Funding comes from the main site sponsors, American Fidelity Insurance company (they provide financial products for educators) and Cisco Systems (an education technology company). Apple, IBM, Microsoft, Gateway, Disney Online, and others have been sponsors and financial supporters.

Searching: Two levels of searching and a simple category browse provide access to the vast resources in the Education World database. The "simple search" box, found prominently at the top of every page, searches for words in the title, or the short description. Entering more than one word in the simple search box presumes an "or" relationship (put in mathematics algebra and you'll get sites with either of those words in the title, URL, or description).

Click on "Narrow Your Search" and you'll get the "Advanced Search" template. Here you can type in the search words and define such things as where you want the terms to be searched (title, description, URL), select a grade level, age of the link (when it was put into the database), narrow it to certain resources (articles, sites, schools, images), and indicate if you want to get only Reviewed Sites, or any sites. There is a caution, though, when you go from Simple to Advanced Search. Typing multiple words in the Advanced Search box defaults not to an "or" search, as with the Simple Search, but to an "and" search. Do the search on *mathematics algebra* in Advanced Search and you'll only get two hits (as opposed to the 620 or so hits from the Simple Search). So, just be sure of what you are searching for.

The subject category browse technique follows the simple, logical, and comfortable Yahoo!-style directory. The 6,500 categories under which sites are grouped fall into broad categories, such as Arts & Humanities, Math, Science, Regional Resources, Special Education, Distance Education, Physical Education. Click on one of the categories and get the sub-headings for the category. Click on one of those to get the listing of links.

What you get: Ten hits per page are retrieved (unless you've set the page for a different number on the Advanced Search page). Hits are displayed in alphabetical order and include the link to the site and, for most of the hits, a brief description of the Web site.

Design: For a site so rich and filled with content, the design is surprisingly clean and accessible.

Other features: Key to the added value of this site are the articles and features that have been written and are exclusively available from Education World. Found on the drop-down menu, there are mailing lists, education employment listings, school listings, site reviews, and event calendars.

Education Index
www.educationindex.com/
Contact: 10200 Alliance Road, Suite 100
Cincinnati, OH 45242
webmaster@educationindex.com

Why we picked this site: Where Education World's focus was on education resources, Education Index's focus is on information to help educate. As they state it, "Our primary goal in publishing the Education Index is to provide learners and educators with access to the best educational Web sites in a variety of subjects and lifestages. Whether you're researching astronomy or political science, theology or business, parenting or health, we want to provide you with quality resources, quickly." Their careful selection and annotation of the sites make up in quality what the resource might lack in quantity.

Created: September 1996 as a service of College View, a software company based in Cincinnati, Ohio.

How many sites: More than 3,000 sites in sixty-six categories.

Audience: Students and teachers.

How sites are selected: Sites can be suggested by users, but the actual sites that get into the directory are reviewed and annotated by the Education Index staff.

How it's supported: CollegeView, publisher of college, scholarship, and career software for professional and consumer use, is the sponsor of this site.

Searching: This is a browse-only site, as there is no search engine on the site. The listings are broken into two main categories, Subject or Lifestage. Select Subject and get fifty or so subject headings to click on. Select one, say, Home Economics, and the list of resource links in that area is displayed.

Select the Lifestage option and get eleven categories, from Prenatal and Infant to College Education-reflecting different educational lifestages. There are also education lifestyles represented in the categories of distance learning, graduate education, and continuing education. Again, a click on the category will reveal the listings for that area.

What you get: The listing for each resource has a link to the site and an annotation about the site.

Design: Very simple, straightforward listing.

Other Educational Scout Sites

The Global Schoolhouse-Link-O-Rama
www.gsn.org/links/
The Global Schoolhouse, from the Global SchoolNet Foundation, actually began in 1984 with FrEdMail (Free Educational) Network.

In 1992, a grant from the National Science Foundation helped launch the Global Schoolhouse online. This is a full-service educational site with forums and chats and news about education. The "Link-O-Rama" is limited, with only 350 or so sites, but they are well selected and well organized.

Ed Web

edweb.cnidr.org/

With its mirrored sites in California, North Carolina, China, and Turkey, the international aspects of this site become readily apparent. Andy Carvin, the creator and maintainer of the site, is clear on the purpose, "to explore the worlds of educational reform and information technology" and dedicated in the commitment to help you "hunt down on-line educational resources around the world, learn about trends in education policy and information infrastructure development, examine success stories of computers in the classroom, and much, much more." His K–12 Resource Guide (edweb. cnidr.org/k12.html) offers a collection of the best education links grouped by Question & Answer Services, Discussion Groups, News Groups, Educational Gateways, Chat Forums for Kids, General and State-Sponsored Educational Networks.

For More Information

Carvin, Andy. "The World Wide Web in Education: A Closer Look." (edweb.cnidr.org/web.intro.html)

Branscomb, H. Eric. *Casting Your Net: A Student's Guide to Research on the Internet.* Needham Heights, MA: Allyn & Bacon, 1997.

Guernsey, Lisa. *College.Edu: On-Line Resources for the Cyber-Savvy.* Chicago: Dearborn Trade, 1997.

Porter, Lynnette R. *Creating the Virtual Classroom: Distance Learning With the Internet.* New York: John Wiley & Sons, 1997.

Skomars, Nancy. *Educating With the Internet: Using Net Resources at School and Home*. Rockland, MA: Charles River Media, 1997.

Provenzo, Eugene F., Jr. *The Educator's Brief Guide to the Internet and the World Wide Web*. Larchmont, NY: Eye on Education, 1997.

Anderson, Catherine, and Christine Freeman, eds. *The Educator's Guide to the Internet: A Handbook With Resources and Activities*. Reading, MA: Addison-Wesley Publishing Co., 1997.

4

Food Resources on the Web

Sure, the Web is multimedia but it is still only bi-sensory. Of the five senses—hearing, seeing, feeling, tasting, and smelling—only two are well satisfied by the Web world's audio files and video downloads. When you're hungry for the other senses to be sated, the Web can come up short. On the other hand, if you want the sensual joys of looking at and imagining fabulous culinary delights and not worrying about the calories, the Web has a smorgasbord of resources to satisfy every craving. So, until Netscape comes up with Smell-o-vision, reading about and looking at food on the Web will have to stave off those hunger pains.

Recipes for any dietary needs (diabetic, low salt, heart-healthy), any foreign delicacy (Thai, Mexican, African), any holiday favorites, or gourmet concoctions can be found on the World Wide Web. There's even a page of delicious recipes using bugs, Iowa State University's Tasty Insect Recipes (www.ent.iastate.edu/Misc/InsectsAsFood.html). Consumer tips, nutritional information, and, if you have trouble getting up from the table (and sitting too much at the computer), diet advice are easy pickings. For those who need advice for entertaining, there are recipe sites with complete menus for any occasion that can calculate for you the amounts you need to serve from 1 to 250 people, and print out a shopping list for you to take to the store!

Web sites with information about food generally come from six different kinds of sources.

- There are corporate sites, sponsored by food companies like Kellogg's (www.kelloggs.com) or Pillsbury (www.pillsbury.com), or like www.shrimp.com from a seafood distributorship in Houston, Texas, that are set up primarily to promote information about and use of their products.
- There are "celebrity sites" for people who are an industry themselves, like master of good taste Martha Stewart (www.marthastewart.com) or Cajun cooking king Paul Prudhomme (www.kpauls.com), that are set up to promote themselves.
- There are online equivalents of classic cooking publications or shows that are online side dishes to the main publication, like Bon Appétit and Gourmet found on the Epicurious site (food.epicurious.com/) or the Food Network's Web site, FoodTV (www.foodtv.com/).
- Food Web sites put together by individuals cover almost any food specialty and are often an online offshoot of someone's particular cooking hobby, such as Diana Rattray's Web site, Diana's Kitchen (www.ebicom.net/kitchen/), with crockpot and Southern cooking recipes as her main items.
- Food-related associations and organizations have Web sites to promote their work and their areas of interest, such as the Bread Bakers Guild of America (www.bbga.org/index.html) or the Vegetarian Resource Group (www.vrg.org).
- Government agencies, such as the Food and Drug Administration (www.fda.gov) or the Department of Agriculture's Food, Nutrition, and Consumer Services (www.fns.usda.gov/fncs/), use the Web to distribute information about food-related issues and concerns and advice to citizens.

The old saying about when you pile up your plate too much, "your eyes are bigger than your stomach," definitely applies to the area of food-related Web sites. If you're not careful, your bookmarks or favorites list will soon be like an overstuffed shopping cart. As with all Web research, being focused about what you want to find will help determine which resources you'll want to use. If you want advice on balanced diets, check out a government or association site. If you want ideas for using a particular product, use their corporate site. If you are just looking for an online coffee klatch about baking, go to some of the personal sites.

For those of you who want to do an online equivalent of strolling up and down the grocery store aisles stocked with food Web sites, check out the growing phenomenon of the WebRing. These voluntary affiliations of similar sites set up a daisy chain of links to other Web sites on a particular topic. If you love to look through bread recipes, join the Breadlover's WebRing; if you're into Vegan cooking, join the Vegan and Cruelty-free WebRing. Once you click to one of the sites, the WebRing icon at the bottom of the page will take you to the next site on the ring. Find food- or cooking-related WebRings at www.webring.org.

When so much of our time and money is spent thinking about, finding, preparing, and eating food, knowing the best places to shop for information can be a savings. Here are a few food information Web sites that can get you started.

Top Great Scout Site for Food

The Culinary Connection
www.culinary.com
Contact: Chefandy@culinary.com

Why we picked this site: Put in a little bit of this, add a dash of that, and you've got a great dish. That's the recipe the folks who cooked up the Culinary Connection followed. This Web site of links delivers recipes, other food sites, newsgroups, even a directory of people who can teach wine courses. Although the practice of pulling the Web sites they link to into the Culinary Connection frame is a little misleading, the links they send you to are well organized. The fact that there is a search capability and some description about the Web sites in the directory makes this site a choice pick over some of the other food information directories.

Created: Started as The Culinary Connection BBS (bulletin board service) on January 1, 1993.

How many sites: Over 1,300 links in the database with an average growth rate of 15–20 new links a week.

Audience: Recipe seekers and cooking hobbyists.

How sites are selected: Sites added to the links database are self-submitted but, says Web site coordinator Andy Biegel, "We try very hard to keep our site G-rated. If a submitted site does not live up to this rating, or if they accept advertising from adult sites, they automatically will not be added. As for content, it is not up to our site to determine what would be beneficial to other users. If it is a culinary-related site with even the smallest amount of useful information to the guest, we will approve it. I personally visit EVERY site submitted for addition."

How it's supported: According to Biegel, "We have been a self-supported BBS/Web site from the beginning. All banner ads on our site are either strategic partnerships, banner exchanges, or content swaps. We are in the middle of a site design makeover, and will soon be opening our online Culinary MarketPlace. When these two phases are complete, we will actively seek paid sponsorships, advertising, and product placement for The Culinary Connection."

Topics covered: There are areas for finding recipes, locating other cooking Web sites, descriptions of cooking-related newsgroups and mailing lists, a glossary of food terms, a calendar of events, directory of associations and organizations, publications, and a roster of wine courses.

Searching: Each of the areas has its own method for finding the links in that area. For example, clicking on the "newsgroups" button gives you an alphabetical listing of food-related newsgroups; clicking on "glossary" displays a list of "A" cooking terms—to look up the meaning of "Bagna Cauda" you'd click on the "B" in the alphabet running down the side of the page.

Two areas, the recipes and the links, each have two ways you can locate resources.

Recipes—Browsing: When you click on "recipes" you get a display page with links to different recipe categories listed in no particular order: Pasta Dishes, Poultry and Fowl, Game Dishes, Salads and Dressings . . . . Click on one of these categories and a page with a long list of recipes is displayed (in no particular order). Click on one of the recipes and you'll see the recipe displayed.

Recipes—Searching: Click on "search" and a search template is displayed where you can type in the ingredient or type of recipe. If you've used more than one term, you can select in a pull-down box either "All terms" (if looking for crockpot recipes for chicken, type in *crockpot chicken* and select "all terms") or "Any term" (if looking for recipes with shrimp or lobster, type in *shrimp lobster* and select "any term").

Links—Browsing: There are sixteen categories on the table you get when you click on "Links" (Beverages, Chef Pages, Educational, Ethnic Links, Events, Magazines, Mail Order, Miscellaneous, Newsgroups, Nutrition, Organizations, Recipes, Restaurants, Software, Types of Food, Vegetarian Links). After each category the number of links in that area is given with a brief description of the area's contents.

Links—Searching: Looking for something in particular? Then use the search box provided. Type in a term, say, *Shrimp*, and the search engine will search the database of links and descriptions. If you want to do a bit more complex search than a single term, click on "More Options" and you'll get a search box to enter the terms, and buttons to select whether you want the terms searched as individual keywords or as a phrase, and a selection for an "and" or an "or" search.

What you get—Recipes: The recipe includes number of people served and time for preparation.

What you get—Links: Organized by categories, the links information provides a hypertext link to the site (brought into the Culinary Connection frame, however), a description of contents on the site, when the site was added to the database, and the number of "hits" made to the site from Culinary Connection users.

Design: The folks behind The Culinary Connection don't want you leaving their site, so they use frames to pull into their site the links they send you to. It can be confusing to users, thinking that the content they are looking at comes from the Culinary Connection. We asked Webmaster Biegel if there had been any complaints about that practice and he said there had not, as yet, and that they would deal with any complaints on an individual basis.

Other features: They are fastidious about making sure the links in the site are fresh; they run an automatic link checking utility once a week. If a link fails to be validated two weeks in a row, it is removed from the database.

Other Food Web Site Directories

GourmetSpot

www.gourmetspot.com/

"GourmetSpot is the first course of the World Wide Web for food lovers. GourmetSpot was designed to break through the information overload of the Web to bring the best food and beverage sites together with insightful editorial in one convenient, user-friendly spot." The number of listings is somewhat limited, but the good organization and nice little annotations about the sites make this a tasty choice for seekers of good food sites.

Food and Nutrition Information Center

www.nal.usda.gov/fnic/

If you have any serious questions or concerns about food and nutrition, go to the experts. The National Agricultural Library's Food and Nutrition Information Center has organized the best links to such topics as Food Safety, Food Composition, Dietary Guidelines, USDA Reports, and an extensive category called "Internet Resources" organized by over 100 topics. Selected by librarians and well organized, this is a useful resource to finding the more credible sites for information about food and nutrition.

Food Info Net

www.foodinfonet.com/

The "most comprehensive Internet site for information and services related to food technology, R&D, and manufacturing. The site combines resources of food companies, research and academic institutions, industry suppliers, government agencies, and non-profit special interest groups." They combine not just the best of the Web in their listings of resources, but also CD-ROMs and books with good information. In addition, the Associations list links to conference information and to Web sites, providing a nice combination of Web-linked resources and relevant associations not on the Web (but with contact information given).

The Kitchen Link

www.kitchenlink.com/

With over 9,000 food and cooking links to food sites on the net, this is an extensive resource but somewhat difficult to wade through. It is well worth a look, though, if you are hunting down an elusive recipe or food item.

Other Food Sites

Calculate measurements (weight, temperature, volume) at the Internet Epicurean Recipe Exchange (internet.epicurean.com/latest/exchange/calculator.index.html).

Are the kids trying to tell you that broccoli has no nutritional value and isn't worth wasting the time to eat it? Use Nutribase's Online Nutritional Database (www.Nutribase.com/) with more than 19,000 food items and their nutritional content. But, also check out their other features: "A weight-loss calculator, a calorie requirements calculator, 'desirable' weight and body fat content charts, a directory of 1,400 food and supplement makers, a listing of healthy food substitutions, a glossary of foods and cooking terms, toll-free numbers for food makers, and 1,000 dieting tips and quotes are also featured."

Maybe you'd like a cooking school on the Net: Hang out with chefs, get recipe ideas, get the latest food news, order products, and take an online cooking class at the Culinary Institute of America's Digital Chef (www.digitalchef.com).

Can't understand what half the items in that new nouveau cuisine cookbook are referring to? Look them up in the Epicurious Food Dictionary (food.epicurious.com/run/fooddictionary/home).

Just what *is* a balanced diet? Find out this and more at the Food and Nutrition Information Center (www.nal.usda.gov/fnic/etext/fnic.html). Check out their list of Internet food resources, which are well organized by topics, such as Allergies, Anorexia, Child Nutrition, Ethnic and Cultural Resources.

Food Safety and Nutrition Information from the International Food Information Council has background material on all flavors of food and nutrition concerns (ificinfo.health.org/infofsn.htm).

Whether you're planning a cozy dinner at home alone or a banquet for 200, the recipes and calculations at Meals For You can help (www.mealsforyou.com). Search the thousands of recipes, display them by time of preparation, calorie content, fat content, recipe instructions, change the number of servings you want, and it will recalculate the amounts needed and provide a shopping list for you. It even recommends a wine to serve. This is an awesome resource for cooks of all skill levels and ambitions.

For More Information

Salkind, Neil J. *The Online Epicure: Finding Out Everything You Want to Know About Good Cooking and Eating on the Internet.* New York: John Wiley & Sons, 1997.

5

Health and Medical Information on the Web

If you're sick, you want to know about what you have and your options for dealing with it. If you're not sick, you want to stay that way. In either case, or if you are a student or writer researching health and medical issues, the Internet is a virtual medical library, a doctor who makes house calls, a support group. But, if you know what's good for you, you'll take researching for health information on the World Wide Web as seriously as a heart attack. With estimates as high as 250,000 health-related Web sites,[1] there is probably no subject area on the Internet as rich in information, misinformation, and disinformation as the area of health and medicine.

By clicking around the Web, you can join a discussion with people interested in heart disease (newsgroup sci.med.cardiology), read articles from medical journals on the latest approved treatments for heart disease (*Journal of the American Medical Association*, www.ama-assn.org/public/journals/jama/jamahome.htm), seek out alternative medicines to the mainstream for treating heart disease (The Emmenagogues: Herbs that move blood and relieve pain, www.planetherbs.com/articles/BloodHerb.html), and read opinions about the validity of those alternative treatments (Quackwatch, www.quackwatch.com).

But, are these rich and varied sources information-full or riddled with misinformation? This is an area of research where your ability to judge the difference might literally be a matter of life and death. Knowing how to evaluate or where to find resources that have done good evaluation is as critical as a catheter to a dialysis patient.

Just as in the pre-Internet days, medical advice and information can be conflicting, even from credible, reliable sources. For example, a co-worker fell off a dock and ended up with a fractured rib. We looked for advice on the Web. Two sites with vast resources of advice and information about illnesses and conditions were located. One, Health Square (www.healthsquare.com), specializes in compiling information from reliable medical sources. Their page of information on rib fractures came from *The PDR Family Guide Encyclopedia of Medical Care*. Under the "What You Should Do" advice, fourth item down was, "Do not wear a rib belt or binder."

Over on ThriveOnline (www.thriveonline.com) the advice for fractured ribs comes from the *Complete Guide to Sports Injuries* by H. Winter Griffith, M.D. Recommended treatment: "Application of a wide elastic wrap or chest binder to decrease movement of the chest muscles and reduce pain with breathing. The binder should be applied around the lower chest beneath the breasts, even if the rib fracture is in the upper chest."

So, wrap or no wrap? The diagnosis for evaluation of medical information on the Internet (or, for that matter, anywhere else) is nicely summed up in the caution note at the end of an information page on MedicineNet: "The content displayed by the physician writers and editors of MedicineNet, Inc., is designed to be educational. Under no circumstance should it replace the expert care and advice of a qualified physician. MedicineNet, Inc., does not give medical advice or care to its viewers. Rapid advances in medicine may cause information contained here to become outdated, invalid, or subject to debate. Accuracy cannot be guaranteed." Your best prescription is to get offline, pick up the phone, and call your doctor!

In the past, patients, and researchers, relied on interviews with medical experts or trips to the local library for information on health-related topics. Those old methods will still be useful. But now you can access some of the basic resources of medical research on the Web.

Medical dictionary: *On-line Medical Dictionary* (www.graylab.ac.uk/omd/index.html).

Medical literature citations: *Index Medicus*, the premier print index to medical literature, has migrated to the Web as PubMed (www.ncbi.nlm.nih.gov/PubMed/) and the Grateful Med (igm.nlm.nih.gov/), which has some other specific databases (i.e., Aidsline) as well as Medline.

Locate a doctor: The American Medical Association's "On-Line Doctor Finder" (www.ama-assn.org/aps/amahg.htm) provides information on virtually every licensed physician in the United States, more than 650,000 doctors of medicine (MD) and doctors of osteopathy or osteopathic medicine (DO). The Doctor Directory (www.doctordirectory.com/) is searchable by region and specialty.

Get information about a drug: The *Electronic Orange Book* from the Food and Drug Administration is searchable at www.accessdata.fda.gov/ob/default.htm. *Merck Manual*: www.merck.com. The bible of drugs, the *PDR (Physician's Desk Reference)*, is available at www.pdr.net (free to doctors, others must pay a fee). A free-to-all guide to drugs is available on the Mayo Clinic's Health Oasis site (www.mayohealth.org/usp/di/uspA-AM.htm) in the MedicineCenter area.

No less than twenty-five guides to health and medical resources on the Internet have been written in the past two years. Bruce Maxwell, author of *How to Find Health Information on the Internet*, says it's all about patient empowerment. Maxwell, author of a guide to federal information on the Internet, too, said, "I got interested in writing the book after health information I found on the Internet saved my life." He had been very sick, had lots of tests done, but dismissed the doctor's diagnosis of what his symptoms showed the illness he was suffering was likely to be. Then he went online to explore a bit further. He went to the National Institutes of Health Web site (www.nih.gov), looked up the illness his doctor had suggested he had and found that the more expansive information available there convinced him that it was what he was suffering from. The information also indicated that immediate treatment was imperative, as the disease could be fatal.

Evaluating the quality of medical information sites can sometimes be counterindicative. It is widely felt that the core standards for site evaluation[2] are:

- Authorship: the affiliations and credentials of the authors and contributors;
- Attribution: sourcing for all the content should be clearly listed;

- Disclosure: Web site "ownership" should be prominently and fully disclosed;
- Currency: dates that content was posted and updated should be indicated;

Unlike some subject areas where the "personal page" registers lowest on the quality thermometer because in the evaluation criteria for "authorship" the page just doesn't have the authority, in the area of medical resources, Maxwell says, the personal pages are sometimes the best. "While it is important to determine official sites and authoritative sites, a lot of the good stuff is put together by patients or their families. They spend a lot of time compiling the results of their personal research and their intimate experience with the management and treatment of the disease can sometimes be invaluable."

The area of evaluation of Web-based health information is not without controversy. In an analysis of evaluation criteria for health sites on the Web in the *Journal of the American Medical Association*[2] the authors conclude: "We applaud the current discussions about quality and hope that they will lead quickly to widespread agreement on a set of core standards that information producers can choose to follow. We are not, however, calling for a single or centralized review process, institution, or agency, except to any extent that appropriate laws or regulations might require. We believe such an approach is neither desirable or realistic, since the Internet is a decentralized, global medium. Nor are we calling for punitive action against those who do not follow such standards. Professionals and the public alike are hungry for quality information, will over time recognize efforts to provide it, and will show their appreciation by pointing their Web browsers to sites that do so. . . . Let a thousand flowers bloom. We just want those cruising the information superhighway to be able to tell them from the weeds."

You'll feel better as you learn about the health-specific search sites available on the Web. Look to the following to cure your medical research ills.

Great Scouts for Health and Medical Information

Healthfinder
www.healthfinder.gov
Contact: healthfinder@health.org
P.O. Box 1133
Washington, DC 20013-1133

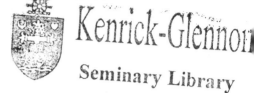

Why we picked this site: This one-stop gateway provides a comprehensive information and referral guide to free health information from federal, state, and local agencies, universities and not-for-profit organizations, as well as selected commercial health care sites. The database of resources focuses on Web pages and Internet sites for organizations but also includes organizations without an Internet presence that will respond to requests for information on health care topics. The rigorous evaluation process each site undergoes before it is added ensures that the information you find, as the mission statement declares, " . . . can help you make better choices for yourself and your family about your health and human services needs."

Created: April 15, 1997.

How many sites: Healthfinder links to over 5,000 web resources.

Audience: Primarily targeted at health care consumers, although medical professionals will find this a useful resource locator.

How sites are selected: A steering committee meets monthly to decide on additions and deletions from the database. Their selection policy considers:
- evaluation of site sponsor,
- quality of the health information,
- technological and design factors, such as accessibility to disabled users.

For more details on their criteria: www.healthfinder.gov/selectionpolicy.htm.

Participating agencies and organizations must be willing and able to respond to information requests from across the nation. Proposed database entries for chosen sites are sent to owners for approval before posting to Healthfinder.

How it's supported: Federal-government supported: your tax money.

Brought to you by: U.S. Department of Health and Human Services.

Freshness: Home page was updated within a week of when it was evaluated.

Topics covered: Over 1,000 specific topics are covered, from abstinence to zidovudine.

Contents: This Web site's database consists of links to and descriptions of information from U.S.-based health care agencies and organizations.

Searching: At the top of every page, you'll find a text search box. Enter a search term and find items in the database of "hand-picked, reliable health and human services resources." Another option is to click on the "Topics A–Z" area on the search box. You'll then click on the letter that starts your topic. A search page will appear with a select box with subjects beginning with that letter. Choose one and click the "select" button or further narrow your focus by selecting a "population" option (men, women, children, teens, infants, minorities, seniors) or by kind of resource (all resources, Web resources only, or organizations only).

What you get: Two listings are given for each topic, Web Resources then Organizations. Some of the retrieved resources have a little U.S. flag next to them, indicating the information comes from a U.S. government agency.

For each of the listings you can link directly to the cited resource or click on "Details" and get:

For Web pages:

- Web address,
- Sponsoring agency,
- Annotation about the site and description of some special features.

For Organizations pages:

- Web address (if available),
- Contact information (address, telephone),
- Description of the agency or organization,
- Links to online resources or citations to print resources available from the agency.

Advanced searching: Be careful: When you put more than one term in the search box, it treats them as a phrase. Indicate connections between words by putting AND or OR between them. For example, typing in *breast cancer* retrieved 33 Web resources and 15 organizations, *breast and cancer* found 36 Web resources and 19 organizations, while *breast or cancer* delivered 175 Web resources and 102 organizations. Variations of words will be retrieved ("disease" finds diseases, diseased).

Design: Simple, clean, low tech.

Other features: News and announcements on latest medical discoveries and events. Hot topics: a listing of the monthly top search topics provides easy linking to the listed resources. Just for You: groups resources by population. Read more about evaluating medical Web sites by clicking on the "Smart Choices" area on the choices bar at the bottom of the page—you'll get links to great guides to medical site evaluation.

Help or FAQ: Click on "Help" in the search box for hints about searching.

Read about it:

Weintraub, Pamela. "How to Get Every Health Fact You'll Ever Need." *Redbook*, November 1, 1997: 124.

Manning, Anita. "Site Sorts Out Tangle of Web Health Information." *USA Today*, April 15, 1997: 6D. (On the *USA Today* Web site archives, www.usatoday.com).

Medical Matrix

www.medmatrix.org

Contact: Dr. Gary Malet, gmalet@healthtel.com

American Medical Informatics Association

4915 St. Elmo Avenue, Suite 401

Bethesda, MD 20814

mail@mail.amia.org

Why we picked this site: "Ranked, peer-reviewed, annotated, updated, clinical medicine resources." That certainly hit all the bases we want covered in a subject-specific search site. This one is exceptionally well organized and its content is constantly being added to and updated.

Created: 1994 when an early Internet Health Science Resources List was converted to HTML and the American Medical Informatics Association, Internet Working Group was formed.

How many sites: As of September 1998, more than 4,000 rated and annotated sites; growing at the rate of 100 to 120 sites per month.

Audience: "Target audience is primarily United States physicians and healthworkers who are on the front line in prescribing treatment for disease conditions." But its ease of use and range of resources linked to make it valuable for all seekers of medical resources.

How sites are selected: Submitted sites are reviewed by an editorial board drawn from the Internet Working Group of the American Medical Informatics Association. The criteria for entry selection and ranking include utility for point-of-care clinical application, quality, currency, and unrestricted access. There is an evaluation survey that is filled out on each site measuring such things as:

- Peer Reviewed (previously evaluated, verifiable, endorsed, dated, current, referenced),
- Application (ability to enhance the knowledge database of the point-of-care specialist),
- Media (use of multimedia),
- Feel (search features, navigation tools),
- Ease of access (reliability, speed of the link),
- Dimension (size, effort, and importance to the discipline).

How it's supported: Academic grants from the biomedical industry including Pfizer Corporation and Organon.

Brought to you by: American Medical Informatics Association, Internet Working Group. The site is posted by Slack Corporation, an academic medical publisher.

Freshness: The dates of submittal to the database aren't given, but sites are constantly being added.

Topics covered: Links lists are organized by specialty/disease, clinical practice, literature, education, healthcare and professionals, computers and technology, and marketplace. Under each of these broad groupings there are specific sub-categories.

Searching: There are two options for searching for resources on the site. Click on one of the topic areas (e.g., Allergy in the Specialty and Disease area, or Patient Education in the Clinical Practice area). The number of listed sites is indicated next to the category name. The retrieved resources are further grouped by News,

Abstracts, Indices, Meetings, Textbooks, Forums, Patient Information, etc.

There is also a search box at the top of each page that searches the database of resources free-text. You'll get more results by searching in the search box than by clicking on the subject words. For example, click on Allergy and you'll retrieve twenty-eight items but type allergy in the search box and you'll get forty-two items (some categorized in a different area but containing allergy in the annotation).

What you get: A listing of links on the topic or retrieved search terms with hypertext links to the site plus a brief annotation about the site. Sites are rated with zero to five stars. Zero is a site with specialized knowledge with suitable clinical content, three stars indicates one of the best specialty sites and a valuable place to go, five is an award-winning site for the Medical Internet.

Advanced searching: No.

Design: Very clean and straightforward site design.

Other features: The mission of the American Medical Informatics Association is "Advancing Health Care Through Information Technology." In pursuit of that mission, they have put together useful criteria and helpful resources on how to evaluate and develop medical resources on the Web.

Help or FAQ: Click on "About Medical Matrix" for more background on the group and the project.

Other Web Sites

There are sites that pull all these types of resources together for a whole portfolio on particular diseases. For example, Mediconsult.com (www.mediconsult.com), which bills itself as "The Medical Web Destination

Patients Use Most," offers a pick list of more than 70 diseases or medical topics. Select one and click on "go" to get to a special page with sections, such as Educational Material, Journal Articles, News, Clinical Trials, Drug Information, links to other useful Web sites, and a link to Medline (the key medical research papers source). Except for the links to other Web sites, the information in Mediconsult is pulled in from other sources, but the source is well documented. For each of these diseases or conditions, there is also a "Support Group" area where you can read messages from others dealing with that medical condition. This offers one-stop shopping for medical information.

For More Information

How to Search for Medical Information (www.ultranet.com/~egrlib/www.htm).

Internet Clinical Medicine Applications (www.medmatrix.org/info/SURVEY.HTML).

Moss, Ralph W. *Alternative Medicine Online: A Guide to Natural Remedies on the Internet.* Brooklyn, NY: Equinox Pr., 1997.

Davis, James, Kathryn Swanson, and Maureen Lynch, eds. *Health & Medicine on the Internet: An Annual Guide to the World Wide Web for Health Care Professionals.* Los Angeles: Practice Management Information Corporation, 1998.

Maxwell, Bruce. "How to Find Health Information on the Internet." *Congressional Quarterly*, August 1998.

McKenzie, Bruce C. *Medicine and the Internet: Introducing Online Resources and Terminology.* New York: Oxford University Press, 1997.

Wolff, Michael. *Netdoctor: Your Guide to Health and Medical Advice on the Internet and Online Services.* New York: Dell Books, 1997.

Endnotes

1. Junnarkar, Sandeep. "Web Sites Warn: Healthcare Information May Not Be What the Doctor Ordered." The New York Times on the Web, March 8, 1998 (www.nytimes.com/library/tech/98/03/cyber/articles/08medical.html).

2. Silberg, William M., George D. Lundberg, Robert A. Musacchio. "Assessing, Controlling, and Assuring the Quality of Medical Information on the Internet: Caveant Lector et Viewor—Let the Reader and Viewer Beware." *Journal of the American Medical Association* 277 (1997): 1244–1245 (www. ama-assn.org/sci-pubs/journals/archive/jama/vol_277/no_15/ed7016x.htm).

6

History Resources on the Web

History on the Web is not just what you can find in a textbook. For seekers into the past, the Web offers infinite space for the words, images, and sounds that make up the history of our civilization. Hypertext adds another dimension—the ability to portray connections among events, theories, personalities, cultures, and disciplines in a non-linear way. With the click of a mouse, even the standard timeline can be turned into a series of links to take you deeper into the past or wider beyond a specific topic to its relationships with events and ideas in other places and times.

In history departments, historical associations, libraries, and archives around the world, scholars, teachers, and students use the Web as a teaching tool, a publishing medium, and a means of communication. University support and government grants have encouraged efforts towards authoritative compilations of historical materials and the tools for accessing them. One of the best examples is the Perseus project at Tufts University, which includes Greek and Latin texts, translations, dictionaries, images, an interactive atlas, and detailed indexes comprising the whole field of classical studies.

Apart from bookstores, publishers, and specialty video distributors, there is little commercial activity in the field of history on the Web. Thus many design and technological innovations—inspired by the potential for electronic commerce in other areas—are absent from this subject topic. As an academic realm, history is text-rich with low potential for random surfers and advertising gimmicks.

But on the Web, history is more than an academic village. The free spirit of the Web opens a channel of communication for a whole community lacking formal affiliations to mainstream academia, but with deep interests and enthusiasm. For history buffs, collectors, fans of historic re-enactment, and independent researchers and theorists, the Web offers a forum, a printing press, and boundless opportunities for expressing alternative points of view, distributing documents, and building sites around personal historic interests, with creativity and even humor.

Here's where you'll find detailed documentation of a vast variety of conspiracy theories, a huge community of genealogy sites, handbooks on historically correct buildings, costumes, vehicles and recipes, diagrams and maps of specific battles and journeys, catalogs of antiques, rare books and collectibles, and enthusiasts' collections of biographic material on personalities throughout history, particularly figures in popular culture not documented elsewhere.

You're out on the Web, so remember that the voices you'll hear may not be reasoned and that an individual's well-produced historical site may be slanted or just plain inaccurate. Watch carefully for bias, check sources of information, and use common sense when you're out in uncharted cyberspace.

Great Scouts for historical materials on the Web fall into two categories: academic source directories and personal lists of links. Our selection will highlight the most ambitious and unique, specifically those with the best search features for locating that historical nugget you're trying to dig up.

Historical Materials on the Web

Biography: From A & E Television Network, Biography.com database puts over 20,000 of the greatest lives, past and present, at your fingertips (www.biography.com/find/find.html); the Dead People Server names people alive and dead, with cause of death and dates (www.dpsinfo.com).

Conspiracies: Browse The Megalist of Conspiracy Theory on the WWW at disinformation (www.disinfo.com) or search the Encyclopedia of Conspiracies at Black-Ops (www.cruzio. com/~blackops).

Databases: For text, Documenting the American South (metalab. unc.edu/docsouth) includes three digitization projects: African American slave narratives, first-person narratives, and Southern literature.

Documents: Scanned documents about a wide variety of historic and popular subjects, many from declassified government sources, including the Unabomber psychiatric report, documents from the investigation of the 1957 assassination of crime boss Albert Anastasia, lots about John F. Kennedy, Robert F. Kennedy, Jacqueline Kennedy Onassis, Elvis Presley, and various other celebrities at The Smoking Gun (www.thesmokinggun.com). The wills of many notable people, including Princess Diana, Marilyn Monroe, John Lennon, Babe Ruth, and Jerry Garcia can be viewed at CourtTV Online (www.courttv.com).

Photographic archives: Visit the Vietnam Multimedia Archives (metalab.unc.edu/vietnam/), photos from World War II and the Civil War at the National Archives (www.nara.gov/nara).

Genealogy: Royal and Noble Genealogical Data on the Web, a pathfinder for royal genealogy, (www.dcs.hull.ac.uk/public/ genealogy/GEDCOM.html); Ingeborg Brigitte Gastel's My Family Research Pages on Descendants of Royal Historical Figures, in which she reveals her family connections to Brooke Shields, Humphrey Bogart, Winston Churchill, Camilla Parker-Bowles, and others (www.worldroots.com/brigitte/royal/royal17.htm).

Maps: Historical Map Web Sites from the Perry-Castañeda Library Map Collection at the University of Texas at Austin points to maps at locations around the Web as well as the extensive digital collection at UT (mahogany.lib.utexas.edu/Libs/PCL/Map_collection /map_sites/hist_sites.html).

News: Today's news is tomorrow's history. Searchable newspaper archives are on the Web in growing numbers, some now stretching back to the early 1980s. For a guide to news archives, visit the news librarians' home page (metalab.unc.edu/slanews/internet/archives. html). Today In History: A number of sites offer daily historical events and birth dates of the famous. Visit HistoryNet (www. thehistorynet.com/today/today.htm).

Oral History: American Slave Narratives at the University of Virginia (xroads.virginia.edu/~HYPER/wpa/wpahome.html). Civil Rights Oral History Bibliography from the Mississippi Humanities Council and the Mississippi Department of Archives and History is a bibliography of oral history interviews on the civil rights movement in Mississippi (www-dept.usm.edu/~mcrohb).

Textbooks: By Thomas Martin, Overview of Archaic and Classical Greek History, at the Perseus Project site (www.perseus.tufts.edu).

CAUTION: History's body of information goes back thousands of years, but the Web is less than seven years old. All of the texts, sounds, and images that comprise the Web of history have been selected and digitized by individuals and institutions with agendas—even selfless, educational agendas—of their own. The Internet is a global library of information, but most of the books are missing because nobody has been inspired to type or scan them in. And, if the books, sounds, articles, images, and documents are still in the domain of international copyright, you won't find them on the freely available Web either. If what you're looking for was in the news (or had an anniversary year) after 1994 or is a popular history topic like the Civil War, you're in luck. But there are just forty-six entries for China's history in the WWW Virtual Library directory of China studies.

Great Scout Sites for History

The Labyrinth
www.georgetown.edu/labyrinth/labyrinth-home.html
Contact: Deborah Everhart
Georgetown University
University Information Services
Washington, DC 20057
everhart@gusun.georgetown.edu

Why we picked this site: The field of history is too large for just one directory to cover comprehensively and thoughtfully. Labyrinth is an excellent model for its coverage of the area of medieval and ancient studies. The site name comes from a quote by Jorge Luis Borges: "I thought of a labyrinth of labyrinths, of one sinuous spreading labyrinth that would encompass the past and the future and in some way involve the stars" (from "The Garden of Forking Paths").

"It's one of the oldest running Web sites in existence," said site co-director Martin Irvine. "It's a portal for anything to do with medieval studies information both for academic users and the general public." He says it's Georgetown University's most popular site.

Labyrinth collects and organizes the amazingly rich resources in this topical area on the Web. This is really OLD material, but it is made new and available to all by the new electronic medium. Irvine said it's one of a handful of humanities sites to receive a seal of approval from the National Endowment for the Humanities, certifying the site as a useful tool for teachers because it provides "premium information" that students from elementary through college can use.

Created: December 1993.

How many sites: "Hundreds," according to site co-director Martin Irvine.

Audience: Students and scholars of Medieval Studies.

How sites are selected: Collaborative effort of academic experts in ancient and medieval studies.

How it's supported: Sponsored by Georgetown University's Medieval Studies program.

Topics covered: Religion, Ancient Studies, Medieval Studies, Byzantine Studies, General Resources. Sub-topics are arranged by country, theme, or type of material.

Contents: The Labyrinth library includes texts in Latin, Old and Middle English, French, Italian, German, Spanish and Iberian, and scholarly monographs, journals, and reviews. Subjects include National Cultures (Anglo-Saxon, Celtic, Iberian, etc.), International Culture (Archaeology, Arts and Architecture, Music, Philosophy, and Theology), and Special Topics (Arthurian Studies, Heraldry, Medieval Women). Pedagogical resources include course materials, language learning aids, software, and multimedia. Professional information covers publications and organizations. There are also links to Medieval Studies text, images, and archival databases.

Searching: Browse or search the directory to retrieve lists of hyperlinks on each scholarly topic. The links are not annotated.

Advanced searching: Argos is the search engine (see the next entry).

Design: The site is text based, with minimal graphics, no frames, and no frills.

Other features: Labyrinth Electronic Center offers conferences and discussion groups.

Help or FAQ: Daedalus's Guide to the Web for help in using the Internet.

Read about it:

Thomason, Robert. "On the Net with Ancient Heroes." *The Washington Post*, November 2, 1995, C7.

Argos

argos.evansville.edu

Contact: Anthony F. Beavers, Managing Editor

Internet Applications Laboratory

University of Evansville

1800 Lincoln Avenue

Evansville, IN 47722

tb2@evansville.edu

Why we picked this site: Argos is what we call a "slice" search engine (Argos calls it a limited area search engine or LASE) that allows you automatically to narrow your search to just the ancient and medieval resources of the Internet. What makes Argos unique is peer review: quality of resources is controlled by a system of hyperlinked Internet indices managed by qualified professionals. Argos has an editorial board representing twelve universities around the globe, including Georgetown University, the University of Cambridge, and the University of Bologna.

Argos searches a small set of academic sites and all the pages to which they link. The sites indexed are accredited and controlled by the editors of the associate sites. If sites are removed from any of the associate pages, they are removed from Argos; if new sites are added to the associate pages, they are added to the index. Thus, poor quality or outdated sites are removed, while Argos can also quickly add new sites and new materials.

A related slice engine from the same folks is Hippias (hippias. evansville.edu), using the same system of peer-review that Argos uses to cover philosophy-related resources.

Created: 1996.

How many sites: 18,000 pages on eleven academic sites with extensive ancient or medieval indexes and all the sites linked to them.

Audience: Students of all ages, teachers, and scholars of the ancient and medieval worlds.

How sites are selected: Sites included on the pages of the associate members are automatically selected for inclusion, with the exception of personal home pages.

How it's supported: Argos was funded by grants from the University of Evansville.

Topics covered: Scholarly resources in the ancient and medieval world.

Searching: A search provides a relevancy ranked list of results with hyperlinked title, the first two lines of the page, and the Web address (URL). A search for the word "Plato" returned more than 500 hits, all of them relating to the Greek philosopher—none of them relating to the software program, towns, or beverages named Plato, which do turn up in a search of the major search engines.

Advanced searching: Searches sub-strings of words (truncation), but not phrases.

Design: Simple, fast, but lacks advanced search features. However, limits on content allow for precise retrieval of relevant information.

Other features: Announcements describing news about Argos.

Help or FAQ: Extensive documentation and explanation of the project.

Read about it:

Beavers, Anthony. "Evaluating search engines for academic purposes." *D-Lib*, December 1998 (www.dlib.org/dlib/december98).

HORUS

Horus Gets in Gear: Horus' Web Links to History Resources

www.ucr.edu/h-gig/horuslinks.html

Contact: James Seaman

History Department

University of California, Riverside

Riverside, California 92521

horus@h-gig.ucr.edu.

Why we picked this site: As Horus creator Dr. Ronald Tobey explains, "Trying to teach the general student about a historical event, such as the Paris Commune of 1871, the teacher tells the student, 'Go take a look at some photographs about the commune. What do they tell us about it?' Browsing enchained links may lead the student to letters, brief biographies of politicians, statues of heroes in provincial towns, photos of old houses for sale, postcards from British tourists to relatives, Department of Health statistics on cholera, genealogical snippets of French immigrants to America, and family photos of heirloom silver. None of this information would probably test any professional hypothesis about the cause and course of the Paris Commune, but it will teach the student a great deal about the event, about its rippling effects through history, and its memorialization in everyday artifacts that help shape the way people view the past. In other words, the World Wide Web is one of the most wonderful teaching resources ever invented."

Created: 1996.

How many sites: Over 15,000 links in 74 categories.

Audience: General historical education—secondary and college and continuing education students. Horus is the Egyptian god who guides the deceased.

How sites are selected: Sites are selected from submissions by the graduate research assistant in charge of the site, James Seaman. According to the site's creator, Dr. Tobey, "Horus' purpose in collecting these sites is to introduce the diversity of educational and research resources available on the Web not ordinarily consulted by historians and history students."

How it's supported: University of California, Riverside Department of History.

Topics covered: Major topic areas are: Histories of Specific Countries, Times and Places, Areas of History, On-line Services About History, and Web Tools. Over sixty-eight topic link collections, including Antiques, Collectibles, Historic and Revival Decorative Arts, Booksellers Specializing in History/Genealogy, Electronic Texts, Funding Sources, Genealogy Pages, Heritage Tourism, Historical Drawings, Illustrations, Maps, and Paintings Online, Living History, Local History, Military History, Oral History, Popular (Mass) Culture/Entertainment/Sports History, Preservation/Conservation/CRM/Restoration, Quantitative Methods and Software for Historians, State Historical Societies, Technology History, Women's History.

Contents: A categorized list of selected, unannotated links in specific historic topical areas organized by topic and theme. You can find sites by using the alphabetical index, browsing by category, or using the search engine.

Searching: A word or phrase search takes you to a directory page on which a word occurs, so often you will pull up many hits to the same page.

Advanced searching: Boolean searching (AND, OR) is available.

Design: Frames keep your browser window within the site, so you can't see a linked page's address or bookmark it unless you open it in a new window—we don't like this. Otherwise the site loads quickly and the organization is clear.

Other features: History polls and forums; Online Services for Historians includes help wanted and genealogical research services, grants, and conferences announcements, study hall discussions.

Help or FAQ: Yes.

Other Top History Scouts

Library of Congress American Memory
memory.loc.gov/ammem
This online gateway to primary source materials on history and culture in the U.S. is provided by the Library of Congress National Digital Library Program, and funded by congressional appropriations and private sector donations. The program is engaged in an effort to digitize documents, films, manuscripts, photographs, and sound recordings that tell the story of American history. This is a vivid, active, and impressive multimedia site and pathfinder that can be searched or browsed. Look here for Matthew Brady Civil War photographs and oral histories from the Works Progress Administration.

WWW Virtual Library for History
history.cc.ukans.edu/history/index.html
A major topical listing for history selected and maintained by the history departments at the University of Kansas and Regensburg University in Germany. This list contains more than 4,000 links organized under 115 topics but lacks annotations or search features. Links to sites providing particularly good access to resources in their fields are indicated.

HyperHistory

www.hyperhistory.com

This site presents 3,000 years of world history with graphics, lifelines, timelines, and maps and links to hundreds of history sites on the Web. There are sections for people, history, events, and maps. Site owners are encouraged to participate by submitting their pages and relevant links to fill in gaps in the world timeline.

Historical Text Archive

www.geocities.com/Athens/Forum/9061/index.html

Originating in 1990 as an anonymous FTP site, the archive provides original material, links to other sites, and electronic reprints of books and is organized by geography/nations and topics. The directory includes a wide variety of texts and links to texts and is searchable by word or phrase. For example, African American texts include the lyrics to "Lift Every Voice and Sing," Frederick Douglass's autobiography, Norman Coomb's *The Black Experience in America*, articles by Henry Louis Gates Jr. and more.

7

Law Enforcement, Crime, and Terrorism Resources on the Web

Usually when people talk about crime and the Internet, it's about fraudulent Internet auctions, pedophiles in the chat rooms, and various ripoffs and scams. In this chapter, though, we'll be discussing resources that help you with "off-line" crime and terrorism. Fear of being a victim of crime consistently ranks at the top of "What do you fear most?" surveys. Political elections have been waged around who has the best response to the public's perception of rising crime. Crime and worries about being a victim remain a major concern even though, according to Justice Department reports, crime is down dramatically with crime rates in 1996 the lowest since data were first collected in 1973 and the crime rate decreasing 9 percent between 1991 and 1996 (www.ncjrs.org/). (To see an overview of crime statistics go to the National Crime Prevention Councils FAQ on Crime Statistics: www.ncpc.org/11stat.htm.)

While national crime rates drop, incidences of domestic and international terrorism seem to be growing, with the bombing of the federal buildings in Oklahoma and the embassies in Kenya and Tanzania being recent dramatic events. Awareness of terrorist activities is important for travelers and businesses overseas. Identification of terrorist groups is a constant challenge.

Law enforcement, crime and crime prevention resources, and information about domestic and international terrorism are all available on the World Wide Web. On the crime front, everything from "Most Wanted" lists (www.MostWanted.org), sex offender registries for Alaska, Connecticut, Florida, Indiana, Kansas, and North Carolina (see a listing of links on CrimeTime, www.crimetime.com/online.html), and local police agency reports of crimes (find an agency at Law Enforcement Online pimacc.pima.edu/dps/police.htm) can be found online.

You can learn how not to be a victim (check out the safety tips for Self, Home, and Family at the National Crime Prevention Council's site: www.ncpc.org/self.htm). You can get a heads-up on how not to get caught doing a crime (find where the speed traps are in different states at www.speedtrap.com). You can even go online to befriend a felon by locating inmates' personal home pages at Cyberspace Inmates (www.cyberspace-inmates.com/state.htm).

In the apparently random and destructive area of terrorism, resources on the Web range from background readings and legislation text from the Center for Democracy and Technology Counter-Terrorism Page (www.cdt.org/policy/terrorism/), to listings with descriptions of more than eighty terrorist groups identified in the State Department's Patterns of Global Terrorism (www.usis.usemb.se/terror/rpt1998/appb.html), to a backgrounder on what to do in the case of a terrorist attack, found at the Federal Emergency Management Agency site (www.fema.gov/library/terror.htm).

What you won't find: Any kind of comprehensive database of police reports or specific crimes across states won't be found online. While you can go to individual police agencies and get crime data, there is not a cumulative source for it. Also, criminal history records can't be retrieved online except for one state, Texas, where you search for a name and get a criminal history report back for $3.15 per report (records.txdps.state.tx.us/dps/default.cfm).

Great Scout Sites for Law Enforcement and Crime Resources

www.Officer.com: The Police Officer's Internet Directory

www.officer.com

Contact: 320 Cornell St.
Roslindale, MA 02131
police@officer.com

Why we picked this site: Their mission: "As a public service, we shall strive to maintain the most comprehensive and user-friendly law enforcement Web site in the world. The Directory shall always be fast, with a minimum of graphics, while still maintaining an aesthetically pleasing interface. We will only accept advertisers that offer law enforcement-related products and services." Who can argue with that? As for authority, it is run by James Meredith, a full-time police officer who lives and works in Boston, Massachusetts. With its honest and ambitious mission, clear organization, and authoritative Webmaster, this is the site to go to for crime links. While it is much more interested in comprehensiveness than selectivity, the good organization of the site allows you to make good choices about which resource to use.

Created: 1996.

How many sites: Over 6,000 sites.

Audience: The site was designed for police professionals but its links would be of interest to anyone looking for crime and criminal justice information.

How sites are selected: Links are scouted out by the Officer.com editors, but also submitted sites are added once they have been examined. They are added to the appropriate area. Links submitted to the site are added in twice-monthly updates (the first and third Mondays of the month).

How it's supported: The site is solely supported by paid advertisers (and only advertisers selling or providing services or products for law enforcement are accepted).

Searching: There are almost 100 different subject categories under which the law enforcement resources on this site are listed. Only seventeen of them are listed on the home page: Agencies, Associations, Computer Crimes, Criminal Justice, Employment, Hate Groups, Investigations, Labor Unions, Listservs, Memorials, Miscellaneous, Officer Down!, Police Officers, Police Supply, Special Ops, Training Events, Wanted. To see the rest, click on "Big Index." When you have narrowed the category to one you want, click on the name and you'll get a listing of appropriate sites.

What you get: Each of the categories is arranged differently, geographically or by further subject breakdown, and then in alphabetical order. Although there are no annotations or descriptions of the links, the organization and categorization are clear enough to make selection of appropriate sites easy. Click on the link and you're off to the site.

Design: The narrative on each sub-directory page and the somewhat cluttered look to the pages make it a little difficult to know what you are looking at. Also, the lack of space between the listings makes it hard to read.

Justice Information Center: National Criminal Justice Reference Service

www.ncjrs.org

Contact: National Criminal Justice Reference Service (NCJRS)

P.O. Box 6000

Rockville, MD 20849-6000

askncjrs@ncjrs.org

Why we picked this site: This site, from a very credible source, is well organized and selective in its linking to resources. With the selected categories, it covers all areas of crime and law enforcement concerns. It has the goal to be one of the most comprehensive sources of information on criminal and juvenile justice in the world. Its role as a "collection of clearinghouses supporting all bureaus of the U.S. Department of Justice, Office of Justice Programs: the National Institute of Justice, the Office of Juvenile Justice and Delinquency Prevention, the Bureau of Justice Statistics, the Bureau of Justice Assistance, the Office for Victims of Crime, the OJP Program Offices, and the Office of National Drug Control Policy" ensures the resources to which you are linked are high quality, credible information.

Created: August 1995.

How many sites: About 1,250 documents, links, and other resources are listed for the ten main categories.

Audience: Criminal justice professionals and researchers.

How sites are selected: Although they get some input from Web site users, most of the links come from surfing by the subject specialists employed by the clearinghouse. The emphasis is on quality and relevance, so only three or so sites are added to the directory each week. New listings are listed in the "New This Week" area; check there for the most current additions. All of the links are checked each month to ensure they are still working.

How it's supported: As a government-sponsored agency and particularly through the sponsorship of the agencies for which it is a clearinghouse (see listing in "Why we picked this site).

Topics covered: Corrections, Courts, Crime Prevention, Criminal Justice Statistics, Drugs and Crime, International, Juvenile Justice, Law Enforcement, Research and Evaluation, Victims.

Searching: You can click and browse the sites or use the search function. To Browse: select one of the above categories and click. For all of the categories but one, there is simply a breakdown of links by Documents, Web Sites, Gopher, FTP, News and Public Affairs and/or Listservs. The Victims category takes you to a listing of sub-categories, which then break down into the types of resources above. To Search: Enter the word you want to have searched into the search box. The search engine will look for documents that contain that word or Web site links with that word in the Web site name or address.

What you get: For the Web Site links, you get an alphabetical listing of the sites with Web addresses. In the Documents links, many of the documents linked to are available in either plain text files or in Adobe Acrobat files (which look like the original document).

Design: Very simple and clean, no frills.

Other features: The National Criminal Justice Reference Service Abstracts Database is available for free on the Web site. It provides summaries of criminal justice literature—government reports, journal articles, books, and more. This is a great deal because you used to have to pay for access on the Dialog online search service or through purchase of a CD-ROM.

Other Crime/Law Enforcement Sites
Law Enforcement Online
pimacc.pima.edu/dps/police.htm
Looking for your state or local law enforcement agency? Look no further. At Law Enforcement Online you'll find links to more than 3,000 agencies, arranged by Federal and National Agencies, State-County-City and Town Law Enforcement, Canadian Law Enforcement, University and College Police Agencies, Military Police, and Criminal Justice Organizations.

Organized Crime

www.crime.org

This somewhat misleadingly named Web site is actually a compilation of links to sources of crime statistics and a tutorial on the analysis of crime data.

Crime Prevention Resources

National Crime Prevention Council On-Line Resource Center

www.ncpc.org/

Home of McGruff the Crime Dog, this site has an array of useful tips, guides, and programs for helping to prevent crime to your person, in your home, and in your community.

Justice for Kids and Youth

www.usdoj.gov/kidspage/

Brought to you by the U.S. Department of Justice, this site for educating children and teens about crime issues is full of facts, quizzes, and resource guides that not just kids but adults too will find useful. There are sections about Internet safety, hate crimes, and how to get involved in crime prevention in your community.

Interesting Crime Coverage Sites

Police Scanner

www.policescanner.com/

Are those "true-to-life" police dramas not real enough for you? Then listen to live police (New York Police Department, Los Angeles Police Department, and the Dallas Police Department), fire (from Dallas), and aviation (from Dallas/Ft. Worth Air Traffic Control) calls. Using RealAudio streams, these calls, with all their crackles and jargon, put you right in the cruiser.

APB Online—The Source for Police and Crime News, Information and Entertainment

www.apbonline.com

Get original reporting on crimes from the APB staff, wire stories on crime, dossiers from the FBI on celebrities and information on missing persons. This "all-crime, all the time" site should serve all your needs for information on high, and low, crimes across the nation.

The Relocation Crime Lab

www2.homefair.com/calc/crime.html

Are you trying to select a new community to move to and you're concerned about the crime compared to where you live now? This handy tool has crime indexes for more than 500 U.S. cities. Just pick the city you are moving from, and find out how its crime rate compares to a city you are thinking of moving to.

FBI FOIA Electronic Reading Room

www.fbi.gov/foipa/main.htm

The Federal Bureau of Investigations has opened up some of its files because of the Freedom of Information Act. They have them here. Click on "Famous Persons" (Lucille Ball, John Lennon, Mickey Mantle, Marilyn Monroe, and others), Historical Cases (Escape from Alcatraz, John Wilkes Booth, The Hindenberg Disaster, Adolf Hitler), Gangster Era (Bonnie and Clyde, John Dillinger, Baby Face Nelson), or "Unusual Phenomenon" to get actual reproductions of the documents used in the cases.

Computer Crime

CyberAngels

www.cyberangels.org

The online version of the neighborhood vigilante group the Guardian Angels, this service, started by Curtis Sliwa, focuses on identifying and preventing various types of online crime. Read their mission statement (www.cyberangels.org/about/mission.html), and then send them a note of thanks. They find the sexual predators, scam artists, and child pornographers on the Net and notify the appropriate police agencies. They give lists of inappropriate Web sites for children to Web site filtering software companies. They are helping to make online a bit safer for everyone without, as they insist, stepping on First Amendment rights. They stand for free, but safe, Web access.

Great Scout Site with Terrorism Links

The Terrorism Research Center
www.terrorism.com/
Contact: TRC@terrorism.com

Why we picked this site: The Terrorism Research Center is dedicated to "informing the public of the phenomena of terrorism and information warfare. This site features essays and thought pieces on current issues, as well as links to other terrorism documents, research, and resources." Although it is not an extensive listing, its listings of links to terrorism resources are targeted and of high quality.

Created: October 1996.

How many sites: Only about 150 links, but all are annotated and carefully selected.

Audience: Students, policy makers, and other interested in terrorism issues.

How sites are selected: The TRC staff has academic expertise in terrorism, information warfare, low-intensity political violence, computer security, cryptography, law enforcement, national security, and defense policy. They select the sites in the directory.

How it's supported: They are not affiliated with any governmental agency or political slant. The Center accepts commercial sponsorship in exchange for advertising space on the Web site. "All proceeds from advertising sponsorships go to the financial maintenance of the TRC Web site."

Searching: The site is divided into two areas: Resources and Research. The links to other terrorism-related Web sites is under the Resources area. Click on the WWW Links label and get a selective and well-annotated list of terrorism resources organized under the categories: Governmental, Academic/Institutional, Other Links. Another listing of links is to documents related to terrorism. Click on Documents and see a listing of well-annotated (but not in any particular order) links to documents and essays.

What you get: A listing of the resources with annotations and links to the cited site.

Design: Very simple and straightforward with no graphics or fancy elements to slow download time.

Other Terrorism Sites

U.S. State Department: Travel Warnings & Consular Information Sheets

travel.state.gov/travel_warnings.html

If you are getting ready to travel overseas, check out the crime and terrorism risk with these comprehensive information sheets. They will denote areas to be careful of and the trend in kinds of crimes against tourists and foreigners.

State Department's Patterns of Global Terrorism Report

www.state.gov/www/global/terrorism/1998report/1998 index.html

This comprehensive report, issued each year in April, is available from the State Department. Find the 1995–1997 reports at the U.S. Embassy in Sweden site: www.usis.usemb.se/terror/index.html.

8

Minority Resources on the Web

When the Web was first available, the popular notion was that the people using the Internet were, for the most part, young, well-to-do, White males. In fact, an early study of Web users, conducted by GVU (Graphics, Visualization, and Usability Center at Georgia Tech's College of Computing) in January 1994, found that 56 percent of the respondents were between the ages of 21 and 30 and 94 percent were male!

This led to the cries of "information haves and information have nots," the creation of a "digital divide" between minorities, which, according to a recent study, continues to exist. In a study conducted in 1999 by the National Telecommunications and Information Administration titled "Falling through the Net: Defining the Digital Divide," it was found that the gap remains wide. The study found that online access rates are about twice as high for Whites (37.7 percent) as for Blacks (19 percent) or Hispanics (16.6 percent). (Read the report at www.ntia.doc.gov/ntiahome/fttn99/contents.html.)

Though these statistics might be disheartening for those who strive for equal access to information, information resources for members of minority and other demographic groups seem to be growing. The Web has become a way for cultural groups and special interests to share their resources, their art, language, stories, and support. In this chapter we will profile those Web scout sites that focus on Web sites that are *not* targeted at the White Anglo male. Look also at the chapter on Social Issues to find resources about diversity and social equality for minority groups. Here we will profile those resources that compile sites designed by, for, and about African Americans, Asian Americans, Latinos, Native Americans, Women, and Gays/Lesbians.

The best of these resources celebrate the unique cultures and concerns of these groups. They provide a community for chat, provide aids to locate services and support, they talk in the language and have the sensibilities of each group represented. As the intro to NetNoir states: "Our mission is simple: To be the #1 Black interactive online community in the world. To achieve that goal, we believe there are fundamental BLACK CULTURAL values that have to be reflected in the programming of our service." In each of the profiled services, the cultural values are reflected in the scout site's design and selection of resources. These services act as a knowing, friendly neighbor and help to make the World Wide Web a community.

They are also interested in helping to correct the demographic picture painted in the more mainstream surveys of Web use. Both the NetNoir and the WWWomen sites are running their own surveys to show the power and interests of what had been minority users of the Web who are developing a stronger voice and greater resources.

Great Scout Sites for Minority Group Resources

NetNoir
www.netnoir.com
Contact: 564 Mission Street, Unit 4
San Francisco, CA 94105

Why we picked this site: "NetNoir Online—the soul of cyber-space." It's a catchy motto, and appropriate for this portal site for Blacks on the Web. There are chat rooms, daily national and international Black-oriented news feeds, resources for specific communities (check out Sistah Connection for resources for Black women), employment opportunities, advice for Black business owners, and shops to buy Black books and art. There is also an extensive area called Black Web, providing links to other sites on the Web with information or resources of interest to Blacks. There are some activist aspects to the site, as well. For example, they are conducting their own survey of Internet usage by asking users of NetNoir to fill out a questionnaire. The goal: "There are many survey results floating around the Internet reporting on how many black people are online, who they are, and what they do. The media publicity surrounding various studies has developed certain impressions among the public. But are they correct?" The enterprising developers of NetNoir hope to find out.

Created: June 1995 by E. David Ellington and Malcolm CasSelle.

How many sites: Over 2,000 and growing at a rate of 4–5 percent a month.

Audience: "Your Home For Black Interactive Culture & Entertainment." Developed for those with an interest in Afrocentric topics and resources.

How sites are selected: Sites are self-submitted and placed into the appropriate categories. Sites are checked for availability about once every sixty days.

How it's supported: Advertising, sponsorships, and e-commerce are the revenue lines supporting the links service.

Topics covered: Arts, Culture, and Film; The Black Diaspora; Business and Career Development; Music; Organizations and

Associations; News and Politics; Black Greeks, Colleges and Alumni; Lifestyles and Hobbies; Personal Web Pages; Shopping, Expos and Fairs.

Searching: When you go to the home page of NetNoir, click on Black Web in the list of choices down the left-hand side. This takes you directly to a search screen for Black Web links—but it's complicated. The initial search gives only the options of locating all links in a particular category from the option box (see above), or you can type in the URL (Web address) of a site, or the site name. This doesn't seem to allow general searches of the directory. But look carefully, click on the Advanced Search link and get an additional search template page with the name and category boxes again, but also a "Description" box. Type a word there and it will look for the word in the brief description given of each site. Be sure to hit the reset button if you are going to do a new search. There are some improvements that could be made to the search functions of this site, but the range of materials available in the directory and the uniqueness of its focus make it worth muddling through some of the ambiguities to find the nuggets.

What you get: A chart of the results is displayed that has the name of the Web site linked, the address and description, a rating, and the category it falls in.

Design: The design of the front page is quite crowded because they have so much to offer, but once you get to the Black Web pages, the design is simply the search boxes.

LatinoWeb
www.latinoweb.com/
Contact: P.O. Box 3877
Montebello, CA 90640
info@latinoweb.com

Why we picked this site: LatinoWeb's goal: "a virtual information center for Latino resources." LatinoWeb's mission: "to empower the Latino community by providing a gateway on the Internet where private, non-profit and public sectors can exchange information freely." We picked this site because it accomplishes both its goal and mission very well. We're not the only ones who think so. LatinoWeb was recently given four stars by *Yahoo! Internet Life* magazine (five stars is the highest possible).

Created: The idea for the service began in March 1995 when they began consulting with Microsoft on the concept of an electronic chamber of commerce for Hispanics. It evolved to this independent service soon afterward.

How many sites: About 2,500 links.

Audience: The Latino community.

How sites are selected: Sites are submitted by the people who create them, but they are reviewed by the LatinoWeb staff before inclusion. They try not to duplicate sites, so if there is one site that lists several sites, they will use that one site instead of individually listing all of the others. About 15 percent of the service links to pages within the service (different features); the rest are links out to other Latino-focused sites.

How it's supported: Advertising and Web design services provide the support. Some of the money generated from online commerce on the site (selling computers, for example) is being funneled back to build better access to the technology in the Hispanic community.

Topics covered: Art, Book Store, Business, Chat Room, Classified Ads, Education, Events, Free Software, Government, Jobs, Music, Non-Profit, Personal Pages, Publications, Search Tools, Sports, Radio & TV, Resources.

Searching: The directory is very simply accessed. Either you can select one of the categories (see above) and browse through the listings or you can type a word or two into the search box and it will find links with those words in the title or description. Typing more than one word in the box presumes an "and" search (i.e., type in "Guatemala art," it will find only listings with both of those words in the description).

What you get: A listing of the Web sites—with the name of the Web site linked to the site itself, and the description of the site.

Design: Very simple, clean, no-frills design.

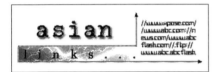

ABCFlash—Comprehensive Asian Links List

abcflash.com/links/

Contact: cyoah@abcflash.com

Why we picked this site: The comprehensive categories, and the clear-cut arrangement of the resources make this site a very useful resource for links to Asian interests in the United States and around the world.

Created: 1997.

How many sites: More than 4,000 sites in 38 categories.

Audience: The Asian American community and those who are interested in finding and using Asian American businesses and products.

How sites are selected: Editors at ABCFlash find and select the sites included in the directory.

How it's supported: ABCFlash's link directory is supported by ABC, the Asian Buying Consortium, whose mission is: "ABC seeks to build the premier membership buying club for North American Asians and Asia Watchers. Through ABC's membership clout, we will seek to be an advocate for our members to continue to provide new discounts and benefits."

Topics covered: News & Business, Society & Culture, Entertainment, Lifestyle, Regional, Reference are the main categories with sub-categories under each.

Searching: There is no search function in the Asian Links directory, which would be a problem if the link categories and sub-categories weren't so well defined. Click on the category for Issues/ Politics, for example, and you'll get sub-categories like affirmative action, health, immigration, multiracial, racism and violence, sexuality, stereotypes. Simply click on a sub-category to get the links listing.

What you get: A listing of the links, many of them with a description of the Web site's contents.

Design: Very simple, clean design.

Index of Native American Resources on the Internet
www.hanksville.org/NAresources/
Contact: kstrom@hanksville.phast.umass.edu

Why we picked this site: With its focus on Native American resources and the clear and structured organization of the links, this site maintains its goal: to provide information by and about Native American people and cultures.

Created: Karen Strom started and has maintained this directory since mid-1994.

How many sites: More than 4,000; 3 to 10 sites are added daily.

Audience: Developed for the Native American community and only secondarily for the general community.

How sites are selected: Links are sent to the directory maintainer, Karen Strom, who then checks them and includes them if they are relevant/useful sites. She also adds sites found in her own browsing through checking the links on good sites to other sites. She also trolls university department sites for electronic texts and relevant information that might not ever be submitted. Commercial sites are generally not included. Sites are checked thoroughly before inclusion for accuracy, tone/attitude. She is stringent in her policy to link only to Native American resources, excluding, for example, works of art with an Indian theme but whose artists are not Indian. The links in the directory are checked each night to ensure that they are still available.

How it's supported: This is entirely an individual effort. The site will be moving to the Heard Museum server in Phoenix from the University of Massachusetts.

Topics covered: Culture, history, language, health, education, indigenous knowledge, Native American art, archaeology, legal, genealogy, government, non-profits, nations, activist sites, books, electronic texts, other indices.

Searching: There are two approaches to accessing the resources of this index. You may click on one of the categories in the table on the home page or else use the search function.

What you get: If you click on one of the categories, you get a listing with good subject divisions under the main category. Look, for example, at Book Sources, and you'll get a links list organized by Books Online, Organizations, Online Journals, Presses, Journals, Book Lists with Native American Content, Home Pages for Native

American Authors, Libraries, Book Stores Online. When you use the search method, the results tell you which categories the terms you searched for appear in and then you click on one of the categories and get the whole list. *Tip:* Use the "find in page" function of your browser to jump to the part of the page where the word you searched for appears.

Design: A simple table and clean white background make this a very uncluttered, easy-to-use site.

WWWomen

www.wwwomen.com
Contact: webmaster@wwwomen.com

Why we picked this site: This Yahoo!-esque site, with the categories in hot pink text, is a winner for so many reasons—the comprehensiveness of the resources, the great organization of the links, and the good spirit shown in why it was created. Read their introduction: "You have just gotten onto the World Wide Web. You are a painter and are interested in learning more about women artists. You go to your favorite search site and put in the key words, 'women artists.' A list of sites come up but somehow you have a vague suspicion that not everything is there. Is there a place where people focus only on finding sites that primarily focus on women?

"Enter WWWomen, the most inclusive, up-to-date search site for women's topics. Searching WWWomen, you can be assured that our team of online surfers (who can verify links as valid and relevant) have compiled the most comprehensive list possible . . . . WWWomen has already sorted through all of the irrelevant and invalid links for you so that you obtain the fastest and most relevant searches possible." That is our ideal description of a scout site— focused, validated, comprehensive, fast, relevant.

Created: The company started in late 1995, and the Web site launched in February 1996. They launched the site because they were looking for women's resources and Yahoo!, at the time, did not have a category for women.

How many sites: More than 20,000 sites are listed.

Audience: "Anyone who is looking for topics relating to women."

How sites are selected: Sites can be submitted and robot searches are conducted of the entire Web to locate women-related resources that can be reviewed and evaluated by WWWomen editors for validity and relevance. "WWWomen accepts sites where the primary focus of the site or resource is related to women or owned by women. If one of the sub-sections of your site has a separate and woman-focused section, we will list the sub-section URL but not the main URL." They also give out the Top WWWomen Site Award using the following criteria (interesting for those of you who are creating a Web site; keep these things in mind . . . .): "Reviewers evaluate each site for content (depth, thoroughness, frequency of updating, community-building, relevant links, generally worth recommending), inspiration (is the site specifically inspirational to women), exploration (well organized and easy to navigate), and presentation (overall appealing design, original graphics, use of leading edge tools/techniques). Content is weighted as 70 percent of the score, inspiration 10 percent, exploration 5 percent, and presentation 15 percent."

How it's supported: It is a privately held company and is using revenues from banner ads and other marketing objectives.

Topics covered: Arts & Entertainment, Women in Business, Community & Government, Women & Computers, Diversity Among Women, Education of Women, Feminism, Health and Safety Issues, Lesbian Visibility, Mothers & Family, Personal Time for Women, Publications, Women's Resources, Science & Technology, Women Go Shopping, Women's Sports, Women Throughout History.

Searching: Just as in Yahoo!, the main categories available and sub-categories are on the home page. Click on one of them to get the listing of relevant hits. The search box on the home page is good if you have one or two words to search by; the default is an "and" search. If you want to do more complex searching (and use other connectors, "or," "not") then go to the Options page. The search finds listings with the word you've searched for in the title of the site, the address, or the description.

What you get: A listing of relevant hits, organized by categories. Each of the listings has the Web site name (linked to the Web site) and a description of the contents.

Design: Reminiscent of Yahoo! with the Category/sub-category table on the home page. This design makes it easy to use and the search functions are well defined.

Other features: Chat rooms and support groups online. Sponsor of the WWWomen's WebRing, linking related women's sites together.

Queer Resources Directory
qrd.tcp.com/qrd/.html/QRD-home-page.html

The Other Queer Page
www.im1ru12.org/toqp/
These two sites are links sites for Web pages of interest to gays and lesbians. Neither of these sites offers much more than broadly categorized links, in no particular order, and with little or no description. Together, they list more than 25,000 resources and provide a great linking service, but they do not have many of the other qualifications for a Great Scout site and so do not get a full profile here.

Other Minority Resources Scout Sites
EverythingBlack.com
www.everythingblack.com/

A Yahoo! style design and good descriptions of the sites help make this a useful resource.

Noir Online
www.noironline.com/
This is no match for NetNoir in terms of scope, but it is a nicely organized site with good categories that can help you find a few of the most relevant sites.

The AfroAmerican WebRing
www.halcon.com/halcon/1ring.html
Links to 1,700 different Afro-American related sites.

CLNet
latino.sscnet.ucla.edu/
One of the earliest sites specializing in this area, their purpose, "Building Chicana/o Latina/o Communities through Networking," is well served by this well-designed site. The resources in the subject areas are somewhat limited, but carefully selected.

NativeWeb
www.nativeweb.org
The strength of this site is its different ways to look for resources available. There is a geographic index, a nations index, and a subject index. With message boards, chat rooms, and other communication links, this is an excellent meeting place for those interested in Native American topics and people. Started in 1993, it moved from one university to another until it got its own Web site in 1997. There are now over 3,000 links, and this is growing at a rate of about 100 a month. This is a site to watch. In November 1998, NativeWeb will become a nonprofit organization, and it is seeking grants and funding to study technology and indigenous nations.

Indian Circle

www.indiancircle.com

This is the beginning of a WebRing of Native American sites. One of the very useful resources is a listing of all the Federally recognized Indian Tribes with links to their Web sites, if they have one. This is run by Seminole Indian Chief Jim Billie.

Cybergrrl's Women'sGuide

home.cybergrrl.com/planet/web/

More of a channel site (bringing in articles, polls, chat, and links onto one page), this resource covers Arts & Culture, Body & Spirit, Business & Money, Education & Career, Family & Community, Girls Only, News & Issues, Recreation & Style, Tech & Net, Women Behind the Web.

For More Information

Ebo, Bosah L., ed. *Cyberghetto or Cybertopia?: Race, Class, and Gender on the Internet.* Westport, CT: Praeger Publishing, 1998.

Gregory, Vicki Lovelady. *Multicultural Resources on the Internet.* Englewood, CO: Teacher Ideas Press, 1998.

Battle, Stafford L. and Ray O. Harris. *The African American Resource Guide to the Internet and Online Services.* New York: McGraw-Hill Book Company, 1997.

Sherman, Aliza. *Cybergrrl!: A Woman's Guide to the World Wide Web.* New York: Ballantine Books, 1998.

Dawson, Jeff. *Gay Lesbian Online: Your Indispensable Guide to Cruising the Queer Web.* Los Angeles, CA: Alyson Publications, 1998.

9

Online Shopping on the Web

Ahhh, online shopping, where the virtual and the real worlds merge when the virtual order is delivered to your real doorstep. I (Nora) first did some online shopping around Christmas of 1992 when one of my sons was a rabid Teenage Mutant Ninja Turtles fan and HAD TO HAVE the Ninja Blimp for his Christmas to be complete. None of the stores in the area had it—they were sold out. But online on CompuServe I was able to find a toy sales area that had it. Christmas was saved! Now there is eToys (www.etoys.com) where you can find toy deals by category or trade name. Parents can avoid the "joys" of dragging acquisitive kids through Toys R Us forever.

As the Internet has moved away from pure academics to more crass commercialism, the opportunities for spending real money in the virtual world of the World Wide Web have grown. Music and books, fruits and flowers, jewelry and junk, computers and cars—all are out there, ready to be bought. It is a buyer's market. Online auctions are a booming business. Maybe the only ones not enthused about online commerce are the mass media, which are extremely worried by the cutting out of the middle man of advertising and the increased direct connection of businesses to their consumers—they need those advertising dollars. From the elite (Neiman Marcus: www. neimanmarcus.com) to the mainstream (Wal-Mart: www.wal-mart.com), retailers are putting their wares online for the busy consumer.

The dark side of this bright online shopping scene is, of course, scams, rip-offs, and the security of online transactions. But, as with so many perceived problems on the Internet, there was a pre-Internet analogy. The Internet certainly didn't create scam artists or credit card fraud. There's a great Dilbert cartoon that deals with online shopping. Two characters are sitting at a restaurant table and one character says, "I would never buy something over the Internet. I'd hate to have my credit card number floating around out there. There are a lot of unscrupulous people on the net . . . ." as he hands his credit card to the waitress, who leaves and comes back in the next frame wearing a mink coat. Hmmmm.

But for those of you concerned about the security of online shopping, here is an explanation of how Web sites are creating secure shopping services. This explanation comes from David Green, Webmaster of CouchPotato, an online shopping guide (see "Other Web Shopping Scout Sites" below).

"Any information you send or receive over the Internet could be intercepted by anyone physically between you and the receiving party. This is where the word 'secure' comes into play. Whenever you enter confidential information into a Web page, make sure that the URL begins with 'https:'. This means that you are using a secure page. Depending on the Web browser you are using, a lock or a key may show up in the very bottom part of the browser when you are viewing a secure page. Look for this bar whenever you enter confidential information! If it is not there, then your information can be intercepted by a third party while in transit!

"Security is accomplished using a method called SSL (Secure Sockets Layer). All information you send or receive when using a secure Web page is encrypted. Anyone in the middle who intercepts the transfer of information will only see gibberish."

So, if you feel safe enough to make an online purchase, be smart enough to select carefully what you are buying. Some of the consumer's best friends are online to help them in making either online or off-line purchasing choices. *Consumer Reports*, from the Consumers Union (www. consumer reports.org/), provides all the great reports and alerts but this is one example of needing to spend money to save money. Consumer Reports Online has a monthly or annual subscription for full access to the contents.

One of the tools to help you make the most of your online spending is the "shopbot." Shopbots are programs that roam the Web and "comparison shop" for you by finding the prices of products on various sites. Look at the Bot Spots listing of shopping bots (www.botspot.com/search/s-shop.htm) to find various online shopping comparison programs to help you locate items and compare prices. There are bots to find the best online book and music deals, ones that scan all the online auction sites to find out what's open for bidding, and C/Net's Online Shopper for finding the best computer deals (www.shopper.com).

ShopFind (www.shopfind.com) is a search engine of over 3,000 online merchants. It goes out and indexes the contents of all those vendors' pages and provides you a listing, with the price, of where the item you are looking for can be purchased. This is fast and easy comparison shopping. Forget about letting your fingers do the walking, let your mouse do the looking!

Types of Online Shopping Aids on the Web

Books: ACSES—Compares the price and availability of books in twenty-five different online bookstores (www.acses.com).

Computers: PriceScan—Pick out the type of equipment or an exact brand name and click to get a listing of the available prices for that hardware on the Web (www.pricescan.com).

Antiques: Antiqnet—Use their database to find the particular items you are looking for and you'll be connected to dealers from around the country. Each item has a photo and detailed description along with the dealer contact information (www.antiqnet.com).

Cars: Car Prices—Their AutoVantage service connects you with auto dealers in your area who have the type of car you are looking for. There is also a used car area (www.carprices.com).

Great Scout Sites for Shopping

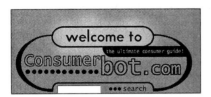

ConsumerBot.com
www.consumerbot.com
Contact: ConsumerBot.
925 Royal Crown Lane
Colorado Springs, Colorado 80906
service@consumerBot.com

Why we picked this site: Billing itself as "The Ultimate Consumer Guide," this is a full-service shopping destination. ConsumerBot. com uses a "channels" design to great effectiveness, providing a variety of types of services and links under a particular category for each of the shopping areas. This site does not limit itself to just those who want to buy, but also provides resources and helpful guides to those who want to provide online shopping opportunities to Web users. Although we usually disdain scout sites that only list those sites that pay a listing fee, this is an exception. One reason is that only about half the sites are in because of a merchant fee payment. Also, because we are talking about commerce, having sites that pay to promote themselves seems appropriate. But, overall, it is the unique and comprehensive design of the pages with their useful links that makes this a standout, even with the paid listings. The folks at "ConsumerBot" realize there are a number of sites that provide links to online vendors. They are working to make this site a "360-degree shopping experience," a "shopping destination," a place where online consumers will return for guidance as well as pointers to merchants. They have succeeded.

Created: Late 1996. Originally called "A Shopping Guide."

How many sites: About 2,600 different merchants.

Audience: Online shoppers and merchants.

How sites are selected: About half of the listed sites are paid entries. There are various categories of paid listings: the higher the merchant fee that's paid, the higher that site will appear on the directory. The other half of the sites are included because they provide that well-rounded shopping channel resource by linking to good content and specific vendors or manufacturers who might not be willing to pay a fee to be listed. As this is a family-oriented site, there are no links to adult products. And, as this is a site that wants return users, satisfied users, it only links to sites that provide secure online transactions.

How it's supported: Merchants pay a fee that supports the site, but a portion of the fee is pooled for "co-op advertising," which goes toward promoting ConsumberBot.com. This promotion of ConsumberBot.com drives traffic to the site and, ultimately, to the merchants' sites. ConsumberBot.com also provides a listing service for the merchants by making sure their sites are entered into the major search engine sites.

Topics covered: There are 15 channels: Around the House, Auction Zone, Books & Calendars, Entertainment, Fashion Zone, Gift Department, Food & Drink, Free Stuff, Health & Beauty, Kids & Family, Services, Sports, Technology Center, Transportation, and Travel & Adventure.

Searching: Click on one of the categories and get the "channel" page for that category, or use the search box to find stores with the term you searched.

What you get: Each of the categories provides different listings, links, and features. Click on the "Around the House" channel, for example, and there are six sub-categories: Arts & Crafts, Furnishings, Home Electronics, Home & Garden, Kitchen Corner, and Tools. Select one of those to get a list of links to stores, recommended sites, and recommended magazines. "Recommended Magazines" links to a service where you can subscribe to a given magazine. The Automotive Channel gives you links to online auto buying sites and links to sites with good information about autos. Down the right-hand side are links to Auto Manufacturers, Automotive Chat channels, and Auto Enthusiasts sites. Check out Sports and get the merchants' links as well as links to Sports News sites, Pro Sports pages, Specialty shops, books and magazines, and sports equipment manufacturer sites. Each of the links listings gives an abstract of the types of things you can buy or find on the site.

Design: The consistent design, with links to all the major categories on the left, the links listings in the center, and the "ephemera" for that particular channel on the right, make navigation and use of the site easy and reliable.

Other features: There are links to information for online consumers and others who want to sell on the Web.

WebMarket
www.webmarket.com
Contact: go2net, Inc.
999 Third Avenue, Suite 4700
Seattle, Washington 98104
webmaster@go2net.com

Why we picked this site: This clever combination of an online shopping sites' consumer guide and a price comparison search engine of online shops makes this site the online shopper's best friend. The great annotations and evaluations of shopping sites and the "consumer guide" with thorough profiling of online merchants gives you all the information you need to make an informed and cost-conscious online purchase.

Created: April 1998.

How many sites: 80–90.

Audience: Price conscious online shoppers.

How sites are selected: The sites that are scanned for price comparisons are the key online shopping sites, selected by Web users and go2net staff.

How it's supported: A project of go2net Inc., which operates other large Web sites, such as MetaCrawler, StockSite, and Silicon Investor.

Topics covered: Apparel, Books & Stationery, Computer Hardware, Consumer Electronics, Department Stores, Games & Toys, General Merchandise, Gifts, Music, Movies & Video, Office Supplies, Outdoor & Sporting Goods, Travel.

Searching: Select one of the categories, say, Outdoor & Sporting Goods, and get a page with several pull-down boxes. Pick from the "Category" list (Climbing, Clothes, Cycling, Fishing, Hunting, Kids, Other, Shoes, Sports, Travel Gear), determine price range (At least, At most), or just type a keyword in the search box.

What you get: The listing of items that fit your profile comes up in chart form with columns for Merchant, Name, Price, Shipping Cost, Product Info, Category, and Availability. You can even sort the results by Merchant Name, Price, or Category. Click on Product Name to see more information.

Design: This deceptively simple and clean design hides a complex database allowing great searchability.

Other features: The Consumer Guide gives profiles of each of the online merchants in WebMarket. Detailed information on the site's shopping features includes whether they have secure transactions, an online shopping cart system, online order tracking service, customer information privacy, gift wrapping service, live customer support, international shipping service, or a product search capability on the Web site. Click on the spyglass icon and get even more information about the online merchant including payment methods accepted and ratings of satisfaction by users of the service.

Other Web Shopping Scout Sites

www.CouchPotatoe.Com

www.couchpotatoe.com

There are so many different directory sites for online shopping, but CouchPotatoe hits on so many of our great Scout site criteria. The listings are well organized in Yahoo!-like categories, there is a stringent review process before sites are added to the links list, and site quality is maintained through a set of requirements for every site included in the directory. What this site lacks in quantity, it has in the quality and rigor in which it maintains the listings. Even though this is a "new kid" on the online shopping block, the potential of the site and the enthusiasm of its creator to "build the best online shopping directory" make this site worth the visit.

CyberSaver Mall

www.cybersaver.com

They, like the CouchPotatoe site, only list stores that offer secure transaction services. They divide the 150 or so merchants they link to into 22 different shopping categories including Art, Crafts and Hobbies, Furniture, Health and Beauty, Optical Site, Ticket Booth, and Travel Center.

@InterMall

www.1mall.com

"Shop the world from your home." The well-organized categories and useful abstracts about each online shopping site's contents make this another of the online shopper's best guides.

For More Information

Lowery, Joseph. *Buying Online for Dummies.* Indianapolis, IN: IDG Books Worldwide, 1998.

10

Politics on the Web

In an age of political spin, the World Wide Web is gaining on traditional media as an ideal place to spin it. By mid-summer 1998, 63 percent of the fall campaigns already had Web sites and 21 percent more expected to have one before Election Day, according to a survey of 270 local, state, and federal candidates, campaign managers, and key staff members in *Campaigns & Elections* magazine (September 1998).

Digital campaigning pre-dates the Web. Early in the 1992 presidential campaign, Jerry Brown chatted live with members of both the Genie and CompuServe online services and Ross Perot distributed his press releases on the dial-up U.S. Newswire service. The Clinton campaign used an electronic mailing list to send the full text of press releases, speeches, and campaign events to a savvy group of subscribers.

"The Clinton and Perot campaign organizations were the first to realize that e-mail and electronic communications could take advantage of the 24-hour news cycle and simultaneously distribute information to campaign operatives," said Mark Stencel, politics editor at WashingtonPost.com. "E-mail is the 'killer app' for campaigning on the Internet." But beyond the presidential hopefuls (and some amusing parodies of their sites), relatively few candidates for other offices had Web sites in 1996.

"Now it's almost unthinkable for a candidate not to have an e-mail address and Web site," said Stencel. Candidate URLs are advertised on campaign literature, billboards, and bumper stickers. Now there are also sites for campaign consultants and the business of political campaigning; you can find out where to buy those buttons and have bumper stickers printed.

Print journalism started to go online with political coverage for the 1996 presidential elections. PoliticsUSA, started by *National Journal* and *The Hotline* in 1995, merged with *The Washington Post* and ABC News the following summer to become PoliticsNow. In 1997 they went their separate ways. AllPolitics from *Time* and CNN launched in 1996.

Early efforts by groups advocating a new era of "electronic democracy" have not yet succeeded in turning the Internet into our nation's new town hall. But these efforts continue to multiply as Web access grows and technology improves. You can register to vote, listen to the candidates debate, and participate in endless and sometimes vituperative political discussions, at a national, local, or global level. "The whole idea is that it [the Internet] will make it easier to have a direct democracy . . . to inform yourself, interact, form a view, and communicate it directly, " said Policy.com co-founder, William R. "Sam" Sneed III.

The act of voting itself is still not implemented anywhere on the Web. But information you need to know to make a decision about how to vote and where and when to do so is now widely available—and presented with increasingly sophisticated technology that makes it easier to find and use. Around the nation, the secretaries of state are increasingly active in making voter and election information available. In the states, the most important political resources can be found at these sites, where you may find collections of election results, candidate lists, text of ballot initiatives, voter guides, and profiles of lobbyists online.

In the political realm, the Web has taken the lead in two of our nation's most highly charged issues—one undeniably for the better, the other, perhaps, for the worse.

Campaign finance—investigations into scandals and debate over possible remedies and reforms—is the subject of a wealth of resources on the Web today. From the Federal Election Commission (FEC) to the secretaries of states to advocacy organizations for reform to journalism's best and brightest computer-assisted reporting specialists, data about campaign finance and spending are being collected in electronic form and made available for viewing, downloading, and searching so that each citizen can "follow the money" and make up his mind about a candidate's campaign practices and potential allegiances to special interest groups or individuals. You can download the entire database of federal campaign filings from the FEC or search it by name, ZIP code, industry, or employer at Tony Raymond's FECINFO site. You can download data for several states from the National Institute for Computer Assisted Reporting or search individual state information at official sites like Hawaii's Secretary of State or the newspaper-supported Virginia Public Access Project. You can look for both data and analysis at the non-partisan Center for Responsive Politics or scan the actual reports at Florida's Secretary of State. With all of this information on money in politics out in the sunshine, reform is up to us as Netizens and citizens.

But another highly charged issue—scandal—has been fueled by the Web's openness. Anyone can publish a rumor or create a seemingly authoritative display of its proof. From diatribes proclaiming conspiracy in the death of Vincent Foster to pre-emptive publication of the Monica Lewinsky story by Matt Drudge's *Drudge Report*, the Web has become our contemporary medium of instant gossip, opinion, and flame-throwing. Even anonymous postings may gain credence as they are stirred up and stewed in the global pot. Keep your mind focused on the source of the information you are reading and hang on tight for the wild ride.

Functionally, the major problem in discovering comprehensive and useful directories of political Web sites is that politics changes every two years. Sites come and go and trying to keep anything current is difficult. "History disappears because Web sites disappear," Stencel said.

Also, most of the directories we found did not include search capabilities, so sometimes the information within them was difficult to find. We've tried to highlight some of the best subject sites, but be aware that you may have to try more than one to get to exactly what you're looking for.

CAUTION: As we've noted above, watch out for the source of your information. Partisanship is intrinsic to politics and all points of view are represented on the Web. Ask yourself: Who has published this and what is their agenda?

Political Materials on the Web

Campaign finance: Center for Responsive Politics (www. opensecrets.org), Campaign Finance Information Center (www. campaignfinance.org), Federal Election Commission (www.fec. gov), FECINFO (www.tray.com/fecinfo).

Polls and polling: The Roper Center (www.ropercenter. uconn.edu).

Parody sites: During the 1996 campaign many sites were started up; in particular there were several with domain names that were *very close* to the candidates' official sites, some of them pornographic as well. Take a look at the (still current) White House (not X-rated) parody at www.whitehouse.net.

Lobbyists: Federal registered lobbyist database at the Center for Responsive Politics (www.opensecrets.org/lobbyists).

News sites: AllPolitics (CNN, *Time*, and *Congressional Quarterly*: www.allpolitics.com); WashingtonPost.com/Politics (www.washington post.com/politics); ABC News.com Political Nation (abcnews.go.com/sections/politics); Roll Call On-line (www. rollcall.com); the National Journal's Cloakroom (www. cloakroom.com).

Political newswires: U.S. Newswire (www.usnewswire.com), PR Newswire (www.prnewswire.com).

Politics business resources: Political Resources Online, a searchable directory of political products and services with over 3,000 company listings (www.politicalresources.com).

2000 Presidential Election: Several sites are already operational, for example, WhiteHouse 2000 (www.niu.edu/newsplace/white house.html).

Scandals: Skeleton Closet, "All the Dirt on All the Candidates—Because Character DOES Matter" (www.realchange.org); the Drudge Report (www.drudgereport.com).

What's missing: Authoritative and current political almanacs, dictionaries, and encyclopedias are still in the realm of fee-based or print-only worlds.

Great Scouts for Politics on the Web

Project Vote Smart
1-888-VOTE SMART
Tracking the performance of over 13,000 political leaders:
President, Congress, Governors & State Legislators

Project Vote Smart
www.vote-smart.org
Contact: Chris Kaltwasser, Director of Online Services
Project Vote Smart
129 N.W. Fourth St. #204
Corvallis, OR 97330
comments@vote-smart.org

Why we picked this site: Project Vote Smart represents a major effort to provide information for decision making by citizens across the nation. The non-profit, non-partisan organization's Founding Board includes prominent national leaders like George McGovern, Geraldine Ferraro, Newt Gingrich, Mark Hatfield, and Bill Bradley. The project is produced by an army of interns, under the guidance of the project staff in Corvallis, Oregon, and Boston, Massachusetts. Research information collected by Vote Smart is based on extensive candidate questionnaires on issues and biographical information and information on performance and voting records from other sources.

Vote Smart is valuable for keeping previous years' history of elections and candidates—some going back to 1995—as well. The directory of links is comprehensive, if somewhat disorganized. Vote Smart's Web Yellow Pages is a free printed Web guide incorporating the links collected at Vote Smart, also available for downloading and browsing at the site. And Vote Smart volunteers will do research for you by telephone on weekdays.

Created: Launched on the Web in 1995 after prior online presence via bulletin board, FTP, and Gopher sites.

How many sites: More than 10,000 links to Web sites and e-mail addresses of politicians, 1,500 issue-oriented links and 3,000 state government and politics links.

Audience: A political tool kit for citizens.

How sites are selected: College student interns and volunteers make up 90 percent of the staff evaluating sites.

How it's supported: A non-profit, non-partisan project funded entirely by the individual contributions of over 50,000 members and foundation grants.

Topics covered: Candidates, Elections, National and State Political Parties, Political Resources, Research and Statistics (Demographics and Maps, Legal Resources, Political Science Resources, Polling), Political Humor, Think Tanks, sites where you can participate. Research the Issues offers links to information on forty-five issue areas, including affirmative action, gun control, foreign policy, seniors, and terrorism.

Contents: Browsable directory of links, integrated with comprehensive, independently collected data from Project Vote Smart's many research projects. Comprehensive state links in several topics make this a basic source.

Searching: No search is available, but the site map helps. Link annotations are descriptive but not evaluative. Not all the links in the directory are annotated.

Advanced searching: No.

Design: Simple text pages with clear delineation between internal information and outside links, but there is so much information on this site that a search feature is sorely missed.

Other features: Biographies: Project Vote Smart has compiled the biographies of over 13,000 candidates and elected officials including the president, members of Congress, governors, and state legislators. National Political Awareness test is sent to all congressional, gubernatorial, and state legislative candidates shortly after each state's primary. During the presidential election year, a special Presidential NPAT is sent to all primary and general election candidates. Candidates who do not return a completed questionnaire "fail" the test. If you don't know who represents you in Congress, just type in your ZIP code on the home page here.

Help or FAQ: Help on navigating the site, FAQ about the site, a site map, and other useful guides are offered.

Policy.com
www.policy com
Contact: William R. "Sam" Sneed III
A2S2 Digital Projects, Inc.
1500 K Street N.W.
Washington, DC 20005
sam@a2s2.com

Why we picked this site: The Policy.com site is a news and information service for the public policy community and citizens in the United States. It offers non-partisan one-stop shopping for policy news, including partnerships with independent policy organizations that provide content directly to Policy.com or who have policy-related content on their sites, and access to news sources, like the Associated Press and UPI. Policy.com offers news, analysis, and links to organizations and research on the issues. "The mission is to empower people as digital citizens to have access to a lot of critical information to take them beyond sound bites . . . not just information but real knowledge related to content," Sneed said. Prominent policy movers and shakers provide content to this site, which is timely, serious, evaluative, and comprehensive.

Created: April 1995.

How many sites: 8,700+.

Audience: "Digital citizens": legislators, policymakers, policy analysts, journalists, professors and students and individuals interested in public policy.

How sites are selected: Policy.com staff follows news industry ethical guidelines to aggregate accurate, comprehensive, timely, non-partisan policy-related news and information from the Internet. They are particularly concerned with balance of ideology and political perspective of providers' information, not with quality of design and presentation of information.

How it's supported: Advertising and sponsorships and partnerships with content providers.

Topics covered: Issues library (over 300 topics), Community Directory, Think Tanks, Advocacy Groups, Associations, Foundations, Businesses, Universities, U.S. Government, Foreign Governments, International Organizations, Media, Other Resources.

Contents: Browse alphabetically or use a form to search a database of five Policy.com areas: Community (database of annotated Web links to think tanks, associations, businesses, advocacy groups, universities, and media), Issues Library (an extensive listing of policy-related articles on the Web), Feature Events (in RealAudio), Policy Calendar (daily listing of events), and Newsstand (reviews of policy-related journals).

What you get: A search provides, for Community listings: description of the organization—usually furnished by the organization—and link to its site. For Issues Library: abstract of the document and link to the text.

Advanced searching: The advanced search form offers separate fielded searches for each of the five areas. You can limit your search by date or twenty-five issues categories, as well as title, keyword, author.

Design: Frame-within-frames design can be frustrating when you link to outside sites. Remember to use your browser's "Back" button.

Other features: Issue of the Week offers detailed coverage of a policy topic in the news. The issues are archived and searchable.

Help or FAQ: Help for searching; extensive editorial guidelines.

Other Top Politics Sites

Politics1

www.politics1.com

Ron Gunzburger, an attorney and political consultant, created this site, which is chock full of listings, many annotated, with terrific illustrations taken from Gunszburger's collection of political memorabilia. There are online memorabilia auctions and a political bookstore here, too.

Jefferson Project

www.capweb.net/classic/jefferson

This guide to political resources online is large and bills itself as comprehensive, but does not annotate or provide criteria for selection. Topics included are Parties, Do-it-yourself Politics, State Resources, Political Parties, Political Humor, The Left, The Right, The Issues, Government Resources, Political Watchdogs, International Resources, Voicebox—Make your voice heard!

Political Information

www.politicalinformation.com

This search engine indexes more than 4,000 political or policy Web sites, allowing targeted searches limited to political information. The sites included cover the topics Campaigns/Elections, Commentary/News, Federal/State Government, Grassroots, Issues, Parties and Organizations, Research Tools and Today in Congress. A search for presidential candidate Bill Bradley pulled up highly relevant sites and put the campaign's home page right on top. This slice of the Web will be growing in the 2000 election year, so we hope this search site keeps on top of it!

Political Science Resources on the Web

www.lib.umich.edu/libhome/Documents.center/polisci.html

Part of the University of Michigan Library Documents Center site (see Chapter 16, Government Information on the Web), this provides extensive annotated searchable links. It is highly recommended.

Political Resources on the Net

www.agora.stm.it/politic

This English-language site, based in Italy, is a searchable directory of more than 16,000 sites linked to political resources around the globe. It's the best international site, and also includes a large U.S. section.

Political Site of the Day
www.aboutpolitics.com
Check here for the best new political sites. The archive of daily selections goes back to 1995.

For More Information

Selnow, Gary W. *Electronic Whistle-Stops: The Impact of the Internet on American Politics*. Westport, CT: Praeger, 1998.

Browning, Graeme. *Electronic Democracy: Using the Internet to Transform American Politics*. Medford, NJ: Information Today/CyberAge Books, 1999.

11

Religion on the Web

Benedictine monks (www.bac.edu/monastery/).

Santeria priests (www.seanet.com/users/efunmoyiwa/ochanet.html).

Sand-painting Buddhists (www.chron.com/content/interactive/voyager/mandala/).

Doomsday cultists (www.heavensgatetoo.com/).

Even the Pope has a Web site (www.vatican.va)!

Sounds like paradise for the seeker of religion information—to have religious and spirituality sites on the World Wide Web covering every sect, creed, doctrine, and belief.

Well, this access is both a blessing and a curse. While the number of religion resources on the Web has been growing, there are still some gaps. Mainstream religious organizations have been a little slow to step up to the online altar. Information provided through their Web sites still tends to be fairly scanty and most religion researchers would be better off contacting the well-oiled public relations offices than scanning the Web. Debra Mason, director of the Religion Newswriters Association, said, "Some of the problem for mainstream religious organizations is they haven't wanted to commit the resources to build up their materials online. In the case of the Vatican's site, however, some of the delay in getting documents and information online is they are trying to provide the material in six different languages; that slows down the time it takes to get it online."

But if you want background or a briefing on some fringe religion, regional group, or cult, your prayers are answered, because religious groups of every type have gone online, providing unprecedented access to materials about their ideas and beliefs. When the Heaven's Gate doomsday cult committed mass suicide, people following the story could go directly to the Heaven's Gate Web site and find statements on their beliefs about the end of the world. Pre-Web, post-suicide access to that material would have been difficult, if not impossible.

Overall, while the types of information available on religion are improving, there are still gaps in resources and difficulties in finding them. As Mason says, "Religion is messy. There aren't a lot of ecumenical sites, places where you can get lots of good information on all the religions." For those wanting facts and statistics on individual groups, sites with reliable statistical information or data on churches and faiths are hard to find. Sorting through which is the official and which is just a fan (sometimes a fanatic) site for a particular church or religion can be challenging.

As for the resources that help you find resources, the offering plate is still pretty light. Though there is a wonderful diversity of religion Web sites— everything from agnosticism to Zoroastrianism—researchers still must pray for some better resources for tracking them. In fact, this is one area where the resources available on Yahoo! might be the most comprehensive. There are over 15,000 listings in the sub-category "Religion" (found under the category Society and Culture).

Otherwise, for the most part, the religious resource Web sites are either not kept current (many dead or moved links), the organization of the page does not aid in locating specific resources, or the sponsor of the site might be seen as problematic for the researcher wanting an unbiased selection of resources. Mason explains, "Most researchers or reporters would look askance at a listing of religion sites put together by someone on the Bahai page. What will their focus be, what is their bias?"

There are a number of large databases of religion sites, many of them Christian-focused. Christian Web site search services, such as Best of the Christian Web: Your Christian Start Page (www.botcw.com/index.shtml) and Goshen (www.GOSHEN.net/), are examples of Yahoo-esque arranged services for locating religion sites. However, their narrow focus (Christian-only sites) and their selection policies (basically, they include any sites that self-submit information), preclude them from being considered valuable resources for locating religion resources, using our criteria.

That said, there are some good religion-specific search sites that are worth a pilgrimage. While none of them seem to have all the features and criteria for an ideal Great Scout subject specific search site, the following have attempted to make the best religion resources on the Internet more reachable.

Top Great Scout Sites for Religion

Virtual Religion Index
religion.rutgers.edu/links/vrindex.html
Contact: Mahlon Smith, mahsmith@rci.rutgers.edu

Why we picked this site: One site that is very useful because of its careful annotation, high selectivity, and the links to useful information buried within a linked site is the Virtual Religion Index. Created by Mahlon H. Smith, a religion professor in the Rutgers University Religion Department, the well-organized, subject-categorized links page gets you to full descriptive annotations. Within the annotations are links to specific pages on the Web site. As Smith says on the site: "This index is designed as a tool for students with little time. It analyzes and highlights important content of religion-related web sites to speed research. Hyperlinks are provided not only to home pages but to major sub-sites, directories, and documents within." While the number of sites is limited, only about 750, the annotations help get you to specific and useful information found within the site. This is a great place to go to get even more specific resource pages (e.g., a link to the Index of Native American Resources on the Internet is in the American Religions-Native America category).

Created: Online since February 28, 1997.

How many sites: Over 750 sites.

Audience: Academics and students and serious researchers of religion topics.

How sites are selected: According to index creator Smith, sites for the Virtual Religion Index come from four sources: his own periodic Web surfing and searches, colleagues' recommendations, alerts from other Webmasters, and recommendations by students and occasional messages from users of VRI.

The criteria of selection are related to the advertised purpose of the index as a tool for academic research. That means the information on listed sites must satisfy scholarly standards for historical accuracy. Sites are listed if they:

(a) post historic documents of primary importance, or

(b) present scholarly analysis or critiques of religious phenomena, or

(c) provide access to official views of major religious organizations.

Sites are not listed if they:

(a) just promote private speculation or religious opinions, or

(b) are primarily designed to proselytize, or

(c) spread false information designed to defame.

Sites that are given priority are those relevant to courses in religious studies at Rutgers and other universities. In some cases sites that are of inferior quality in terms of presentation are not listed if the same material is available in a superior format at another Web site.

How it's supported: Part of Rutgers University's Religion Department.

Topics covered: Academia, American Religions, Ancient Near Eastern Studies, Anthropology and Sociology of Religion, Archeology and Religious Art, Biblical Studies, Buddhist Tradition, Christian Tradition, Comparative Religion, Confessional Agencies, East Asian Studies, Ethics and Moral Values, Greco-Roman Studies,

Hindu Tradition, Islam, Jewish Studies, Philosophy and Theology, Psychology of Religion.

Searching: Determine which of the categories your interest would fall in and click on the category label to see the listing of Web sites for that topic area.

What you get: A very complete annotation and link to the Web site home page or specific page within the Web site.

Design: If you are a frames fan, this page has that format—subject categories down the left scrollable frame, the links, and then the sites linked to in the right frame. But don't worry, if you are not a frames fan, scroll down on the right-hand frame of the home page and click on "If you prefer a full screen format, click here."

Other features: Submit your e-mail address in the box at the end of the Web site listing pages to receive notification when the page is updated.

Help or FAQ: The Webmaster is very responsive to questions, otherwise this straightforward resource has no particular help files or FAQs.

RELIGIOUS RESOURCES ON THE NET

Religious Resources on the Net

www.aphids.com/relres/about.htm
Contact: Susan Brumbaugh, susan@aphids.com

Why we picked this site: Religious Resources on the Net started in April of 1995 as part of a Web site that indexer Susan Brumbaugh was developing for her local church in Boulder, Colorado. It grew from a one-page listing of fewer than fifty entries to a fully-developed database containing, now, over 3,000 entries. Susan considers this a moderated Web site in that sites can be submitted, but not all are selected. A very nice feature is the link to other Christian and Religion resource sites—if you've searched her database and want to try another, click on one of the six other search sites (including Goshen, CrossSearch, 777.net) and your search term will be passed over to that site for a search.

Created: April 1995.

How many sites: Over 3,500.

Audience: People seeking religion sites of varying types, of varying value.

How sites are selected: Sites are self-submitted but reviewed by the Webmaster and not all are included. "I reserve the right not to list certain sites (usually either because the content is not religious or because I strongly disagree with the content)."

How it's supported: The principals of this resource also run a Web design and development company, specializing in church-related design. This supports the resource; the resource advertises their company.

Searching: There are two ways to access the sites:

Browse the categories: There are fourteen major categories (Art, Bibles, Commercial, Directories, Electronic Communities, Miscellaneous, Music, Organizations, Publications, Reference, Seasonal, Web Development, Young Adult, Youth). Select one from the pull-down menu box and then pick whether you want to see the sub-categories or see all the selections for that listing. In all there are over 160 subject categories.

Search box: Enter the search terms, select whether you want the terms found in the titles, descriptions, or URLs.

What you get: The alphabetical listing of retrieved sites includes the linked title of the Web site (click on it to go directly to the Web site) and a "details" link you can click to find out more information about the site before you visit it, including (if available) the URL, title, category(ies), description, and contact e-mail.

Design: Very simple, clean, no-frills design.

Other Religion Sites

Religions & Scriptures
www.wam.umd.edu/~stwright/rel/index.html
For tracts, doctrines, and texts from specific religions, this site links to fourteen religions' Web resources pages and direct links to the scriptures or sacred writings.

New Religious Movements
cti.itc.virginia.edu/~jkh8x/soc257/profiles.htm
Wonderfully detailed profiles of over 100 sects and quasi-religious groups (from snake handlers to Amway) give background on history and beliefs.

The Geography of Religion
www.morehead-st.edu/people/t.pitts/mainmenu.htm
Click on one of the fifteen icons representing the world's major religions and get a chart with the demographic distribution of adherents to the religion plus a well-sourced essay about the major tenets of the religion with hyperlinks to further explanation. The "Other Religions" links give you brief listings of links to Web resources on a variety of religions.

Religion News Service
www.religionnews.com/
"For more than 60 years, Religion News Service has been an authoritative source of news about religion, ethics, spirituality, and

moral issues." And now it's on the Web. Look here for the latest news compiled by the RNS network of worldwide correspondents.

American Religion Data Archive
www.arda.tm
Coming out of Purdue University, this unique collection of quantitative studies about American religious practices was compiled for four reasons: to preserve data, improve access to data, increase the use of data, and allow comparisons across data files. Taken mostly from public opinion polls, this site hits on all four goals and provides a primary source for getting demographic and attitudinal information about Americans and their religious beliefs.

For More Information

Cobb, Jennifer J. *Cybergrace : The Search for God in the Digital World*. New York: Crown Publ., 1998.

Gold, Laura Maery. *Mormons on the Internet*. Rocklin, CA: Prima Publishing, 1997.

Green, Irving. *Judaism on the Web* (On the Web Series). Indianapolis, IN: IDG Books Worldwide, 1997.

Groothuis, Douglas. *The Soul in Cyberspace*. Ada, MI: Baker Book House, 1997.

Zaleski, Jeff. *The Soul of Cyberspace: How New Technology is Changing our Spiritual Lives*. New York, NY: HarperCollins, 1997.

Romm, Diane. *The Jewish Guide to the Internet*. Northvale, NJ: Jason Aronson Inc., 1997.

12

Social Issues
on the Web

Abortion, adoption, affirmative action. Animal rights, children's rights, civil rights, firearms rights, human rights. Immigration reform, health care reform, tax reform, welfare reform. Population, pornography, privacy. Bioetchics, capital punishment, cloning, euthanasia, drug policy, and secondhand smoke. Hate.

Whether it's food for thought or fodder for e-mail flames, all sides of the story on any of today's key issues can be found on the World Wide Web. Unlike the traditional media, the post office, or physical library collections, the Internet facilitates the publication and dissemination of ideas beyond the limits of borders, cost, or even good taste.

Controversy fuels the Web and gets fed by its loud response. Results of studies and surveys may present the verifiable truth; one voice can claim its case based only on belief. And no seal of credibility will mark the difference. As the joke says, "On the Internet, nobody knows you're a dog."

Prestigious think tanks from the Urban Institute to the Cato Institute to the Brookings Institution and the Rand Corporation offer selections from their influential writings on contemporary issues. University departments present scholarly publications and links to social science data. Foundations post the research results of studies they've funded, as do government agencies, and legislative bodies. Political parties and candidates publish their stances, advocacy groups issue calls to action, and individuals post their opinions. On the fringe, there are sites and people advocating personal views that you may find disturbing, as well.

Magazines, newsletters, and e-zines addressing the issues may be free or subscription-based online. Non-U.S. and non-mainstream viewpoints are now available, if you can find them.

Activism is alive on the Web. You can follow a calendar of upcoming protests at Protest.net or select from the company and product boycotts on the Boycott Board. You can send e-mail comments to officials or sign virtual petitions. Across the Web, home pages display an array of electronic ribbons and badges of support or opposition to causes.

Volunteerism is alive on the Web, too. At Impact Online, the VolunteerMatch service matches volunteers with non-profits in several communities across the U.S. and in the new area of volunteering online. The Virtual Volunteering Project at the Center for Volunteerism and Community Engagement at the University of Texas encourages and assists organizations in developing volunteer activities that can be done via the Internet. If you're concerned about an issue, see what you can do to help.

You can make contributions to some charities via the Web and visit the home pages of many more. Check into the groups soliciting your charitable contributions at consumer interest sites, like Guidestar and the Internet Non-Profit Center, which offer databases of information about philanthropic organizations.

Debates on the issues are lively and engaging at the many sites that offer message boards, Web forums, and chat. Some are hosted by moderators or guest experts; others are free-for-alls. Learn the lingo; RKBA is the right to keep and bear arms. If you're expressing opinions online, writing succinctly, civilly, and well gives your message more credence.

CAUTION: Extremist groups promote their opinions, too. In the fall of 1998, media attention focused on the Creator's Rights Party Pro-Life Christian Anti-Abortion Web site, which displayed lists of physicians who perform abortions with the names of murdered doctors crossed out. Militia groups, White supremacists, anti-Semites, and the whole range of radical political ideologies, as well as alternative sexual, religious, and social viewpoints, have space on the Web. Some subject-specific guides will not list sites advocating violent or illegal acts; others provide listings so that these groups can be monitored by concerned Netizens.

What's missing: Although it's difficult to find information about a controversial issue by using generalized search engines, it's also difficult to find balanced information by using a single subject-specific guide. Frequently, the advocacy of the person or organization producing the directory shows their bias. We've selected some of the best from all sides, but you'll still need to be conscious of where the information comes from. Policy.com (www.policy.com), described in the Politics chapter, is a good source for social issues as well as political debate.

Social Issues Materials on the Web

Activism: Protest.Net lists progressive and leftist protests, meetings, and conferences worldwide (www.protest.net). Boycott Board is a bulletin board listing consumer boycotts (www.2street. com/boycott).

Charities: Search for information on more than 650,000 nonprofits and charities at Guidestar (www.guidestar.org), locate organizations at the Internet Non-Profit center (www.nonprofits.org), or find out about standards in philanthropy from the National Charities Information Bureau (www.give.org).

Discussions: Check for Web forums about your issue of interest at Forum One (www.forumone.com), for newsgroups at Deja.com (www.deja.com), and for e-mail discussion (listservs) at Liszt (www.liszt.com).

Hate group monitors: Hatewatch (www.hatewatch.org) is a Web-based not-for-profit that monitors the growing and evolving threat of hate groups on the Internet. The Hate Directory: Hate Groups on the Internet (www.bcpl.lib.md.us/~rfrankli/hatedir.htm), compiled by Raymond A. Franklin, includes Web sites, file archives (FTP), mailing lists (Listservs), Newsgroups, Internet Relay Chat (IRC), and Electronic Bulletin Board Systems (BBS).

Humanitarian relief: Reliefnet is a non-profit organization dedicated to helping humanitarian organizations raise global awareness and encourage support for relief efforts via the Internet (www.reliefnet.org).

RKBA: The right to keep and bear arms, and the opposing views of gun control advocates, are widely discussed and documented viewpoints on the Web. Visit rkba.org for files and links to arms rights and liberty information on the Internet.

Think Tanks: Brookings Institution (www.brookings.org), Cato Institute (www.cato.org), Heritage Foundation (www.heritage.org) and its TownHall conservative portal and community (www.townhall.com), Rand Corporation with abstracts of research searchable back to the 1960s (www.rand.org), Urban Institute (www.urban.org), offering access to a multi-year research project and database focusing on health care, income security, job training, and social services.

Volunteering: Impact Online (www.impactonline.org) offers VolunteerMatch service for matching volunteers and non-profits in Virtual Volunteering Project to encourage volunteer work online (www.serviceleader.org/vv).

Top Great Scout Sites for Social Issues

AAAS Directory of
Human Rights Resources
on the Internet

AAAS Directory of Human Rights Resources
on the Internet
shr.aaas.org/dhr.htm
Contact: Stephen A. Hansen, editor
Directory of Human Rights Resources on the Internet
Science and Human Rights Program
Directorate for Science & Public Policy
American Association for the Advancement of Science (AAAS)
1200 New York Avenue, N.W.
Washington, DC 20005
shansen@aaas.org

Why we picked this site: The AAAS's Science and Human Rights Program has built a database of hundreds of organizational Web sites around the world providing content and contacts relating to the broad topic of human rights and its many sub-topics. Among groups in Third World countries and smaller non-governmental organizations (NGOs), Internet access and use has grown tremendously in the past two years, according to editor Stephen A. Hansen. "It's a step forward in the human rights community," Hansen said. This directory and its printed counterpart allow individuals and organizations a way to find smaller and more remote NGOs. Each entry in the database is detailed, complete, and relevant to the topics included in the directory. The directory is updated frequently and sites are checked and updated regularly.

Created: November 1995.

How many sites: 500+.

Audience: Human rights researchers and the general public.

How sites are selected: Self-submitted for review by editor. Site must be human-rights-based organization; political issues are avoided.

How it's supported: American Association for the Advancement of Science.

Topics covered: Include Censorship, Children, Civil Rights, Conflict Resolution, Death Penalty, Electronic Privacy, Freedom of Expression, Humanitarian Assistance, Indigenous Peoples, Journalists, Landmines, Political Prisoners, Racism, Refugees, Religious Freedom and Minorities, Sexual Orientation, Torture, War Crimes, Women's Rights, and more. The directory also offers a section on Web tools.

Contents: Browse by Site Name, Topical Focus, Geographical Focus, and Language or search by keyword for listings of entries in database. Separate search words by commas.

What you get: A database entry contains a description and purpose of the organization and Web site, date posted and updated, complete contact information with e-mail and URL. You may sort listings by relevance or date.

Advanced searching: Search by exact word or thesaurus term.

Design: It's quick and each page is labeled for easy navigation.

Other features: Sections of the site are now available in Spanish and French.

Help or FAQ: No.

Read about it:
Hansen, Stephen A. *Getting Online for Human Rights*. Washington, D.C.: American Association for the Advancement of Science, 1998.

WebActive

WebActive Directory
www.webactive.com/webactive/directory/
Contact: Sam Tucker, Publisher
WebActive
1111 Third Avenue, Suite 2900
Seattle, WA 98101
webactive@webactive.com

Why we picked this site: "Connect with a cause" is the slogan of the WebActive Directory, part of the WebActive audio and video news project from the streaming media technology company Real-Networks, Inc. This is a large and actively updated directory of activist and issues sites. It is weighted towards "progressive" or left/liberal sites, but includes a section "The Wrong Side of the Web," which highlights comprehensive and representative conservative sites.

Created: January 1996.

How many sites: 2,200+.

Audience: "Progressive activists."

How sites are selected: Submitted sites are reviewed and selected by WebActive staff. According to publisher Sam Tucker, "We select sites that fall under a broadly-defined progressive umbrella. Some of the large headings under which we consider sites for inclusion are: democracy, freedom and self-determination; diversity and community; and our material well-being."

How it's supported: Supported by banner advertisements and revenue from RealImpact Web development and consulting company (www.realimpact.net). WebActive is a project of RealNetworks, Inc., the makers of RealAudio and RealVideo.

Topics covered: Forty topics under the categories Democracy, Freedom and Self-Determination, Diversity and Community, Our Material Well-Being, and special topics like Activist Tools, Animal Rights, College Activism, and Progressive Businesses. Includes AIDS/HIV Issues, Children's Issues, Civil Rights, Housing and Shelter, and Social Justice.

Contents: Browse the topical or alphabetical listings or search by keyword or phrase.

What you get: Dated brief descriptions of selected sites with hyperlinks to the sites organized alphabetically.

Advanced searching: No.

Design: Plain text; pages are long lists so they may take some time to load.

Other features: "New and Updated Listings."

Help or FAQ: No.

Other Top Social Issues Scout Sites

Death Penalty Information Center
www.essential.org/dpic
This is a comprehensive site offering information and resources on the issue of capital punishment, including resource materials and links, state-by-state review of the death penalty, bibliographies, news, and international developments.

Social Science Information Gateway (SOSIG)
sosig.esrc.bris.ac.uk
SOSIG is a searchable networked online database catalog of thousands of Internet resources in the social sciences, with descriptive annotated entries and direct links to them. Each has been selected

and described by a librarian or academic in the United Kingdom and the collection is aimed at the academic researcher and scholar. Selection criteria are extensive and detailed; evaluations are made in terms of content, form, and process. For social issues the major topic covered is Social Welfare with sub-topics for Addiction, Children and the Family, Community Work, Disability Issues, Elderly, Homelessness, Insurance, Mental Health and Mental Illness, Poverty, Social Assistance, Social Health Care, Social Problems, Social Services, Social Work, Unemployment, and Youth Welfare.

Ultimate Pro-Life Resource List

www.prolifeinfo.org

A comprehensive listing of right-to-life resources and sites on the Internet. Topics include Organizations, Adoption Resources, Politics, Opinions, Educational Factsheets, Health Information, and Abortion Alternatives. This site states plainly that, "We do not list those organizations that adopt a militant approach or support violent or illegal activities."

World Animal Net Directory

worldanimal.net/wan.htm

This database of animal protection societies around the world has over 10,000 listings and links to more than 2,000 Web sites. You can search by geographical region or by categories, which include Anti-Vivisection, Bird, Cat, Dog, and Horse Protection, Animals in Entertainment, Animals in Transport, Farm Animals, Fur, Genetic Engineering, Marine Animals, and Wildlife, as well as information on shelters, sanctuaries, and other facilities around the world.

13

Travel Resources on the Web

Want to travel without leaving your chair? Crank up your browser. You can climb Mount Everest (www.everest.mountainzone.com/), travel the Nile (www.adventureonline.com/rtn/ about.html), go on an expedition to Antarctica (www.terraquest. com/antarctica/). Or, if you will actually be on the move, the travel resources on the Web can help you find a place to stay, locate the best fare or route, and advise you about dangers or cautions when going.

I located a bed and breakfast in a tiny village in Northumberland, an idyll of country living, through the Internet. I booked a daylong bus tour to Stonehenge and to see crop circles through a Web site. I rented a floor in an old Dutch row house on one of Amsterdam's grand canals through the Web (and got a 10 percent discount). Every step of the traveler's process, from dreaming to booking the reservation, can be done easily and effectively through the Internet's travel resources.

When checking out travel sites, however, be careful of the source of the material. An information-rich site might be a promotional site pushing a particular chain of hotels or travel options. You'll be more likely to get less biased information from state or local tourist bureaus operated by the government (but, be aware that they will be pushing the glories of travel to their locale, that's their job!). The information sites that individual transportation companies have created are invaluable when tracking travel options, but they won't give you all the possibilities. Even those sites that seem to compile possible itineraries from a number of carriers don't cover all the airlines.

There are specialty travel sites for backpackers to bicyclists to B&B aficionados. Most of the sites exist through the sales and promotion of travel services. Other sites full of good travel information contain only original material, like Discovery Channel's Travel Channel Web site (www.travelchannel.com/travelhome.html). Some compile information from a variety of sources and present a full package of "recycled" material. Just be aware of what you are looking at and where the information comes from. Then click away, pack your bags, and make some memories.

Great Scout Sites for Travel

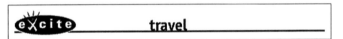

City.Net

www.city.net/destinations/

Contact: Excite, Inc.

555 Broadway

Redwood City, CA 94063

Why we picked this site: One of the criteria for selecting great scout sites is "does this site help me find the answer to any question I might have on a subject?" For City.Net's resources and organization, the answer is a big Yes! If you have questions about a country you are going to and want to locate resources on the Web that might have the answer, City.Net has found them and has organized the links in a logical way. Although City.Net is a portion of the larger Excite "portal" search service, one of the "omni-search" services we are trying to find alternatives to, this portion is an excellent travel resource and deserves to stand out.

Created: 1996.

How many sites: There are more than 5,000 featured travel spots, but each has multiple links to outside Web sites.

Audience: Whether for business or pleasure, this guide is designed for the traveler.

How sites are selected: The Excite Directory Team searches and selects the best Web sites for the channel they are editing. Submissions are carefully reviewed and selected only if they fit into the category or destination. Relevance of the content of the site is the highest criterion used in selection.

How it's supported: This is one of the many "channels" provided by Excite, which has a software sales- and advertising-based revenue support.

Brought to you by: Excite.

Freshness: There is no date stamp on the pages, and spot checks found about a 20 percent "no find" rate. They should use their robot to go out and check these sites more frequently.

Topics covered: Once you select a city or region or country you want to have profiled, you get links to Fact Sheets, What to Do, Where to Stay, Travel & Tourism Sites, News & Media Sites, Community Sites. There are also special sections for cruises and tours, business, family, and outdoor adventures.

Searching: There are a couple of ways to find the links on the site. The index column has a list of regions (Africa, Asia, Australia/Oceania, Caribbean, etc.) with some specific countries underneath. If one of the countries you are interested in is listed, click on it to get right to the country-specific links page. If it isn't listed, click on the continent or region link to get a clickable map to more specific places in the area.

It takes some finding; you must scroll down the page, but there is a search box into which you can type a country or city. This search function is actually searching the titles of the links on the profile pages. If, for example, you type "family," you'll get results: *Excite Travel: Family Travel*, and *Excite Travel: Olathe*—click on *Olathe* and you'll see you retrieved that site because one of the links on the page is to *"Kansas City Family-family events calendar."* Be sure to use quotation marks ("xx xxx") around a phrase; for example, a search for San Antonio is interpreted as an "or" search (and will retrieve San Antonio AND Cabo San Lucas), but the "San Antonio" search will just get you that beautiful old city in Texas.

What you get: If you are searching for a country or state, you'll get a clickable map with links to more specific sites. Under the map is a current weather report for specific cities. Before you get to the links listings, you'll get an article full of useful background information. The links listings to relevant sites for that area fall under the broad categories of General Information, Guides, a listing of specific cities or countries. The more travel-specific information links are in a column to the left, with clickable categories for: What to Do, Where to Eat, Where to Stay, Travel & Tourism Sites, News & Media Sites, Community Sites. Some of these categories are subcategorized, but many just give you the listings. There are no annotations; clicking on one of the listings takes you right to the Web site, but the sites linked to are well selected and organized.

Advanced searching: None.

Design: This is a very commercial service and one of those "portal" services that is trying to do everything for everyone, which makes for a busy page. Once you find your way around, however, the clarity of organization of the links makes up for the clutter of the page.

Other features: The whole Travel Channel, City.Net, is designed to facilitate all the traveler's needs. There is an online reservation and fare-finding service, maps, and even links to books that might be of interest.

Help or FAQ: None.

Fodor's Resource Center
www.fodors.com/resource/
Contact: Fodor's Travel Publications, Inc.
201 East 50th Street
New York, NY 10022

Why we picked this site: What book are you likely to pick up at the bookstore if you're going to make a trip? One of Fodor's over 290 excellent travel guides. Their clear and practical advice to the traveler has been in print for the past sixty years, and now it's online. Fodor's Travel Online Editor Chelsea Mauldin explains the goal of the Resource Center well: "There's a wealth of travel information on the Web, but if you've ever spent hours wading through dubious, oddball sites, you may have wondered if you're dealing with too much of a good thing. To ease your way, we've selected the best sites in dozens of travel categories, then supplemented these links with tips and ideas from Fodor's best-selling guidebooks." And that's just what they've done, combined the best of the Web with the best of Fodor's. Travelers, both virtual and real, thank them.

Created: February 1996.

How many sites: About 1,000 very well selected sites.

Audience: Travelers seriously planning a trip and needing advice.

How sites are selected: All of the sites are carefully selected; information resources the editors want to use to supplement the Fodor's travel advice are sought out. As editor Chelsea Mauldin said, "We have an editorial viewpoint in our books, also on the Web. We don't take material that is submitted by providers in our guidebooks; all the material is provided by our writers and editors; same for our Web links. People ask all the time if their site can be listed. Generally the answer is no, unless it happens to be one of the kinds of information resources we would be looking for to enhance the section of the guide." In each section of the guide, the advice text comes from one of their print publications, then specific information sources that would complement that section are located through "intense surfing, following other compilers' link lists, wandering through the search engines and Internet directories." Sometimes specific guide sections were created to showcase a particularly good Internet resource (for example, a section on subways is being added in order to help people link to the great Subways page: www.reed.edu/~reyn/transport.html). Mauldin's philosophy for the Resource links area is to help find the best of the comprehensive listings rather than to try and provide a comprehensive listing herself.

How it's supported: Fodor's Travel Publications, the largest publisher of English-language travel information in the world, is a subsidiary of Random House. The Web site is considered an arm of their publishing efforts and a marketing/sales outlet for their print guides. The editors see the online material teasing to their books and the books linking to the online resources.

Brought to you by: Fodor's Travel Publications.

Freshness: They use a "linkbot" to run weekly checks of the links.

Topics covered: There are twenty-four categories, but more are being added all the time: Air travel, Bus travel, Cameras & computers, Car rental, The Channel tunnel, Children & travel,

Consumer protection, Customs & duties, Disabilities & accessibility, Ecotourism, Electricity, Health, Insurance, Language, Lodging, Money, National parks, Packing, Passports & visas, Pets & travel, Tour operators, Train travel, Visitor information, Volunteer & educational travel, When to go.

Searching: There is no searching, only selecting. Pick one of the categories (see "Topics covered" for a listing) and browse their well-organized selected links. Each of the categories has different subcategories. Air Travel, for example, has links woven through the helpful travel advice narrative to such topics as Aircraft Layouts, Airline Safety, Online Booking Services, Carriers (an alphabetical list of links to all the carriers organized by regions), Charters, Consolidators, Couriers, Cutting Costs (links to budget ticket services online), Discount Pass Retailers, advice on how to enjoy your flight, and how to complain if you don't. Some categories, such as Consumer Protection, supplement the excellent Fodor travel advice with links to a couple of online resources.

What you get: See above.

Advanced searching: None.

Design: We're not a big fan of frames, but this is framed in a useful, easy-to-use way. The travel categories list scrolls in the left-hand frame and the article with links appears on the right. Clean and easy to read.

Other features: The whole Fodor's Travel Online Web site is the other useful feature. Great articles, searchable forums for travelers, and a fare-finding service make this a one-way ticket to the best travel advice around. Be sure to check out the "Create your own mini-guide" area. Select one of the ninety-nine cities and check the boxes on "Where to Stay," "Eating out," "Fodor's Top Picks," or "Essential Information" to get a custom-made guide to that city.

Help or FAQ: None.

Other Useful Sites

TravelWeb

www.travelweb.com/

Don't you wish someone would give you really good advice about where to stay when you have very specific needs? You want a place in a reasonable price range that has a golf course nearby and babysitting facilities. Don't you wish you could locate a source where you could plug in the place you want to get to, the date and time you want to travel, and all the possible routes would come up (with links to profiles of the type of plane you will be flying on if you pick that flight)? The TravelWeb folks have made your dreams come true. Their site makes finding and reserving your best travel itinerary so easy you'll be picking up and flying away before you know it. Although their links to other travel sites, found in the "Resources" area, are fairly skimpy, they are well organized. The key feature is the plug and find search for accommodations and flights that lets you specify details about your requirements and find the best fits.

Rail Serve

www.railserve.com/

Links to everything about the railroad, from model trains to the Orient Express, organized in Yahoo!-esque sub-categories. The "modified" date and number of links in each section is a great help.

How far are you going? Use the *How Far Is It?* calculator at www.indo.com/distance/. Plug in two cities' names and get the mileage between them.

How are you going to get there? Where are you going to stay? Check out your options for air travel on more than 360 airlines and places to rest your travel-weary head in tens of thousands of hotels worldwide in TravelWeb's databases (www.travelweb.com/ TravelWeb/index.html). Or, if you are going to drive, plot out the route to take and where to stop along the way with AutoPilot from FreeTrip (www.freetrip.com) or CyberRouter at (www.delorme. com/cybermaps/route.asp).

What are you going to do once you get there? Get some advice from the tourist office, find the phone, address, e-mail and URL of country and state official tourism departments in the *Tourism Offices Worldwide Directory* (www.mbnet.mb.ca/lucas/travel/). Also, check out the excellent online version of the *World Travel Guide* (www.wtg-online.com/) for thorough profiles of every country in the world including advice on accommodations, national holidays, travel restrictions and requirements.

What should you be careful of? The State Department's Travel Warnings and Consular Information Sheets give essential background on conditions of travel in various countries (travel.state.gov/ travel_warnings.html).

Need shots? If you are going to exotic lands, be sure to be aware of any particular health concerns. Travel Health Online (www. tripprep.com/index.html) compiles, by country, general information, health precautions, disease risk summary,and official health data.

What's that going to cost in pesetas? Find out what that hotel rate will be in the local currency or in your home currency with the Currency converter (www.oanda.com/converter/classic). Find and calculate 164 different world currencies.

How do you say that in . . . ? Try these two pages of links to all manner of dictionaries and get help translating over thirty languages (rivendel.com/~ric/resources/dictionary.html and www. travlang.com/).

For More Information

Pack, Thomas. *10 Minute Guide to Travel Planning on the Net*. Indianapolis, IN: Que Education & Training, 1997.

Dempsey, Elizabeth. *How to Plan Your Dream Vacation Using the Web*. Scottsdale, AZ: The Coriolis Group, 1997.

Shapiro, Michael. *Nettravel: How Travelers Use the Internet*. Cambridge, MA: O'Reilly & Associates, 1997.

Holleman, Gary. *Travel and Hospitality Online: A Guide to Online Services*. New York: John Wiley & Sons, 1997.

Dummies Technology Press. *Travel Planning Online for Dummies*. Indianapolis, IN: IDG Books Worldwide, 1998.

Part II

Business & Professional Resources

14

Business and Management Resources on the Web

The Web is ready to get down to business.

Trucks speed across the interstates displaying company URLs. Television commercials end with advertiser Web addresses superimposed on the bottom of the screen. Cereal boxes and soft drink cans tout corporate home pages. Banks, investment companies, stock exchanges, and major business publications invite your virtual visits. And when you take up these invitations, experience the virtual marketplace of the future: secure servers processing monetary transactions and marketing departments collecting your preferences.

The 21st century World Wide Web? A brave new world where we'll buy products from online catalogs, pay bills, track packages, conduct banking or investment transactions, and attend business meetings without leaving home or even picking up the telephone. We'll be able to look for tools and training resources to help us work better or pound the virtual pavement for new and better jobs. We'll seek assistance and advice on starting a new business. We'll find products, services, and customers in huge databases of company and personal directory information.

You don't have to wait for the new millenium to do your business on the Internet. In many places online, the office is already open and virtual corporate real estate is rapidly expanding. Even if your business doesn't yet have a storefront or cubicle in a corner of cyberspace, the Web offers a global business library, commercial bulletin board, financial newswire, and management class-room at your fingertips. Business decisions rely on information, with currency and speed of delivery of equal importance to its value, depth, and reliability. But, like other subject areas on the Web, there's already too much business information to capture, digest, and analyze. Where do you start?

Major business media have invested heavily in Web sites to display or sell their value-added information products. From the venerable *Wall Street Journal* to the successful upstart *Bloomberg News*, to *Forbes*, *Fortune*, and *Money* magazines, and the Web versions of popular financial cable television networks like CNBC and CNNfn, news and numbers relating to financial markets, company events, and government economic releases are multiplying. Most of these information products have long been used by corporate and library subscribers to proprietary fee-based services. But these highly competitive commercial information services now aim to attract the small business and consumer markets with easy-to-use Web interfaces. For "intermediaries," information specialists like librarians and corporate researchers, the easier interfaces are welcome, although some feel that their professional livelihood may be threatened by the push to get every computer user to do his or her own research. As you'll find when you do it yourself, business research is more than entering search terms; evaluation of the veracity and reliability of the information that pops up and analysis of the content are necessary, too.

Beyond the print publications and online services that have moved to the Web, there are also new business information sources built just for an electronic audience, like the NewsPage news service and search engine and the popular TheStreet.com, a must-see source of news and market commentary for any financial professional, according to *The Washington Post* financial researcher, Richard Drezen. There are also Web financial advisors like the Motley Fool that compete with traditional investment services for a share of the apparently limitless market for investing advice and information. Great Scout sites for investing are described in our chapter on Personal Finance.

CAUTION: Be prepared to pay for the business information you value. The daily Wall Street Journal Interactive, TheStreet.com, NewsPage, and many other business sites require subscription fees for services and documents, too.

If you want to dig deep into business research, go to the source. Stock markets, from the New York Stock Exchange, AMEX, and NASDAQ to markets around the globe, have developed sites with both depth and currency of information on the stocks traded there. If you want information about a company, go to the company's own home page for the latest on corporate changes and products, as well as company history, executive biographies, and headquarters contacts. You can seek out companies and their products in online yellow pages and product directories across the Web. For retail shopping online see the Great Scouts described in our Online Shopping chapter.

For economic trends and business conditions, the free information collected by the U.S. government via the Securities and Exchange Commission, the Federal Reserve Board, and the Labor and Commerce Departments come highly recommended by both Drezen and Time Warner Inc. financial researcher, Patricia Neering. EDGAR (Electronic Data Gathering, Analysis, and Retrieval) is the name of the project that collects and disseminates the required electronic filings of information from every publicly traded company in the United States. SEC filings from EDGAR appear on several sites on the Web in different formats, and include information on each company's financial performance, the compensation of their corporate executives, and lots of other tidbits worth taking the time to study.

For findings on economic and business trends that won't require the high costs of investment firm analysts' research reports, Drezen and Neering recommend that you try your topic on the pages of the regional Federal Reserve Bank boards, where the excellent reports are free.

Whether you're looking for government assistance for a small business or angel investors for your high-tech startup, guidance and opportunities can be found on the Web. And if you're thinking about starting up a Web-based business, you'll find plenty of help. Start by checking to see if your preferred domain name has already been claimed or quickly register it online.

You can visit the nation's top schools of business administration and use the resources of their libraries online, or look for educational opportunities from management programs and associations.

Offered here are the best scout sites for starting out on your search for company, management, and economic information on the Web. Bookmark these and visit them regularly; change is constant in the area of business and on the Web.

Business Materials on the Web

Careers and employment: CareerPath offers a searchable database of employment listings from more than sixty newspapers and a Résumé Connection service for creating and posting résumés online (www.careerpath.com). CareerWeb is a free site where you can post your résumé and search a database of current openings for professional, technical, or managerial jobs (www.cweb.com). JobWeb from the National Association of Colleges and Employers has extensive resources for new college graduates and students seeking employment, internships, and career guidance (www.jobweb.org).

Company finance: The Venture Capital Resource Library gives you lots of help and pointers to sources of money for company financing as well as sources of investment for venture capitalists (www.vfinance.com). The U.S. Small Business Administration site offers information and help on starting, financing, and expanding your business (www.sba.gov).

Directories: CorpTech directory for high technology companies offers free database searches of companies by name or stock symbol and a people-finder for company executives, with a free capsule company report (www.corptech.com). Free membership at the Thomas Register of American Manufacturers' site allows you to search by company, name, product, and brand name in a directory of over 155,000 companies and view product catalogs (www.thomasregister.com).

Encyclopedias and glossaries: The interactive International Financial Encyclopaedia (www.euro.net/innovation/Finance_Base/Fin_encyc.html), and the New York Stock Exchange Glossary of Financial Terms (www.nyse.com).

Federal Reserve publications: Visit the Board of Governors of the Federal Reserve System (www.bog.frb.fed.us) for statistics and articles from the *Federal Reserve Bulletin*, the Board's National Information Center for comprehensive data and information on financial institutions (www.ffiec.gov/nic), or the twelve regional Reserve Banks, each of which publishes statistics and analysis relating to its respective region and the national economy (www.bog.frb. fed.us/otherfrb.htm).

Libraries: Harvard Business School's Baker Library (library.hbs. edu), Lippincott Library of the Wharton School (www.library. upenn.edu/lippincott), British Library of Political and Economic Science at the London School of Economics (www.lse.ac.uk/blpes).

Lists: Forbes World's Richest People (www.forbes.com/tool/ toolbox/billnew/index.asp), Fortune 500 (www.pathfinder.com/ fortune/fortune500), Inc. 500 (www.inc.com/500), Black Enterprise 100 (www.blackenterprise.com/).

News: TheStreet.com fee-based news and analysis service with free areas for markets and resources (www.thestreet.com), Bloomberg News (www.bloomberg.com), Wall Street Journal Interactive Edition—fee based subscription with free two-week trial (www. wsj.com), CNBC business news (www.cnbc.com), CNN Financial Network (www.cnnfn.com).

SEC filings: First, consult the excellent "Guide to SEC Filings" from Disclosure, Inc. (www.disclosure.com). You can search for the text of filings at Disclosure, at Free Edgar (www.freeedgar.com), or at the source itself, the Securities and Exchange Commission (www.sec.gov/edgarhp.htm).

Stock exchanges: American Stock Exchange with live video from the trading floor (www.amex.com), NASDAQ (www.nasdaq.com), New York Stock Exchange (www.nyse.com), Istanbul Stock Exchange (www.ise.org), Tokyo Stock Exchange (www.tse.or.jp/ eindex.html), and almost 100 more.

Great Scout Sites for Business

Dow Jones Business Directory

businessdirectory.dowjones.com
Contact: Glenn Fannick, Senior Producer
Dow Jones & Company
P.O. Box 300
Princeton, NJ 08543-0300
Glenn.Fannick@dowjones.com

Why we picked this site: This directory achieves the highest marks for quality and presentation among the evaluative and descriptive guides to subject-specific sources. The criteria and standards for selection of sites reflect the solid reputation of Dow Jones as a resource for business information. Sites are restricted to high-quality, free or low-cost resources on the Web in the subject areas covered. Sites are selected for reliable information and ease of use; no low quality information will be found here. An extensive maintenance process ensures that addresses are fresh and that selected sites continue to provide consistent value. Senior producer Glenn Fannick states, "We run software to check the links twice a month. But more importantly we have staff that continually monitor what's happening in the business world and how that impacts related Web sites. So, as soon as a major corporate merger is completed, for example, we check the two company sites to see what changed (if anything) and report about it as soon as possible. If we hear a news organization relaunched its site, we address that immediately and rereview the site."

The reviews are complete and insightful and rankings are given for key attributes. A broad selection of resource types for industries, including companies, mailing lists, reference aids, and links to associations and organizations make this selective site our top pick.

Created: October 1996, relaunched with new design in August 1997.

How many sites: 1,700+.

Audience: Business professionals and the general public.

How sites are selected: Sites are selected by Dow Jones editors and freelance writers based on Dow Jones editorial criteria. Sites are evaluated for content (depth, currency, use of technology and accuracy), speed (tested with a variety of modems, network connections, and browsers at varying times of day and week for response), navigation (ease of use, including a standard of just three clicks away from the information you're seeking), and design (big graphics, garish colors, and "frivolous" hyperlinks are eschewed). Scores for each of these categories range from 1 to 10; scores below 5 indicate performance is substandard in that area; above 8 indicates exceptional performance.

How it's supported: Free site from premium provider Dow Jones is supported by advertising.

Topics covered: Careers, Companies in the Dow, Economy, Financial Markets, Government & Politics, Industries, Law, Public Records, News, Personal Finance, Reference, Small Business.

Contents: Rated, signed reviews of high-quality business and financial market Web sites. Each concise review describes both the up and down sides of each site. Reviews are edited by Dow Jones staff—a superlative job.

Searching: Browse the categories or enter a search term into a search box for quick retrieval of results. Each brief result listing includes "key reasons to use this site" and cost and a compilation of the score of the site based on Dow Jones criteria. Read the review or go directly to the site via a hyperlink. Reviews are dated and signed.

Advanced searching: The advanced search allows you to sort your hits by rankings for title, total score, or individual scores for content, speed, navigation, and design. You may also search the full text of reviews with Boolean logic (AND, OR).

Design: Consistent and clear; response is fast.

Other features: "In the News" presents daily topics of current business interest with Web links to relevant sites. A separate category of available sites for companies included in the Dow industrials, transportation, and utilities indexes are included.

Help or FAQ: Yes, detailed FAQ with search feature. The rating system and standards for selection are described fully. The names of editorial employees are listed on the "About Us" page.

Hoover's Online
www.hoovers.com
Contact: Gordon Anderson, Editor in Chief
Hoover's, Inc.
1033 LaPosada Drive, Suite 250
Austin, TX 78752
ganderson@hoovers.com

Why we picked this site: Hoover's Online is our top pick for company information. This authoritative publisher of business information offers a lot of free information on all publicly traded and many private U.S. companies as well as large foreign companies organized in the simplest of all manners—just search by company name. Smaller private companies are not included. Your search retrieves both Hoover's own editorial content and externally linked company information. The members-only area is available to paying subscribers, but when a company turns up in Hoover's free area, you can count on getting basic company information, home page and subsidiary links and more, including financials, links to SEC filings, competitor information, company news, and executive listings and biographies. Capsules are concise and informative; if the company is listed here, you're in luck.

Created: 1995; prior to the Web, portions of Hoover's Company Information were licensed to Lexis-Nexis (1991) and America Online (1992).

How many sites: More than 400,000 links to information on 13,500+ public and private companies and 45 industries in the U.S. and worldwide.

Audience: Business professionals, investors, and the general public.

How sites are selected: For publicly traded companies: includes every U.S. company traded on the New York Stock Exchange, American Stock Exchange and Nasdaq, more than 1,200 Nasdaq Small Cap Market (SC) companies, as well as a number that trade over-the-counter (OTC) or on Pink Sheets. Private companies: every non-public company with annual revenues greater than $500 million. Foreign companies: emphasizes those with large U.S. operations and provides complete coverage of those with sales of more than $20 billion and in future all companies with sales greater than $10 billion and all companies on the FT 100, SBF 120, DAX 40, Milan 30, Nikkei 225, and Hang Seng Index. "Links are selected by our editorial team based on the quality, breadth, and depth of information available, as well as the usefulness of the information to our customers," said Hoover's spokesperson Stephanie Dodds. There are more than 100 researchers, writers, and editors combing the Web for company news and information on Hoover's editorial team.

How it's supported: Free information supplied by business publisher as part of a subscriber site; advertising and paid memberships.

Topics covered: Company information for every U.S. company traded on the New York Stock Exchange, American Stock Exchange, and Nasdaq National Market System, more than 1,200 U.S. companies traded on the Nasdaq Small Cap Market, more than 1,500 of America's largest private companies and other non-public enterprises, more than 1,000 other private companies and more than 1,400 of the most influential non-U.S. companies.

Contents: Company Capsules contain the legal name, headquarters address, telephone and fax numbers, Web site address and link to a list of the company's subsidiaries, as well as a description of the company's products and operations and ownership, links to the Company Capsules of its top three competitors, and industry information. Links to current news and to company press releases are also provided. In addition, key numbers and market information, including stock exchange, ticker symbol, links to stock quotes, the most recently available annual sales and net income, and number of employees are provided. Rankings from the Fortune 500, the Forbes Private 500, or Hoover's 500 are provided if available. The sales figures for some private companies are estimated or approximate. Up to five of the company's top executives are listed.

Searching: Search by company name, ticker symbol, keyword or person's last name to retrieve company capsules, financials, and company news. Each company retrieved includes the contents described above, as well as additional information for Hoover's fee-based subscribers.

Advanced searching: No.

Design: Each page is chock-full of information and links, but still easy to navigate; use of tabs is innovative.

Other features: Company of the day, "Lists of Lists" links to ranking lists compiled on external Web sites, IPO Central sub-site for information on initial public offerings, including an alphabetical list of all IPOs filed electronically since May 1996.

Help or FAQ: Extensive Help Center available, with aids to content, searching and technical issues.

Other Top Business and Management Sites

Price's List of Lists
gwis2.circ.gwu.edu/~gprice/listof.htm
George Washington University librarian Gary Price maintains a clearinghouse of sites that present information in the form of rankings of different people, organizations, companies, etc. Includes the Top 100 Banks in Latin America, Nielsen U.S. TV Market Rankings, 250 Richest Towns in America, Top 50 Women-Owned Businesses, and much more.

International Business Resources on the Web
ciber.bus.msu.edu/busres.htm
Maintained by Tunga Kiyak at the Michigan State University Center for International Business Education and Research (CIBER), this searchable directory of annotated links is organized by region, country, and business topic. It offers useful sites for international trade, foreign company directories and yellow pages, and a multitude of statistical resources worldwide.

Scout Report for Business & Economics
wwwscout.cs.wisc.edu/scout/report/bus-econ/index.html
This must-see biweekly Web publication publishes selective annotations of recommended Web sites as well as a current awareness

service, selected by the librarians and content specialists at the well-regarded Internet Scout. Sections include Research, Current Awareness (lists of new documents available on the Web), Learning Resources, New Data, General Interest, and In the News. The listings are compiled into a searchable database at the Scout Signpost. It's also available via e-mail.

Livelink Pinstripe
pinstripe.opentext.com
A "slice" search engine for business-related information only, from the Ontario-based OpenText Corporation, Pinstripe searches for information on the pages of URLs recognized by reliable business sources. Updated every two weeks, Pinstripe's structure is based on the North American Industrial Classification System. You can search for one industry, several industries simultaneously, or all 150 slices. Sophisticated search features are available. The database is still small but the service is unique.

For More Information

Seybold, Patricia B. *Customers.Com: How to Create a Profitable Business Strategy for the Internet and Beyond*. New York: Times Books, 1998.

Hamel, Gary and Sampler, Jeff. "The E-Corporation: More than just Web-based, it's building a new industrial order." *Fortune*, December 12, 1998: 80+.

Ojala, Marydee. "Beginning all over again: where to start a search." (The Dollar Sign column) *Online*, May 1, 1998: 44.

Martin, Justin. "Changing Jobs? Try the Net. The Internet Is a Far More Powerful Job-search Tool Than It Was Just Months Ago. Now You Can't Ignore It." *Fortune*, March 2, 1998: 205+.

15

Countries and Regions of the World on the Web

In its early years (say, four years ago), referring to the hypertext, multimedia information space of the Internet as the "World Wide Web" was a misnomer. It really was the "United States Wide Web." Even though one of the earliest teletext systems, Minitel, was a French project, and the number of computer users per capita is higher in Iceland than in the U.S., until recently, few countries outside the U.S. had much in the way of information or representation on the Internet. In fact, most of the information that was available about foreign countries came from U.S. government or international agencies' sites, such as UNESCO.

But that is no longer true. Governments around the world have awakened to the power of this medium for information distribution about their country. Entrepreneurs of all types have made niche publications and sites about the unique products and places of their countries and use the Web to attract tourists, businesses, and customers. A recent study by Andersen Consulting found that European business use of the Internet in 1997 was two years behind the U.S. but in one year has almost caught up. Now, there is no country, from Andorra to Zimbabwe, that doesn't have some sort of Web site with information and resources about itself.

The main disadvantage when using non-U.S. sites is that the naming nomenclature that has become standard for U.S. sites, because of the vast numbers, is not in use in most countries. The clues the U.S. Internet site address suffixes give (.gov for government, .com for commercial, .org for non-profit organization, .edu for education, .mil for military) are not available in most non-U.S. Web site addresses. With the exception of the United Kingdom, which has a version of these "type of site" designations in place (.ac for education, .co for commercial), most countries rely only on the two-digit country code (see the list at the end of this chapter).

Information about individual countries includes official government sites, non-governmental organizations, and sites created by individuals in those countries about the country. Businesses operating in different countries are also putting their promotional information online, but they generally use the generic .com suffix rather than their country code, particularly if they operate internationally.

One of the challenges in using international Web sites is the language issue. For so many years the complaint, legitimately, was that the Web was almost exclusively English. Even reading the few Web sites in some other languages was hampered by the need to download special character sets. But now with the range of languages represented on the Web, and the ease of use because browser software has come to include these special characters, the Web is truly polyglot. However, with a nod to the predominance of English language speakers on the Internet, many international sites have multi-language options on their sites.

If you really, really need to see a rough-cut translation of a non-English Web page, the innovative, if inaccurate, AltaVista-sponsored translator, Babelfish (babelfish.altavista.digital.com/) will translate text or a Web page in French, German, Italian, Portuguese, or Spanish to English, or English to those languages. Don't rely on this translation, though, for serious correspondence. Translate the following into Spanish and then translate the Spanish back into English and it truly sounds like Babel:

Good afternoon, I am so very happy to be here with you. It beats working! It is always enjoyable to share good ideas with smart people.

This becomes, in Spanish,

Buena tarde. Me plazco tan muy estar aquí con usted. Bate el trabajo! Y es siempre agradable compartir buenas ideas con la gente elegante.

And this becomes, back in English:

Good it takes, I so very please myself to be here with you. It beats the work! And he is always pleasant to share good ideas with elegant people.

So, just remember, translator beware!

Not all countries offer the wide range of information available in the more Internet-progressive countries. In some cases there is a cultural reluctance to make information freely available, particularly from the government. Go to the Argentinean Web sites and you'll find information from all the political parties and activist groups, but little from the government itself. In the area of political and governmental information on international sites, determining the source of the information, and the "spin" they are likely to place on it, is particularly important.

A recent trend for most countries has been the development of a country-specific "Yahoo!-esque" Web site with resources about that country. Some of the major U.S. search sites, like AltaVista and Yahoo!, have created their own country-specific services. In other countries, a good scout has come up with the links related to the country and made them available. While not all the countries have grown an entrepreneurial site like that yet, for those countries where a good directory site is located, the organized links will help you tap into the myriad and exotic resources that our friends across the oceans are creating. The Web is truly a World Wide information Wonder.

Great Scout Sites for International Information

The Virtual Tourist
www.vtourist.com/
Contact: interaction.de GmbH
Haid-und-Neu Straße 7
76131 Karlsruhe, Germany
vtourist@interaction.de or tk@interaction.de

Why we picked this site: Why didn't we put this one in its obvious category, tourism sites? Well, because it is much more than just resources about tourism and travel in the countries of the world. Despite its rather limiting name, this site is a combination atlas, Web site guide and geography book. The unique features and readily displayed facts, plus the unique design and navigation of the site make for an interesting international, and national, resource. It's only right to have a scout page for international Web sites come from outside the U.S. This German site is available in English and German with French and Spanish versions coming soon.

Created: 1994 by Brandon Plewe. The site was bought by inter-action.de GmbH in August 1998.

How many sites: More than 100,000.

Audience: The general Internet community.

How sites are selected: The site gets resources through a number of methods. The original compilations came from Brandon Plewe's work. New sites are added by Internet hunters employed by inter-action.de. In addition, they get about 100 e-mail messages per day from people wanting to submit a site. These self-submissions are checked for relevancy and quality before they are added. Usually sites that just promote some individual business are not included.

How it's supported: interaction.de, a German Internet design and software engineering company, funds the building and maintenance of the site; it is their main on-going project. They will be selling banner ads on the site.

Searching: There are two ways to access the links. To browse the sites available, you click not on a keyword or category label as in most sites. On the Virtual Tourist, befitting its geographic subject, you click on a map of the world to get to one of the eight regions you want. Click on Asia, for example, and a detailed map with labels pointing to different countries is displayed. Select one of the countries and you get a smaller map of that country along with a profile of the country from the *CIA World Factbook* and the links available for that country, divided into City links and General links. This navigation scheme becomes a mini-geography lesson, learning the location on the world map and the general characteristics of each country on your way to the links.

The search method for locating links is simply a search box where you can put in terms. Multiple terms typed into the search box are read as an "and" search, so if you want links with information about hotels in Singapore, type in "singapore hotels." The search looks for words in the title or description of the links in the site. A select bar will be added to the search function soon. This will let you pick a continent, then a country, and then put a topic or keyword in the search box and it will automatically restrict the search to the region you are interested in.

What you get: Using the browse method, clicking by map to the country you want, you get to a country page with links divided by City and General. Clicking on a City gives you links specific to that city. The General links listing includes the link to the site and a brief description, written by the interaction.de staff, about the contents of the site. There is also a splay of icons to the left of the country profile page that indicate sub-categories of links available about the country: Entertainment, Business, Officials, Culture, Travel. If there are links available about that country in that sub-category, you can click on it and get the list of links. If that sub-category does not have any listings, there is a line through it.

In the search method, the results of the search are displayed in a useful way. Type a word in the search box, and the results are displayed with the sub-categories and countries listed down the left with the links and descriptions on the right. You can see immediately if the link is to a relevant area.

Design: The geographic theme with the map navigation is fitting to the site, and having the icon clues about available links is interesting. Befitting an international Web site, the universal and non-text-based navigation aids will make it easier for people from around the world to use the site with ease.

The Argus Clearinghouse
www.clearinghouse.net/
Contact: Argus Associates, Inc.
221 North Main Street, Suite 200
Ann Arbor, MI 48104
clearinghouse@argus-inc.com

Why we picked this site: The Argus Clearinghouse is one of the great compilation sites, with a twist. They provide links to value-added resource guides developed by other individuals and submitted to the Clearinghouse. They then evaluate the guides, giving seekers of resources on particular topics a few guides to those resources. People & Places is one of the thirteen Clearinghouse categories and is a compilation, in their words, "of guides on topics pertaining to cities, states, provinces, countries, and other regions of the world, their peoples and cultures, and travel information." While the number of links to guides provided is not extensive, it is their selectivity and careful evaluation that make this a good example of a scout site.

Created: 1993 by Louis Rosenfeld, author of *Information Architecture for the World Wide Web*.

How many sites: 1500 guides are rated and available in the Clearinghouse.

Audience: "A resource that brings together finding aids for students, researchers, educators, and others interested in locating authoritative information on the Internet."

How sites are selected: The Clearinghouse is highly selective in their inclusion of guides to the site: Only 5–10 percent of the guides submitted are included. There is a set of guidelines for people who want to submit a subject guide to the Clearinghouse. Human editors review the sites to ensure they are appropriate and to do the evaluation (which includes such elements as: Level of Resource Description, Level of Resource Evaluation, Guide Design, Guide Organizational Schemes, Guide Meta-Information). Each of these evaluation areas is rated with one to five check marks.

How it's supported: Argus Associates is a non-profit venture run by a small group of dedicated individuals.

Searching: From the main menu, select the People & Places category. You'll then get a list of sub-categories by continent and a listing of travel and regional information. Not all of the continents have guide categories. In South America, for example, only Bolivia is represented. When you click on a sub-category, you get a further breakdown of regions available. Clicking on one of those brings up the list of guides and their evaluation.

What you get: Each guide entry has the address where the guide is available, keywords about the guide, information about who compiled the guide, the rating given, date it was rated, and the date it was last checked by the Clearinghouse staff. Each guide is checked at least once a year to see if the guide is being maintained. If it is not, it is removed from the Clearinghouse.

Design: Very simple, clean, no-frills design.

Other features: Each month, the outstanding resource guide submitted to the Clearinghouse is given the "Digital Librarian Award." You can find the current and past winners at www.clearing house.net/dla.html.

Search Engines: Localized Search Engines

BIG Search Engine Index

www.merrydew.demon.co.uk/search4.htm

This straight-forward directory links you to the search engines that cover forty different countries.

infobel: International Telephone Directories

www.eu-info.com/inter/world.asp

What started as EuroInfo is now the world's available white pages (for looking up people), yellow pages (for looking up businesses) and fax directories all on one site. Select the country you want from the pull-down box, select from the look-up resources available for that country, and type in your request. This is one of the great compilations on the Net that help make the world a little smaller and more accessible.

Hieros Gamos

www.hg.org/hg.html

This site is profiled in the chapter on legal resources but it is worth mentioning again for its comprehensive, if somewhat confusing, links to resources about every country. The focus is on legal resources, but the links to country-specific information resources (like the Yahoo! listing of the country and country directories) are relevant to our topic here. We like the name of the site, "hieros gamos (Greek): harmonization of seeming opposites, e.g., sun and moon, earth and sky, mercury and sulfur and, in the case of the Internet, electronic and written information."

World POPClock Projection

www.census.gov/cgi-bin/ipc/popclockw

So just how many people are out there in the wide world? Keep track with the World Population Clock from the U.S. Census Bureau.

Internet Country Codes

AD	Andorra	CL	Chile
AE	United Arab Emirates	CM	Cameroon
AF	Afghanistan	CN	China
AG	Antigua and Barbuda	CO	Colombia
AI	Anguilla	CR	Costa Rica
AL	Albania	CS	Czechoslovakia (former)
AM	Armenia	CU	Cuba
AN	Netherlands Antilles	CV	Cape Verde
AO	Angola	CX	Christmas Island
AQ	Antarctica	CY	Cyprus
AR	Argentina	CZ	Czech Republic
AS	American Samoa	DE	Germany
AT	Austria	DJ	Djibouti
AU	Australia	DK	Denmark
AW	Aruba	DM	Dominica
AZ	Azerbaijan	DO	Dominican Republic
BA	Bosnia and Herzegovina	DZ	Algeria
BB	Barbados	EC	Ecuador
BD	Bangladesh	EE	Estonia
BE	Belgium	EG	Egypt
BF	Burkina Faso	EH	Western Sahara
BG	Bulgaria	ER	Eritrea
BH	Bahrain	ES	Spain
BI	Burundi	ET	Ethiopia
BJ	Benin	FI	Finland
BM	Bermuda	FJ	Fiji
BN	Brunei Darussalam	FK	Falkland Islands
BO	Bolivia		(Malvinas)
BR	Brazil	FM	Micronesia
BS	Bahamas	FO	Faroe Islands
BT	Bhutan	FR	France
BV	Bouvet Island	FX	France, Metropolitan
BW	Botswana	GA	Gabon
BY	Belarus	GB	Great Britain (UK)
BZ	Belize	GD	Grenada
CA	Canada	GE	Georgia
CC	Cocos (Keeling) Islands	GF	French Guiana
CF	Central African Republic	GH	Ghana
CG	Congo	GI	Gibraltar
CH	Switzerland	GL	Greenland
CI	Côte D'Ivoire	GM	Gambia
	(Ivory Coast)	GN	Guinea
CK	Cook Islands	GP	Guadeloupe

Internet Country Codes

GQ	Equatorial Guinea	LK	Sri Lanka
GR	Greece	LR	Liberia
GS	S. Georgia and	LS	Lesotho
	S. Sandwich Islands	LT	Lithuania
GT	Guatemala	LU	Luxembourg
GU	Guam	LV	Latvia
GW	Guinea-Bissau	LY	Libya
GY	Guyana	MA	Morocco
HK	Hong Kong	MC	Monaco
HM	Heard and McDonald	MD	Moldova
	Islands	MG	Madagascar
HN	Honduras	MH	Marshall Islands
HR	Croatia (Hrvatska)	MK	Macedonia
HT	Haiti	ML	Mali
HU	Hungary	MM	Myanmar
ID	Indonesia	MN	Mongolia
IE	Ireland	MO	Macau
IL	Israel	MP	Northern Mariana Islands
IN	India	MQ	Martinique
IO	British Indian Ocean	MR	Mauritania
	Territory	MS	Montserrat
IQ	Iraq	MT	Malta
IR	Iran	MU	Mauritius
IS	Iceland	MV	Maldives
IT	Italy	MW	Malawi
JM	Jamaica	MX	Mexico
JO	Jordan	MY	Malaysia
JP	Japan	MZ	Mozambique
KE	Kenya	NA	Namibia
KG	Kyrgyzstan	NC	New Caledonia
KH	Cambodia	NE	Niger
KI	Kiribati	NF	Norfolk Island
KM	Comoros	NG	Nigeria
KN	Saint Kitts and Nevis	NI	Nicaragua
KP	Korea (North)	NL	Netherlands
KR	Korea (South)	NO	Norway
KW	Kuwait	NP	Nepal
KY	Cayman Islands	NR	Nauru
KZ	Kazakhstan	NT	Neutral Zone
LA	Laos	NU	Niue
LB	Lebanon	NZ	New Zealand (Aotearoa)
LC	Saint Lucia	OM	Oman
LI	Liechtenstein	PA	Panama

Internet Country Codes

PE	Peru	TH	Thailand
PF	French Polynesia	TJ	Tajikistan
PG	Papua New Guinea	TK	Tokelau
PH	Philippines	TM	Turkmenistan
PK	Pakistan	TN	Tunisia
PL	Poland	TO	Tonga
PM	St. Pierre and Miquelon	TP	East Timor
PN	Pitcairn	TR	Turkey
PR	Puerto Rico	TT	Trinidad and Tobago
PT	Portugal	TV	Tuvalu
PW	Palau	TW	Taiwan
PY	Paraguay	TZ	Tanzania
QA	Qatar	UA	Ukraine
RE	Reunion	UG	Uganda
RO	Romania	UK	United Kingdom
RU	Russian Federation	UM	U.S. Minor Outlying Islands
RW	Rwanda		
SA	Saudi Arabia	US	United States
Sb	Solomon Islands	UY	Uruguay
SC	Seychelles	UZ	Uzbekistan
SD	Sudan	VA	Vatican City State (Holy See)
SE	Sweden		
SG	Singapore	VC	Saint Vincent and the Grenadines
SH	St. Helena		
SI	Slovenia	VE	Venezuela
SJ	Svalbard and Jan Mayen Islands	VG	Virgin Islands (British)
		VI	Virgin Islands (U.S.)
SK	Slovak Republic	VN	Viet Nam
SL	Sierra Leone	VU	Vanuatu
SM	San Marino	WF	Wallis and Futuna Islands
SN	Senegal	WS	Samoa
SO	Somalia	YE	Yemen
SR	Suriname	YT	Mayotte
ST	São Tome and Principe	YU	Yugoslavia
SU	U.S.S.R. (former)	ZA	South Africa
SV	El Salvador	ZM	Zambia
SY	Syria	ZR	Zaire
SZ	Swaziland	ZW	Zimbabwe
TC	Turks and Caicos Islands		
TD	Chad		
TF	French Southern Territories		
TG	Togo		

16

Government Information on the Web

"Our Constitution is in actual operation; everything appears to promise that it will last; but in this world nothing is certain but death and taxes," Benjamin Franklin wrote in 1789. Thanks to the U.S. government from which it arose, the Internet is in actual operation and promises to last. Government is expanding its strong Internet presence to the World Wide Web, even as commercial sites explode.

From death—the Morbidity and Mortality Weekly Report, to taxes— Internal Revenue Service tax forms, government information thrives and multiplies daily on the Web. Governments generate mass quantities of information and publish millions of pages annually. The Web allows for paperless publication and mass dissemination of the results of agency research, data collection and regulating, congressional speechifying and legislating, consumer publication programs, and whatever else goes through the government process. Be aware that at some agencies you may have to pay. Just because the information is on the Internet doesn't mean that it's free, even if it's from your government.

You can view high resolution images of each page of the *Constitution* and the *Declaration of Independence* at the National Archives, read the minutes of your city council's meetings, search the holdings of the Library of Congress, and listen to the president or governor speak. You can investigate a specific airplane's ownership or President Kennedy's assassination. The Central Intelligence Agency has a special "Secret Zone" for kids complete with cute spy dog photos (and a barking audio!) and a warning that your kid's visit there may be monitored (www.cia.gov/cia/ciakids/safe.html). You can also find information about foreign governments at many sites on the federal Web, including the CIA and the Departments of State, Defense, and Commerce. In fact, there's so much information from government agencies already on the Web—and so much more coming on in the future—that it's impossible to keep up.

Fortunately, there are subject-specific sites, search engines, and guides to help you exercise your right to access your governments—federal, state, county, and local. Even in this well-covered area, however, the search sites are of varying quality and use. Within the government community, several sites offer coverage and features that overlap or display startling gaps. Our government is so huge that it can't even keep track of itself, so many of the best search sites are organized and maintained by knowledgeable citizens outside the government, in non-profit organizations, university libraries, and more remote outposts.

Because there are so many sites to consider when categorizing the government Web, some of the search sites stop at the level of listing links to agency home pages. Although these sites can be very useful, they can't help you plumb the depths of the varied content that may reside on an agency's pages. Information on death benefits can be found at the Social Security Administration, statistics on mortality can be found at the Centers for Disease Control, and an account of the funeral ceremonies for the Unknown Soldiers of World War II and Korea is recorded in a text at the Department of the Army Center for Military History. Tax information may be federal, state, or local.

So even death and taxes aren't certain on the Web. If you don't know the name of the agency that is hiding your particular nugget, your digging can be frustrating or fruitless. We hope our selection of search sites will help you make your way through this excess of information with a little more ease and grace by focusing on those that offer topical access, descriptive evaluative annotations, or subject-specific search engines to point to the specific information you need.

In particular we hope to provide guidance on how to get to topical information across the boundaries of agencies and political geography. If you're looking for evaluations on how welfare reform is working in the states, or trying to find out how another locality is dealing with a problem that your town is struggling with, the topical gateways described below can help.

CAUTION: If you like to read this kind of information in printed form, be prepared to lose that luxury in the future. The Web provides your government with the opportunity to publish more economically to a wide audience without paper; increasingly the printed versions are being abandoned for digital formats. Printing out a full copy of a congressional hearing, budget document, or census report can use up a lot of one-sided paper and jam up the printer's works. Related to this issue is the replacement of "old" information by new and updated pages. When there's no paper copy, the older digital document may disappear forever. We used to call this "history." In the case of government e-mail and computer files, citizens have filed suit to demand that this type of information be retained and archived. Other types of information should be kept from deletion as well. Researchers, be aware!

Federal Government Materials on the Web

Archives: The National Archives provides information about our nation's treasured documents and links to the presidential libraries around the country (www.nara.gov).

Biographies: Uncle Sam: Who's Who in the Federal Government offers links to biographies and photos of Cabinet members, Supreme Court Justices, and other top government officials, from the library at the University of Memphis (www.lib.memphis.edu/gpo/whos3.htm).

Consumer information: The Federal Information Center provides a wide range of consumer publications from A to Z (fic.info.gov).

Directories: Government Information Exchange (GIX) aims to be one-stop shopping for contact information throughout the government (www.info.gov).

Government publications: U.S. Government Printing Office GPO Access (www.access.gpo.gov/su_docs/aces/aaces002.html).

Legislation: THOMAS is the U.S. Congress Web site, offering searchable text of bills, laws, *Congressional Record*, and much more (thomas.loc.gov).

Maps: The U.S. Geological Survey is our nation's mapmaker and offers an interactive map browser of the National Atlas of the United States where you can locate and map more than two million geographic names (www.usgs.gov).

Presidential documents: Premier site for the executive branch, with full-text archives from January 1993 of all presidential speeches, press releases, press conferences, executive orders, and a tour of the White House (www.whitehouse.gov).

Statistics: Bureau of the Census is one of the best government sites on the Web, offering up the demographics and business statistics of our nation (www.census.gov).

Tax forms: IRS (www.irs.gov/forms_pubs/).

ZIP codes: Search for ZIP codes at the U.S. Postal Service (www.usps.gov).

What's Missing

- Each agency decides what to put on its Web site, so you may not find what you're looking for even if you know it exists. Send the agency an e-mail to request that it be made available.

- Although there's a lot of request for feedback, there's not much real interactivity on the government Web. Commercial sites and individuals seem to be doing a better job than governments do at asking viewers for their opinions, providing open discussions, allowing electronic commercial transactions, and answering e-mail.
- Information about Native American tribal government is not easy to find. Although there are 575 federally recognized Indian tribes and Alaska Native villages, fewer than 20 are linked to the Web directory at Codetalk, at the U.S. Department of Housing and Urban Development (www.codetalk.fed.us).

Great Scouts for Government

Federal Government Resources on the Web
www.lib.umich.edu/libhome/Documents.center/federal.html

Contact: Grace York, Coordinator
Documents Center
The University of Michigan Library
Ann Arbor, Michigan 48109-1205
graceyor@umich.edu

Why we picked this site: Look through the eyes of an expert documents reference librarian at the world of federal government information. She'll point you to the site or document that will give you an answer. That's what Grace York at the University of Michigan Library Documents Center has been doing on the Internet since the Gopher days in 1993. Federal Government Resources is part of a larger Web site, Government Resources on the Web (www.lib. umich.edu/libhome/Documents.center/govweb.html), that has sections on foreign, international, Michigan, and state/local government, as well as Documents in the News, Documents Librarianship, political science and statistics, and class assignment pages for UM students. What makes this site our top pick are the brief, evaluative descriptions for each of the selections, including tips on what's important on the site and how to use it. You can browse or search the listings with a search engine that is updated weekly. The directory is easy to navigate (both frames and non-frames versions), current, comprehensive, and just plain useful.

Created: Predecessor Gopher site started in May 1993; Web site started in April 1995.

How many sites: 250 pages in whole site, 30 to 200 site entries per page.

Audience: Reference staff of University of Michigan Library Documents Center and UM students.

How sites are selected: Selection is based on potential use in answering real reference questions. York writes: "Items are selected from the various Scout Reports, messages posted on GOVDOC-L, recommendations by other Webmasters, and material found while answering a question or preparing a class assignment Web page . . . . The only way to keep up with federal information is by knowing the federal information infrastructure and checking the 'Browse Titles' option on the GPO Access web site."

How it's supported: University of Michigan Library.

Topics covered: Agency Directories and Web Sites, Bibliographies, Budget, Civil Service, Copyright, Executive Branch, Executive Orders, General Accounting Office, Grants, Contracts and Auctions, Historic Documents, Judicial Branch, Laws and

Constitution, Legislative Branch, Office of Management and Budget, Patents, President, Regulations, Taxes, White House.

Contents: Guides to both Web and non-Web information, including material available at the University of Michigan Library (but useful because the same materials will be available in other libraries closer to you). Browse the directory or search the contents of the pages.

What you get: A search provides the title of the site or resource (including those old-fashioned books), links to Web sites, and a brief bulleted description. Some entries include the specific answer; for example, the entry for Kenneth Starr includes his address and telephone number, as well as a link to his biography.

Advanced searching: SWISH is a shareware program available on the library's Web server. It lacks proximity locators (e.g., you can't search a phrase), but it re-indexes the site once per week so the SWISH index is very current. A link to an AltaVista search is offered as well.

Design: Very simple, clear, text-based, quick to load.

Other features: "Documents in the News" highlights topics in the news, with an archive back to 1995. "What's New" adds sites just about every day. A special collection of the text of President Kennedy's 214 executive orders, accessible by date, keyword, title, and number, is a unique collection on this site. There is also a comprehensive resource for government documents librarians.

Help or FAQ: Search help is available.

Read about it:
York, Grace, (with Rita Wilson). "Government Resources on the Web: Will It Change Public Services?" *Library Hi Tech*, v. 16, (1998): 60–70.

FedStats

www.fedstats.gov

Contact: The gateway does not provide contacts, except for the ubiquitous "Webmaster"; however, it is coordinated by the Interagency Council on Statistical Policy, Office of Management and Budget, Executive Office of the President (www.whitehouse. gov/omb).

Why we picked this site: FedStats is the one-stop shopping gateway to the incredible wealth of statistical information gathered by federal government agencies. The information available through FedStats is maintained and updated solely by federal agencies on their own Internet servers. Through this gateway, you can search across agencies to find statistics on topics that may be covered by several separate statistical programs. Agencies represented in the database include the Bureau of Economic Analysis, Bureau of Labor Statistics, Bureau of Justice Statistics, Bureau of Transportation Statistics, Bureau of the Census, Energy Information Administration, Economic Research Service, Environmental Protection Agency, National Agricultural Statistics Service, National Center for Education Statistics, National Center for Health Statistics, National Science Foundation, Office of Management and Budget, Internal Revenue Service, and the Social Security Administration. Statistical information pages from more than fifty additional federal agencies are also linked from the FedStats directory.

"FedStats takes advantage of Internet technology to make federal statistics more accessible," said Sally Katzen, administrator of the Office of Management and Budget's Office of Information and Regulatory Affairs when the site opened in 1997. "Today, a high school student with a modem in Boise, Idaho, has better access to federal statistics than top officials in Washington had five years ago."

"The public release of FedStats in May 1997 has been a phenomenal success by providing one-stop shopping for all federal statistics. Continued interdisciplinary research may not only permit users to find the statistics faster and easier but may also help users understand how best to use the statistics. FedStats may, therefore, become an icon for improving the quantitative literacy of all Americans" (from Tupek, cited below).

Created: May 1997.

How many sites: 70 agencies.

Audience: Federal agencies and the public.

How it's supported: U.S. government: your tax dollars.

Freshness: Unfortunately, the pages on the site are not dated, but the links out to the participating agencies are usually fresh.

Topics covered: Agriculture, Crime, Demographics, Economic, Education, Energy, Environment, Health, Income, Labor, National Accounts, Natural Resources, Safety, Transportation.

Contents: Agencies (fourteen agencies that make up the Interagency Council and more than fifty others that provide statistics with descriptions of the types of data collected), programs (topical arrangement), contacts (people who are responsible for collecting and analyzing statistics at the agencies), Fast Facts (link to the latest demographic and economic statistics from the White House Federal Statistics Briefing Rooms and the full text of the *Statistical Abstract of the United States* in PDF format), Regional Data (sites that provide regional statistical compilations on indicated topics), searchable press releases from eleven agencies. For example, safety statistics are maintained by the Bureau of Labor Statistics, the Consumer Product Safety Commission, OSHA, and Mine Safety and Health Administration.

Searching: Search or browse the A–Z list of topics for the entire list of participating agencies or search by keyword in the sites of the Interagency Council representatives (the largest statistical agencies). TOPIC search software by Verity Inc. is used on Fed-Stats. You can choose which agencies to search or search all fourteen. The A–Z list is easier to use than the site's search engine. The basic search involves relevancy ranking. TOPIC searching is different from what you may be accustomed to using on other search engines. If words are entered next to each other, TOPIC will look for them as a phrase; if you want to add words to your search, separate them with commas. Basic search instructions are on the search page; you can't miss them.

What you get: The search results page gives you a ranked listing of hits with the title and URL and key passage of text on the page where your keywords appeared. The link will take you directly to the document at its agency site.

Advanced searching: A user guide to advanced searching is available for using Boolean operators (AND, OR) in searches.

Design: Low tech, simple; most pages fill just one screen; where frames are used, they are clumsy, so choose the no-frames option. The site map is useful for navigating the sections of the site.

Other features: "Fast Facts" links, which allow users to visit either the Federal Statistics Briefing Rooms or online versions of the most frequently requested tables from the *Statistical Abstract of the United States* and the *State and Metropolitan Area Databook*. Detailed feedback questionnaire.

Help or FAQ: Only for searching.

> **CAUTION:** Many of the documents, when you get to them, are in PDF (Portable Document Format) and you must have the free Adobe Acrobat reader installed on your computer to view the information in them.

Read about it:

Tupek, Alan R., National Science Foundation, and Cathryn S. Dippo "Quantitative Literacy: New Website for Federal Statistics Provides Research Opportunities." Bureau of Labor Statistics, *D-Lib Magazine*, December 1997 (www.dlib.org/dlib/december97/stats/12tupek.html).

Berinstein, Paula. *Finding Statistics Online: How to Locate the Elusive Numbers You Need.* Medford, NJ: Information Today, Inc. (Cyber-Age Books), 1998.

State and Local Information

U.S. State & Local Gateway
www.statelocal.gov
Contact: Don Elder, Adviser
National Partnership for Reinventing Government
Don.Elder@npr.gov

Why we picked this site: U.S. State & Local Gateway is a federal interagency project that coordinates information about state and local government issues on federal Web servers, in collaboration with Vice President Al Gore's National Performance Review. Much of this online federal information was hidden deep in the Web sites of a multitude of separate agencies, but this site is the Great Scout that points you to the topic and the page you're seeking.

"This is one of several federal Web sites that are known as gateway or portal sites," said NPR adviser Don Elder. "It's an online resource for federal programs, projects, funding and grants."

We pick the State & Local Gateway for its unique mission, topical arrangement, simplicity,and ease of use. There's also a Non-Profit Gateway for federal information of interest to non-profit organizations (www.nonprofit.gov/index.html) coordinated by the White House Office of Public Liaison.

Created: Fall 1997.

How many sites: Web sites of more than thirty federal agencies and seven state and local organizations, including the Council of State Governments, Internation City/County Management Association, National Association of Counties, National Council of State Legislatures, U.S. Conference of Mayors, and the National League of Cities.

Audience: This Web site was developed to give state and local government officials and employees, academics, businesses, and professionals easy access to federal information on state and local topics.

How it's supported: U.S. government, sponsored by National Partnership for Reinventing Government.

Topics covered: Subjects include Administrative Management, Communities/Commerce, Disasters/Emergencies, Education, Environment/Energy, Families/Children, Health, Housing, Money Matters, Public Safety, Transportation/Infrastructure, and Workforce Development. Current Issues include Brownfields, Performance Measures, Sustainable Communities, Welfare Reform, Year 2000, and Plain Language (a government-wide group working to improve communications from the federal government to the public).

Contents: Under each subject are these topics: News, Frequently Asked, Contacts, Related Links, Reference Materials, Funding, Best Practices, Tools, TA/Training, Laws/Regulations.

What you get: Browse the directory by topic or subject or current issue to retrieve a list of links (some annotated) to relevant Web pages on appropriate agencies and organizations sites.

Advanced searching: No site search, but links to available government-wide search engines (GILS and www.info.gov) are provided. Searches for the subject title in a relevant agency database and retrieves list of databases available for searching at agencies.

Design: Text-based, easy to use, integrated design.

Other features: Reference Room, a library of important documents; Customer One-Stops, which provides links to federal interagency gateways and search sites; and Contacts, which links to agency phone directories and e-mail addresses.

Help or FAQ: "Frequently Asked" section links to FAQs and other guides to the gateway's topics and agencies.

StateSearch
www.nasire.org/statesearch
Contact: Amy Hughes, Assistant Director
NASIRE
167 W. Main St., Ste. 600
Lexington, KY 40507
lread@amrinc.net

Why we picked this site: StateSearch is designed to serve as a topical clearinghouse to state government information on the

Internet. StateSearch is a creation of NASIRE, the organization representing chief information officers of the states. "It's one-of-a-kind when it comes to Web-based state information," said Amy Hughes, NASIRE's assistant director. "State governments have recognized its value by providing links to StateSearch from their own Web sites." StateSearch offers an easy way to find the name of a state agency for the topic you're seeking and quickly get to it. Sometimes the Great Scouts are just that simple.

Created: 1995, redesigned in December 1998.

How many sites: 2,310+.

Audience: Government officials and the general public looking for information from individual states across the nation.

How it's supported: NASIRE, a non-profit membership organization.

Topics covered: The thirty-two categories include Agriculture, Arts Commissions, Auditors, Corrections, Criminal Justice, Disabilities Agencies, Economic Development and Commerce, Education, Employment Services, Energy, Environment and Natural Resources, Finance and Administration, Governors, Health and Human Services, Information Technology, Judicial, Legal Opinions, Lieutenant Governors, Older Adult Services, Purchasing/Procurement, Regulation and Licensing, Revenue, State Constitutions, State Homepages, State Legislatures, State Libraries, Tourism, Transportation, Treasurers, and the Year 2000 Officer.

Contents: Index, not searchable; no annotations, but subject arrangement.

What you get: For each category, you retrieve a page that lists, by state, department, or agency, names with live links to their Web sites.

Advanced searching: No.

Design: Simple, just a list of sites for each state under each topic.

Other features: No frills.

Help or FAQ: No.

Other Top Government Sites

Federal Web Locator
www.law.vill.edu/fed-agency/fedwebloc.html
The Federal Web Locator is a service provided by the Villanova University's Center for Information Law and Policy and is intended to be the one-stop shopping point for federal government information on the World Wide Web. The site matches the structure found in *The United States Government Manual*. It's the ultimate site for finding agency Web sites, but there are no annotations or evaluations. Also offers a search feature and "What's New" that's updated frequently and very useful. The place to go for a listing of nearly every government site.

FedWorld
www.fedworld.gov
FedWorld is probably the oldest and leading U.S. government electronic information site and we have to mention it, but it is confusing and difficult to use. Some of the most important information you can find here includes many federal fee-based products. FedWorld was a pioneer in electronic bulletin board and file sharing; the dial-up BBS and FTP sites are still maintained.

State and Local Government on the Net
www.piperinfo.com/state/states.html
The place to go when you're looking for official U.S. state and local agency sites, this is a comprehensive up-to-date, well-organized list

of links, but it does not offer descriptions, annotations, or topical access. Contents for each state include a State Home Page, State Directory, Statewide Offices, Legislative Branch, Judicial Branch, Executive Branch, Boards and Commissions, Counties, Cities, Other (for example, in New Jersey, the State League of Municipalities). The "glimpse" search engine provides easy access to the links on sub-pages.

Top Federal Government Search Engines

GovBot

eden.cs.umass.edu/Govbot

The Center for Intelligent Information Retrieval (CIIR) GovBot has gathered more than a million Web pages from U.S. government (.gov) and military (.mil) sites around the country. You can search the GovBot database by using a simple form. GovBot uses the InQuery search engine, which offers many useful advanced features that require commands that are different from most search engines. Read the Help and Hints for a thorough explanation. This search engine brings up an enormous amount of information, but it can be confusing. Many of the hits seem to come from Department of Defense (.mil) sites.

Government Information Locator Service (GILS)

www.access.gpo.gov/su_docs/gils/gils.html

The Government Information Locator Service (GILS) is a decentralized gateway to databases containing records identifying public information resources (both electronic and non-electronic) throughout the federal government, describing information available in those sources, and providing assistance in obtaining information on those sources. It's like a searchable card catalog of information maintained within a large selection of federal agencies, including the CIA, Treasury Dept., Federal Reserve Board, Selective Service System, and a score more. GILS started at the U.S. Geological Survey, but our favorite entry point to the decentralized database is at the U.S. Government Printing Office (GPO). Not all agencies have mounted their GILS records on the GPO Access server and some are not easily accessible. Other databases at GPO can be searched via GPO Access at www.access. gpo. gov/su_docs/dbsearch.html.

For More Information

Maxwell, Bruce. *How to Access the Federal Government on the Internet.* Washington, D.C.: Congressional Quarterly Inc., 1998.

Andriot, Laurie. *Internet Blue Pages: The Guide to Federal Government Web Sites.* Medford, NJ: Information Today, Inc. (CyberAge Books), 1999.

17

Law on the Web

Since Moses came down from the mountain with Ten Commandments inscribed on stone tablets, the laws of Western civilization have been based on written word and precedent. Contemporary legal research requires the utmost attention to details of prior judicial opinions and decisions from the bench, as well as keeping up with the most recent developments and interpretations in courts and legislatures around our nation and—as the international marketplace expands—around the globe. Attorneys, legal paraprofessionals, and law librarians use their specialized research skills to pursue the specific cite or fact that will make or break a case in court or settlement.

The volume of legal information generated in this increasingly litigious society is staggering. A corresponding growth in the field of information technology has responded to the needs of the legal community for text storage and retrieval.

As computers entered the commercial market in the post-World War II information boom, legal researchers turned computer power towards the dilemma of managing the indexing needs of the law. In the late 1950s and early 1960s, John Horty, Director of the University of Pittsburgh Health Law Center, experimented with entering text of statutes on punch cards. By making the text retrievable by Key Words In Combination (KWIC), Horty invented "computer-assisted legal research," according to Pittsburgh law professor Bernard J. Hibbits.[1]

The development of legal information retrieval software continued as the Mead Data Central subsidiary of the Mead Corporation in 1973 introduced Lexis—then a database of full-text federal statutes and case law and a few statewide databases—to the legal market. At the same time, the West Publishing Company began development of the WestLaw text database. In the 1980s, the two companies entered into serious competition for subscribers to computer-assisted legal research products. West's uniqueness was in its proprietary abstracts and citations of case law, Lexis' in its flexible and speedy text-retrieval software and the size of its database, still outstanding even in our days of terabyte-sized Web indexes. The addition of law review material to both services increased both the comprehensiveness and timeliness of the body of materials covered.

What made these services possible and profitable was the availability of legal materials in the public domain: The text of opinions and legislation are our governments' public documents and thus freely distributed. In those early days of information retrieval, the keepers of mainframe computers held the keys to the information kingdom, and profited enormously as a result of their foresight and investment in technology and marketing. Lexis and WestLaw continue to dominate the legal research realm and also to charge handsomely to recoup enormous investments in both brain and computer power. And the model for the legal market—charging back research expenses to the client—continues to support law firms' use of these Cadillacs of information retrieval.

The Web is instigating a sea change in the legal information world. As the cost of computer power declines and access to online information via the Internet expands, governments and academic institutions are making legal documents and review articles available at no or low cost as an information service to the public—as well as passing them on to the commercially enhanced megadatabases. There are an up side and also a down side regarding integrity and usefulness of these Web legal databases. Instead of a global search of all case law or legislation, a Web researcher has to discover and search individual databases by jurisdiction, publication, or time frame as available on the Internet: One-stop shopping versus point-and-click hunt-and-peck. And, although the body of legal information on the freely available Web is growing quickly, it is still hit or miss. The law is complex and voluminous; that's why there are so many attorneys.

If you're looking for information or assistance with the law, there are an ever-wider variety of free and fee-based sites on the Web that can help. Providers of legal materials on the Web include federal and state courts and agencies, law schools, bar associations, law firms, commercial legal information services like Lexis-Nexis and WestLaw, advocacy groups and individuals—from jurists and experts to hobbyists and gadflies. *Caveat emptor!*

"The Web is not a replacement for a lawyer by any means," said FindLaw co-founder Stacy Stern. "There are complicated issues that a lawyer will know. For example, if you're looking at a legal form or article on a law in Georgia, the law will be different in California. That's something really important that a consumer may not notice. When you're going to a doctor or a lawyer, do a little research first to have an educated discussion."

CAUTION: Don't depend on the Web for your legal defense; get professional help. Be aware that lawyers advertise, too; self-promotional sites may not be the best place to go for reliable legal advice.

What's missing: An essential legal reference tool, *Black's Law Dictionary*, 6th edition, is not available on the Internet, although it can be purchased at cyberbookstores. Jury trial verdicts are not available, but companies that track verdicts for a fee or provide litigation support services, such as jury research and consultation, advertise these services. Legal textbooks are not available on the Web, although students' posted class outlines can often be found. Disbarments and disciplinary actions against lawyers are difficult to locate except by hit-or-miss. For example, names of Texas attorneys or judges mentioned in disciplinary actions published in the Texas Bar Journal and disciplinary actions taken by the District of Columbia Bar can be found. Here's a real service for consumers that we hope will be provided on the Web in the future.

The Great Scouts for law will help you become a more educated consumer as you make your way through the online legal maze of what's on the Web and what's not.

Legal Materials on the Web

Advocacy groups: American Civil Liberties Union (www.aclu.org), Adoption Policy Resource Center (www.fpsol.com/adoption/advocates.html).

Attorney directories: West Legal Directory (www.lawoffice.com) and Martindale-Hubbell Lawyer Locator (www.martindale.com/locator/home.html).

Consumer information: American Bar Association Legal Help Center (www.abanet.org/public/home.html).

Disciplinary actions: *Texas Bar Journal* (www.lawlib.uh.edu/ethics/attydiscipline/index.html), DC Bar (www.dcbar.org/public_consumer/discipline.html).

Discussion list and forums: Web law lists and discussion groups from Washburn University School of Law Library (www.washlaw.edu/listserv.html).

Law education and employment information: Law School Admission Council (www.lsac.org), legal jobs listings and job hunting information from Law Journal Extra (www.lawjobs.com).

Law reviews: University Law Review Project—includes searchable text of hundreds of law review articles (www.lawreview.org).

Legal forms: Power of Attorney for Health Care from Choice in Dying (www.choices.org), business license applications from the District of Columbia Department of Regulatory and Consumer Affairs (www.dcra.org).

Opinions and case law: Supreme Court Opinions 1893—from FindLaw (www.findlaw.com/casecode/supreme.html), Opinions of the Supreme Court and the Court of Appeals of Virginia (www.courts.state.va.us/opin.htm), or try your own home state.

Transcripts and documents: Famous cases like O.J. Simpson, Paula Jones, Unabomber, Oklahoma City bomber from Court TV (www.courttv.com).

Lawyer jokes: Court Humor and Lawyer Jokes from CounselQuest (www.CounselQuest.com/jokes.htm). An example: While summing up the State's case against the alleged despicable conduct of the defendant, the Prosecutor addressed the jury, "Ladies and gentlemen—all I can say is that if Moses had known the defendant, there would have been two or three more Commandments."

Great Scout Sites for Law

FindLaw
www.findlaw.com
Contact: Stacy Stern, Co-Founder
FindLaw
2850 Middlefield Rd. #205
Palo Alto, Ca 94306
info@findlaw.com

Why we picked this site: FindLaw gets four stars in the Great Scout galaxy of subject-specific searching. Not only does it have Yahoo!'s clean look and feel, it provides subject content and extra features that take it beyond a search site to a full-service legal information site.

"We were inspired by Yahoo!," said FindLaw's Stacy Stern. "We think they're great." Stern and co-founders Tim Stanley and Martin Roscheisen attended Stanford University where Jerry Yang and David Filo started Yahoo! in 1994.

FindLaw offers its own "slice" search engine, LawCrawler, which lets you search for legal information in both its own deep resources and out on the global Web. Databases of Supreme Court slip opinions dating back to 1893 and Federal Circuit Court slip opinions, as well as a networked search of all law review articles currently available on sites across the Web, can be searched from this singular location.

Stern sees FindLaw and the Web as complementary, not competitive, with the traditional legal databases. "The Web is not of the same quality as the incredible legal directories," she said. "It's not as comprehensive, not as reliable. Slip opinions are not 'officially published' and we have nothing like sheparding or autociting."

But FindLaw offers a community, which makes it an authentic Internet citizen. Avoiding commercialization (although advertisements contribute to its support), FindLaw combines academia, the legal profession, government sources, and Netizen participation for the best of all purposes. The LegalMinds section archives the postings to legal discussion groups (listservs). Here you can sift through the opinions and ruminations of contributors to specialized legal discussions. "It's a great way to locate a lawyer," Stern said.

Created: Online since January 1, 1996.

How many sites: 25,000.

Audience: Attorney, law students, general public.

How sites are selected: Paid staff of lawyers and law students select from submitted sites and pro-actively seek out useful sites and legal forms.

How it's supported: Advertisements (including commercial legal publishers like Lexis and West), partnerships like JusticeMail, and joint academic projects including the University Law Review Project.

Topics covered: Legal subjects index includes practice section categories for more than thirty-five practice areas, including Entertainment and Sports Law, Family Law, Health Law, Property Law and Real Estate, and Tax Law. Other features include cases and codes, a legal jobs database, career center, law schools, legal associations, foreign law resources, and legal news from Reuters.

Searching: LawCrawler, powered by AltaVista, searches contents of site, as well as law-related sites on the Web, a collection of Supreme Court opinions since 1893, U.S. Constitution, U.S. Code, Federal Circuits, and a special collection of law review articles. Boolean searches (AND, OR) are supported.

What you get: Your search of FindLaw's Guide retrieves listings of FindLaw categories and sites. Category listings include links to texts of relevant laws and documents, journals, newsletters and articles on the Web, mailing lists (with subscription information), Usenet newsgroups and message boards, links to government agencies, and law firms within the relevant legal practice area.

Advanced searching: Specialized searches include LawCrawler's search of legal sites across the Web, an archive of Supreme Court opinions since 1893, federal circuit opinions, legal mailing list and discussion group archives, and U.S. government sites.

Design: The page looks and feels like Yahoo!. Clear, clean, fast-loading and easy to navigate.

Other features: LegalMinds makes it easy to access public-interest mailing lists on the Web. Law reviews on the Web from the University Law Review Project are searchable via LawCrawler. Additional features include links to law firms on the Web (free home pages for law firms are offered), Continuing Legal Education credits for online courses, and free e-mail via @justicemail.com.

Help or FAQ: Help and information includes FAQs on how to find case law online and searching for legal information with LawCrawler.

Read about it:

Rampe, David. "Legal Resources on the Web." *The New York Times*, May 12, 1997, (www.nytimes.com/library/cyber/sites/051297 sites.html).

Counsel Quest

www.counselquest.com
Contact: Paul Ward, Vice-President, Development
Counsel Quest
4602 East Thomas Road
Phoenix, AZ 85257
paulward@law.com

Why we picked this site: Counsel Quest's standard is uniqueness and quality rather than quantity of site listings. "Content is king," said Counsel Quest vice president, Paul Ward. "The format doesn't matter, the content of the material does." This scout doesn't include repetitive similar listings; only the best sites for each topic are selected, so that all the listings in the subject sections are "recommended." We also like this site for its cleanly designed tree structure and ease of use. Counsel Quest is a Great Scout for business users, students, and consumers seeking quick and easy directions to legal information on the Web. The Counsel Quest guide is now part of the Law.com legal portal at www.law.com.

Created: 1994.

How many sites: NA

Audience: Consumers and the legal profession.

How sites are selected: Professional staff, overseen by attorneys, reviews submissions and pro-actively and highly selectively seeks out new sites. Criteria include usefulness and quality of content and uniqueness of site. Law firms are listed without preference. Links are checked weekly.

How it's supported: Banner advertising: Counsel Quest was bought by law portal Law.com in August 1998.

Topics covered: Archaic Laws, Documents and Tribunals, Articles, Newsletters and Columns, Attorneys and Firms, Bar Associations, Codes and Statutes, Constitutions, Courts and Opinions, Employment Resources, Federal Resources, Humor, International Sites, Law Schools, Legal Forms, Legal Research, News, Publishers, Reference Desk, Services, State Resources, Usenet Newsgroups. Under Legal Research there are practice area sub-sections (including business and consumer law, criminal law, family law, immigration law, and more) in several areas that point to Web resources, news articles, and legal studies and education (including class notes, exams, and more).

Searching: Browse the expandable outline, where sites are arranged alphabetically by title, or use the site's excellent HotBot-powered search engine for relevance rankings.

What you get: Site name, address, and link for each listing. The listings are selective but not annotated, except for handy descriptions of what's available on the Legal Forms sites and indication of sites you have to pay for.

Advanced searching: HotBot search engine has all kinds of bells and whistles and also provides pre-cooked search paths to federal and state government and agency sites.

Design: Unique and easily navigable outline design offers sub-topics as open-and-close folders. Clear large type makes for easy viewing.

Other features: No.

Help or FAQ: Good help only for search engine.

Other Top Legal Sites

Heiros Gamos
www.hg.org
This is a portal and searchable Web directory combining law and government listings for more than 50,000 Web sites. It provides searchable global directories of associations, societies, publishers, law schools, and vendors to the legal profession and links to Web sites in more than 200 subject areas. This is a huge site but lack of annotations and hectic framed design make it more difficult to use than some other sites.

Internet Legal Resource Guide and LawRunner
www.ilrg.com, www.lawrunner.com
This is a guide to over 3,000 selected law-related Web sites in 238 nations, islands, and territories and a collection of resources including a legal forms archive, and extensive information about law schools and legal education, including law studies abroad. "The selection criteria are predicated on two principles: the extent to which the resource is unique, as well as the relative value of the information it provides." This is the home of the LawRunner legal research tool, which provides pre-designed query templates for intelligent searching of AltaVista's legal and government sites and other selected legal databases on the Web.

WashLaw Web

www.washlaw.edu

From the Washburn University School of Law in Topeka, Kansas, this is a categorized list of links to law resources. Also at Washburn is RefLaw: The Virtual Law Library Reference Desk (www.washlaw. edu/reflaw/reflaw.html).

Center for Information Law and Policy

www.cilp.org

Contains an extensive body of federal case law, regulations and legislation, including the Federal and State Court Locators and the FLITE database of U.S. Supreme Court decisions from 1937–1975.

For More Information

Heels, Erik J. and Richard Klau. *Law Law Law on the Internet: The Best Legal Sites & More.* Chicago, IL: American Bar Assn., 1998.

Endnotes

1. Hibbits, Bernard J. "Last Writes: Re-assessing the Law Review in the Age of Cyberspace." *New York University Law Review* 71, 615 (1996), (www.law. pitt.edu/hibbitts/lastrev.htm).

18

News and Publications on the Web

Sure, the motto for *The New York Times* is "All the news that's fit to print." But for many print news products, the saying might be, "All the news that fits, we print." The constraints of the "newshole," the space available for news (after the ads have been counted in) or the time slot for broadcast news, have been the limitations many organizations have dealt with in delivering their product, news, to consumers. That and the limited delivery range—all the news we can get to your doorstep by morning or in your viewing area—have all changed with the growth of digital news delivery through Internet and World Wide Web publications.

Now you can see a story in your hometown paper and check out what they said about it in the hometown where the event took place. Terrorist bomb in Ireland? Check out the *Irish Times* (www.ireland.com.ie). Money crisis in Russia? Read the *Moscow Times* (www.moscowtimes.ru). Earthquake in Southern California? Follow it in the *Los Angeles Times* (www.latimes.com).

It's not just the daily news coverage that you might want. Archives of past news stories are increasingly becoming a feature for news Web sites. Did someone tell you about a great article in *The New York Times* this week? Go to their Web site (www.nytimes.com) and look for it. Want to find out if anyone else has written about a topic your newspaper has been featuring? Use one of the cross-publication searches on the Web to find other stories.

Electronic news archives started to be developed in the late 1970s when newspapers moved from hot type (poured lead) production methods to "cold type"—computer generated production pages. The output from the news production allowed organizations to capture the news text and put it in databases that allowed them to be searched. For the first decade and a half, however, only those who subscribed to expensive database services, like Lexis-Nexis or Dialog, could tap into these past files of stories.

That has changed in the past few years as newspapers have looked to their Web sites as a way to market access to past news stories. While only a small portion of the 4,000 or so newspapers worldwide with online editions have access to their past stories, the number who are making these resources available and the services that are being created to help you tap into these databases has been growing steadily.

Reading news stories on the Web from credible news organizations is one answer to the question all Web users should ask themselves, "Can I trust this information?" For the most part, the information that appears on a news Web site is the same as that which appears in the print version. There are often some supplements to the print information, additional photos or links to past news stories on the topic, or links to outside Web sites with relevant information. These can help those news-hounds who want to sniff out more material on a story they are following closely.

In the case of television news, the multimedia aspects of Web pages are an ideal fit. On the anniversary of Princess Diana's death, the package on CNN Interactive (www.cnn.com) included a Web page laid out with text and photos, links to videos you could view on your computer, links to past stories and videos of coverage, links to related sites, and links to photos of people or places named in the text. To make this a full-service resource for those interested in this particular news event, there is even a box at the end of the package with links to books on the topic available from Barnes and Noble.

News organizations, used to working with a particular medium (print or broadcast), are still trying to figure out the idiosyncrasies of publishing on the Web. Some of the things that can be done online have repercussions for the news consumer, of which you should be aware. The "constant updating" capability of online publications means a story you saw on the Web this morning might not be there this afternoon, and there might not be any record of it having been there (not everyone is archiving their Web sites' material). The dating that is done of material on news Web sites is often misleading; they might change the date of publication of the Web page to reflect the current day but the story will actually have been on the site for several days. Some news organizations are loath to send you off their site to other Web sites so they might pull into their site documents or information that they want to supplement their news story. This can be a problem, particularly for a dynamic document that might undergo some changes. A good rule of thumb for information-seeking on the Web is to try to get it from the source that originated the document.

We may be in the heyday of newspaper and television news on the Web. For a while it was almost a fad to crank up a Web version of your publication and the rush to cyberspace meant that almost every part of the world had an online news presence. But now the economic realities of creating a new product for a new medium has hit many corporate pocketbooks and some fledgling online publications have had their funding dry up. Advertisers, the mainstay of print and broadcast news organizations' revenue stream, have been somewhat reticent in moving their business online (or they have been creating their own online sites and have cut out the "middle man"). Part of the challenge, too, is that Web publications find that many of the users of the site are former residents of the area who use the expanded circulation area that the Web allows to keep up with hometown news—but this doesn't help sell the local advertisers on the benefits of Web advertising to drum up local business.

For smaller, regional publications and alternative news outlets, the Web has meant expanded awareness of their publications by an online audience. "News junkies" are in a golden age of access. If you are interested in what's going on in San Francisco, you can read the two mainstream hometown papers (the *Chronicle* and the *Examiner*), the local business journal, a weekly (the *Beacon*) and a daily legal publication (Cal Law), an alternative paper, and even a Jewish regional newspaper. That's not enough? Well, connect to one of the fourteen San Francisco area television Web sites or over sixty AM/FM radio station Web sites.

An interesting development, too, for news seekers is the practice of packaging news stories from a variety of sources on a news event. Yahoo! does one of the best jobs of this. In its quest to be a one-site-serves-all-needs portal service, its home page (www.yahoo.com) has a sidebar called "In the News," which links to several top stories and provides a line-up of stories and resources to follow the story. In the offerings for a Swissair airplane crash, for example, there were stories from the Associated Press and Reuters, ABC, CNN, and Fox News, *The Globe and Mail*, *Toronto Star*, *The New York Times*, *The Washington Post*, and PR Newswire. There is a sidebar with links to RealAudio and video clips and links to Usenet newsgroups where people are likely to be talking about the event. For even more background, it links you to related sites, such as the Swissair Web site, Federal Aviation Administration, and a site called Crash Detectives, which tells you how airline crashes are investigated. If you want to drill deeply into one news story, Yahoo! gives you the resources.

Do you want to find the options for reading/seeing/hearing local news, even when you're not local? Do you want to tap into the virtual newsstand and get news from around the globe? There are a number of news Web site directories that can help. That's the good news. The bad news is that none of them appears to be complete. Spot checks of country listings of news sources from three key directories have significantly different numbers of publications listed (for example, listings of South African newspapers in MediaInfo's—20, in the Ultimate Collection—18, in AJR NewsLinks—9, and each has some the others don't have). With this area, as with so many, it's a case of "so near and yet, so far." No one resource has become the one-stop shopping spot for news access, but there are some noble efforts that we will profile. In the case of news browsing and locating all the relevant resources, it is the combination search, checking into a number of different directory sources, which will get you the complete picture.

We'll look at two different types of cybersources for news research—directories that link you to the locales on the Web for newspapers, radio, television, and magazines, and services that let you research the material in multiple publications.

Top Great Scout Sites for News

The Ultimate Collection of News Links
pppp.net/links/news/
Contact: PPPP.net
Via Carlo Poma, 2
00100, Rome, Italy
U.S. headquarters: 708 3rd Avenue
New York, NY 10017
pppp@pppp.net or info@pppp.net
webmaster@pppp.net

Why we picked this site: We usually look askance at "The best, the biggest, the ultimate . . . " type tags, especially when they are self-named, but in this case "The Ultimate Collection" is appropriate and not over-reaching. If you are looking for local news or regional publications on specific topics, look no further.

Created: September 1996.

How many sites: Over 10,000.

Audience: Seekers of local news for places all over the world. It is also useful for people wanting specialty publications from particular countries and areas.

How sites are selected: Sites are self-submitted but checked by the editors of the site.

How it's supported: PPPP is a Web design and management company.

Searching: The only access to the records at this point is by geography. Countries are organized by continent in the left frame. Scroll to the continent, click on a country, and the results from the directory of publications appear in the right frame.

What you get: The Main Menu frame is headed by a flag of the country, the date the listing was last modified, and a notice that the links were checked and good as of a certain date. Underneath is a subject categorized listing of publication types, over 110 categories (grouped under Newspapers, Art & Entertainment, Automotive, Business, Computer, Culture & Society, Current Issues, Health, Home, Industry Trade Publications, Pets & Animals, Religion, Science, Sports, Travel). If there is a publication in that country or state that falls into one of the subject categories, there is a hyper-link to the publication's description page. The indication of how many links in that category is very helpful.

When you click on one of the subject categories, for example, Newspapers (at the top of the list), you'll get the listing of publications in that category, in alphabetical order by publication name. (We wish they didn't consider "The" as the first word of the name in the listing!) Next to the name is the city where it is published. Click on the publication you want and a new browser window will open up to the address.

Design: If you don't like frames, you won't like this site. Except for our bias against frames, this is a clean and clear-cut design. The automatic link check is a great feature that ensures that you get the site you want when you click.

Editor & Publisher
www.mediainfo.com/emedia/

Contact: The Editor & Publisher Company, Inc.
11 West 19th Street
New York, NY 10011-4234
212-675-4380

Why we picked this site: There are several media directories with links to newspaper, magazine, and broadcast sites, but E&P's MediaInfo is the smoothest at finding them all for an area in a logical and easy-to-use way. The brainchild of Steve Outing, an early pioneer in tracking online media, this directory has been around since late 1994. Although he has moved on to other projects, his baby has grown up nicely and is learning some new tricks. The fact that there are some information sheets about the sites being linked to is helpful—this isn't just a listing of links with little background information.

Created: Late 1994.

How many sites: More than 11,000 records. To see the current statistics on the databases in the directory, go to www.mediainfo.com/ephome/npaper/nphtm/statistics.htm.

Audience: People who want to search for media Web sites or to browse media Web sites by media category or geographic region.

How sites are selected: Most of the information in the database on media outlets comes from submissions. The criterion, according to the submissions page, is, "Only media sites and media associations that fit into the six categories listed below (newspaper, magazine, radio, TV, syndicate/news service, city guide, association) are currently being added to the database. The database does not contain links to personal Web sites, company information sites or advertising brochures. Submissions of non-media sites will be discarded." Submitted links are checked by the staff before they are included in the database. There is an extensive form with information on the publication and the Web site, some of which becomes part of the background information sheet retrieved during a search.

How it's supported: *Editor & Publisher* is the trade publication for the news business. This service supports their print publication and is a new outlet into online news.

Topics covered: Journalism associations, city guides, magazine, newspaper, news services and syndicates, radio and television Web sites.

Searching: There are three types of access to the resources in this directory:

Browse by geographic area: If you want all the media outlets for a particular area, this is the technique to use. Select one of the areas (Africa, Asia, Canada, Caribbean, Europe, Latin America, Middle East, Oceania, United States) and you'll get a page with further geographic breakdown (state or country). Select one of the regions and then select the Media Type you want to have displayed (newspaper, magazine, television, etc.). There is a select list at the bottom of the retrieved directory page that lets you jump to the listings for another Media Type for that region.

Browse by media type: If you want to find all the television stations in a region, use this technique. Select a media type: associations, city guides, magazines, newspapers, radio, news services and syndicates, and television. You'll then be asked for the region in which you are interested in locating those resources. Click on the region and a list of the Media Types for that area is displayed.

Advanced search: Click on "Advanced Search" or go to www.mediainfo.com/emedia/advanced.htm. You'll get a search template page where you can select or type in information that covers the Media Type and/or Geographic Location you are interested in. Select boxes for "Media Type," "Geographic Location," and "Publication/Station Frequency" let you specify such things as "Newspapers in Georgia, Florida, or South Carolina that have a daily publication." You'll get an alphabetical listing of the publications that meet the criteria. You can also type the criteria in the search boxes provided for "Name," "City," and "Site Type." Want publications with "Post" in their names in any country? Type "Post" into the "Name" box, select all the countries (by holding down the "control" key as you select) in the "Geographic Location" select box, and hit search for a complete listing. Want any kind of media in Tampa? Type in "Tampa" and select all the Media Types. The search permutations possible with the advanced search are limitless.

What you get: Click on a category or do a search and you'll get a list of sites with basic information about each site: the name of the publication or company, the name of the site (with a link to the information page on that site), the city and state or country, the frequency of the publication (how often it is published), and the site type (i.e., business, general interest, sports). The media category of each site is symbolized by a small graphic at the beginning of each listing, which is helpful if you are doing a listing of all media in a particular region. The following is a legend of the graphics used for the different media categories:

A   Newspaper and Journalism Association Web Sites

C   City Guide Web Sites

M   Magazine Web Sites

N   Newspaper Web Sites

R   Radio Web Sites

S   Syndicate and News Service Web Sites

T   Television Web Sites

Once you get the directory listing, selecting one of the site name links takes you to an information page about the site that includes

Company Name, Location, Service Name (linked to the service itself), Service Type, Frequency, Update Frequency, Date Launched, Entry (about the site) Last Updated, Affiliation, Description of the Site, Content Notes (Local News, Weather, Sports, Technology Coverage, Games, Lifestyle/Entertainment), Advertising Information, Availability of an Archive of stories, and availability of Classifieds online.

Design: The one fault of this site, so rich in information about news sites and flexible searching of the sites, is that there are so many clicks involved in getting to the sites themselves. Other than that, the design is straightforward and easy to use.

Specific Media

If you are interested in simply looking for one particular medium, going to a single medium look-up directory can be a good idea. Here are some.

The MIT List of Radio Stations on the Internet

wmbr.mit.edu/stations/list.html

Listing over 8,000 radio stations and constantly updated and checked, this is the ultimate listing of radio on the Web. Search for stations by Call Letters, Frequency, City, State, or Format type. Two databases will be searched: FCC licensed radio stations and information on radio stations with Web pages. The results are sorted by radio stations on the Web and then radio stations in the FCC database. The results list for stations on the Web link you directly to the Web station (a lightning bolt symbol to the right of a listing indicates the station is a bitcaster and broadcasts its audio signal on the Internet). The results list for FCC licensed stations links you to the FCC information (call letters, frequency, city of license, transmitter location—linked to a map, transmitted power, and the date the record was last updated).

Search by geographic location in the U.S. with the search template. Fill in the City or State, Latitude and Longitude, radio band, or stations within a certain number of miles of your location. If you want to find radio stations for foreign countries, click on the listing for Africa, Asia, Europe, Middle East, South America, Oceania/Australia and find links to Web-available radio stations by country (a nice little feature is the flag of each country at the beginning of the listing).

PubList.Com
www.publist.com

PubList provides a comprehensive directory of information about more than 150,000 publications and more than 8,000 newspapers around the world. According to the description on the site, the information comes from "authoritative sources like R.R. Bowker's *Ulrich's(tm) International Periodicals Directory* and *Editor & Publisher International Yearbook(r)*. For the end-user, this means more immediate access to comprehensive publication information and relevant supporting services, making research efforts on the Web more efficient and effective." And it does. This elaborate site is truly a gold mine of information about publications. Not only does the listing give you specifics about a publication, it also leads you to others on the topic. The information about each publication answers any questions a seeker might have about ordering (International Standard Serial Number, publisher information, contact names, numbers, and e-mail), use (rights and permissions information), and advertising.

You can browse by title or subject or publisher, or use one of the search fields (title, ISSN, description, or publisher) by clicking on "custom search." The only bump in the smoothness of the access to publications is that online availability is noted, but not facilitated—if there is a Web site there is no link to it, just a listing of the address.

Ultimate TV

www.ultimateTV.com/

Find stations in the U.S. or around the world with this full-service television information site. Click on U.S. and get a search template with a select box for states or a search box for call letters. The results list will give you, sorted by city then station, the link to the Web site for that station. Click on World TV for an alphabetical list of countries with links to the stations available on the Web from that country.

Searching for News Stories

NewsTrawler

www.newstrawler.com

From their information sheet: "NewsTrawler is a service brought to you by Commun-e-kay Marketing. We are a company based in Sydney, Australia, and we launched the service in June 1998. This service was developed in order to fill a perceived need for searching the archives of news sources spread across different continents. A parallel search technology was designed to enable simultaneous search from a single point of contact. The search technology is scalable and new information sources can be added very easily."

They had the perceived need right—seekers of news stories were having to hop around the Web and go from site to site looking for stories or rely on some of the limited news Web search engines, such as NewsBot (www.wired.com/newsbot) and NewsHub (web.NewsHub.com/), until NewsTrawler came along.

This service lets you select from hundreds of online publications around the world and enter a search. You can search in publications within one country (currently twenty-four countries are available) or search across countries. You can search in particular categories (journals, newspapers, magazines, Web references, Web-based news services) or across categories. Select one of the categories or regions, click on the publications listed and type in your search terms. Click "Trawl" and the parallel search function will go out, find the stories that match and give you the results by publication. This is a brave step into the future of one search for many sources. It is a welcome new service.

Electric Library
www.elibrary.com
If you want information from magazines, books, maps, newspapers and newswires, TV or radio transcripts, or pictures whether they are on or off the Web, check into Electric Library. It is a subscription-based service, but the search function is free. If you want to see one of the results found in your search, the registration form will pop up (or if you have registered and asked to have your password remembered, you'll go right to the material). It is a remarkably comprehensive service that is easy to use, and has abundant resources and lots of features that make the browsing of the relevant materials you find easy. Electric Library truly makes the idea of the virtual library on your desktop a reality.

For More Information
Want to keep up with what news outlets are doing online and off-line? Read the insider information on these Web sites:

The Antenna: The Broadcaster's Guide to the Internet
www.theantenna.com/

AJR Newslink
www.newslink.org/
The American Journalism Review's Web page on daily happenings in the news business.
See also:
Magne, Larry and Phil Schoen. *Passport to Web Radio: Music, Sports, News and Entertainment from the Hometowns of the World.* Penn's Park, PA: International Broadcasting Service, 1997.

19

Personal Finance on the Web

Money matters.

Surfing the World Wide Web for fun may provide a pleasant afternoon's entertainment. Searching the Web for a particular nugget of information may offer the thrill of the chase and the fleeting satisfaction of success. But when your mission is locating and gaining in-depth knowledge about a subject that really matters to you, the Web can help you reap the continuing rewards of lifelong learning.

Money matters. And money matters are the focus of a riot of terrific, fair, mediocre, and downright lousy Web sites—among them many that are not free of charge. Personal finance is one of two subject areas on the Internet today where users are now prepared to pay to get more details—the other topic is sex. But you'll find plenty of good free or inexpensive information, many practical tools, and much educational material to study, if you know where to look. Below are some great scout sites to point the way to the Web's many resources on making, saving, and investing your assets. You may not get rich quick, but you'll get a wealth of information to help make better decisions about personal finances.

Cyberspace is now part of our daily personal financial lives. With more and more ease and security, we can bank, take care of mutual fund and retirement account transfers, and deal with brokerages online. More than 600 banks were offering electronic banking in 1998 and Dataquest research group predicts that the figure could double within four years. But personal finance is more than investments and banking; it also includes car buying, home buying, retirement planning, paying for college, and consumer credit.

And, even if you don't yet trust electronic transactions, the Web is a fast, convenient way to get a wide range of useful stuff, for example, the locations of bank ATMs and branches, listings of properties for sale or rent in your town or across the country, comparison shopping for insurance, loan, mortgage, and interest rates, and directory listings for real estate agents, home inspectors, contractors, movers, and much more. Tax forms, filing instructions, and taxpayer tips and advice are available from government revenue agencies and commercial tax preparers online.

The technology of the Web also makes it easy to use a growing number of free interactive business tools that do calculations for you online, including currency converters, loan and mortgage payment calculators, education cost analysis, and comparisons of cost-of-living by city or by year.

These tools take up just a small corner of the cyberacreage devoted to personal finance. Most of the space is occupied by investment information and money news from all over, from stock tickers, quote services, indices, and trend charts to company and industry research reports and financial pundits' predictions, tips and gossip about initial public offerings, technology startups, and foreign markets. We have described in our chapter on Business and Management Resources where information about public and private companies and their executives and corporate activity is available from official company sites, as well as from Securities and Exchange Commission filings, research analyst reports, and other sources. There's also a vast quantity of advice, much of it free, from a wide range of advisors and market watchers (both professional and amateur) via newsletters, home pages, audio programming, e-mail, discussion groups, and chat rooms.

"The old saying 'you get what you pay for' rings true with a lot of the free information on the Internet," said Richard Drezen, *Washington Post* financial researcher. "So *caveat emptor*."

In addition to reputable (but unguaranteed) advice, there are also scams and financial skullduggery and shenanigans on the Web, just as there are offline. Official remedies for misconduct and rip-offs are available online, too, with financial industry regulatory boards, Better Business Bureaus, and government agencies on the lookout and at the ready for consumer reports and appeals for help.

The financial supersites hope to serve all your needs and they're a good place to start. Yahoo! Finance, CBS MarketWatch, Microsoft Investor's Web site, and the Motley Fool offer news headlines and articles, delayed prices, analysis, personal portfolios, reference tools, links, expert columns, and advice. They also have partnerships with providers of real-time prices, research reports, and other fee-based features. These portals hope to keep you searching, browsing, and buying within their services.

There's a lot more beyond the portal doors, and great scouts sites can guide you across the frontiers and the fringes of what's out there and what's new. The great scouts test the links and chart the untested waters for you. If, like many people these days, you're taking charge and taking care of your personal finances and nest egg for the future, the Web offers practical help, guidance, and advice. But it's your money, so be careful and vigilant while you ride the waves.

What's missing: Free stock quotes are on 15-minute or more delay. For real-time quotes you'll have to subscribe to a fee-based service.

Personal Finance Materials on the Web

Associations: American Association of Individual Investors is an educational site for helping individuals manage their assets (www. aaii.org). The National Association of Investors Corporation is a non-profit organization site providing educational materials on investing for investment clubs and individual investors (www.betterinvesting.org).

Banks: Bank Directory & Consumer Banking Guide offers clickable maps for locating banks in the U.S. and around the world (www.banksite.com), or try the directory of more than 2,000 banks at BankWeb (www.bankweb.com).

Consumer protection: The Stock Detective uncovers scams and "stinky stocks" (www.stockdetective.com). Better Business Bureau has a central Web server for the U.S. and Canada (www.bbb.org).

Glossaries: InvestorWords provides definitions for over 4,000 financial terms and includes 15,000 links between related terms (www.investorwords.com). Campbell R. Harvey's Hypertextual Finance Glossary contains over 2,500 entries and is available at both Professor Harvey's Duke University site (www.duke.edu/~charvey) and at Yahoo! Finance (biz.yahoo.com/f/g/g.html).

Financial supersites: CBS MarketWatch (www.cbsmarketwatch. com), Microsoft Investor's Web site (www.investor.msn.com), Microsoft's Money Central (moneycentral.msn.com), Motley Fool (www.fool.com), Yahoo! Finance (quote.yahoo.com). Money Online is an interactive supersite filled with news, tools, advice, and discussions and chat from the pages and staff of the popular personal finance magazine (www.money.com). An archive of the magazine going back to 1986 is available free. Special features include the annual report on best places to live, safest cities, choosing charities, a college guide to over 1,300 schools, and lots of tools for keeping track of your finances and planning for the future.

Insurance supersite: Insurance News Network includes insurance company ratings and insurance industry reports from Standard & Poors (www.insure.com).

Internal Revenue Service: The IRS has a top-flight site with lots of information and services for taxpayers, including online forms for downloading and publications, statistics, Frequently Asked Questions, and even a sense of humor (www.irs.gov)!

Toolkits: Forbes Toolbox includes financial indices and ranked lists, a Growth Flow Calculator, Fund Expense Calculator, and Tax Rate Calculator (www.forbes.com/tool/html/toolbox.htm). MSNBC's Investment Toolkit for personal finance includes a mortgage payment calculator, asset allocator, net worth calculator, income tax estimator, cash flow worksheet, and retirement planner (www.msnbc.com/modules/commerce/newtoolkit/). Homefair's calculators include the salary calculator comparing U.S. cities' costs of living and the moving calculator (www.homefair.com).

Great Scout Sites for Personal Finance

InvestorGuide
www.investorguide.com
Contact: WebFinance Inc.
2006 Gallows Tree Court
Vienna, VA 22182
Tom Murcko, murcko@investorguide.com

Why we picked this site: There are many directories and guides to the vast, varying, and constantly changing body of financial information on the Web, but InvestorGuide states a goal that agrees with our Great Scout standards. "InvestorGuide exists to help you combat these new problems. By imposing order on the chaos, by making it easy for you to find just what you need, and by focusing on the high-quality, free (or low cost), objective information, this site transforms the Web from an interesting way to kill time into a powerful tool that helps you take control of your money and your financial future."

InvestorGuide is more than links. It enhances the sub-topics with informative descriptions. In the Retirement section, for example, there are definitions and tips provided for 401K plans, Social Security benefits, and retirement calculator tools. And Investor-Guide also focuses on the use of the Web for learning, with educational resources highlighted throughout its sections. There are some biases revealed on these pages (InvestorGuide has doubts about the viability of the Social Security system in the future) but the opinions offered won't hurt you.

Created: June 1996.

How many sites: 7,000+.

Audience: Individual investors and consumers.

How sites are selected: InvestorGuide's staff selects and annotates links.

How it's supported: Advertising-supported.

Topics covered: The three major areas covered are investing, personal finance, and learning.

Personal finance includes car buying, home buying, paying for college, retirement, Roth IRA, loans, credit, insurance, taxes, advisors, kids and money, and electronic commerce. There are also links to over fifty newsletters, public company home pages, and stock research links, charts, and quotes.

Contents: Browse the topics and sub-topics or search the site by keyword. Topic and link annotations basically follow a pattern for each of the subjects named above. For the Retirement topic, for example, there are sub-topics like IRAs, Social Security, After Retirement, Estate Planning, Roth IRAs, and Taxes with descriptions and links and functional links like Calculators, Discussion Groups, Learning, Organizations, Software and Answers (from the Answer Center).

What you get: When you browse, the "most useful" sites are featured on top.

Advanced searching: SmartSearch search engine feature uses HotBot technology to search other financial sites for business news, educational information, and articles about investing.

Design: Consistent page design keeps navigation easy; contents are described on top of the page and a navigation toolbar stays on the left. There are "See also" links to related pages and a site map.

Other features: The InvestorWords glossary and Investorville community with message boards are affiliated with InvestorGuide.

Help or FAQ: Help pages are available. There's also an Answer Center, with a collection of over 1,000 investing questions and answers.

CyberInvest
www.cyberinvest.com
Contact: Kassandra Bentley, President
CyberInvest.com
5959 Corporate Drive, #2000
Houston, TX 77036
kbentley@cyberinvest.com

Why we picked this site: CyberInvest stands out from the familiar guides because its mission is to offer comparisons among the personal finance and investing Web sites. CyberInvest gives you the details you need about each site it picks in more than twenty topical "guides" and presents them in a standardized table layout so you can easily distinguish the comparisons and make up your own mind. For example, you can compare online brokers by lowest commissions, by minimum initial investment, by commissions of $13 or less, by the top ten market share leaders, or by brokers that have been rated #1 in at least one of the popular surveys. And it's kept up to date: According to founder Kassandra Bentley, "the guides are updated frequently—any time we receive notification from the sites themselves that something has changed or when we run across a change or a new site that seems guide-worthy."

Created: 1997, from charts developed for Kassandra Bentley's book *Wall Street City: Your Guide to Investing on the Web.*

How many sites: 300+ in the guides; hundreds in the LinkSoup section.

Audience: Individual investors and consumers.

How sites are selected: Highly selective: The sites are rigorously investigated and presented in great detail. Guides are updated regularly; the last update is indicated on the top left of each guide.

How it's supported: Advertising and sponsorships.

Topics covered: Banking Online, Bonds, Brokers/Trading Online, Company Research, Education, Global Investing, Interest Rates, Investing Supersites, Investing 'Zines, IPOs & DPOs, Market Monitors, Mutual Funds, News, Personal Finance, Portfolios, Stock Prospecting, Technical Analysis, LinkSoup, Guides in the Works.

Contents: Each guide is a table with detailed information in rows and columns. There are links to each of the sites included in the tables. For "Banking Online" the comparisons are available for nineteen banks (with link to each bank and a toll-free number for phone contact), about Online Banking (comparing Web access, software access, and access cost), Bill Paying (comparing cost per month and conditions), Credit Card Access and Extras. The Personal Finance guide compares Web sites that offer personal finance tools and resources.

What you get: Each topic has a separate page with links to the guides available and to related Web sites and articles. The guide pages themselves are compact comparisons with subject-appropriate column headings, often abbreviated. Most of the guides present the sites in alphabetical order, but the Online Broker guides allows you to sort and rank by several variables, like lowest commissions, largest market shares, top ratings from business periodicals, and more.

Advanced searching: No, but there's a link out to Northern Light for a pre-cooked Web search on each guide topic.

Design: The site's home page is busy; we think the guides should be central to this page, rather than the news, quotes, and other portal-type information. Move on quickly to the comparison tables, which are chock full of information; unfortunately, this means the print is really small, but the details are worth the attention you have to pay to read them. The comparison tables may be wider than the portrait orientation of your printer. If you want to print out these useful tables, you'll need to change your print preference to landscape view or use a smaller font.

Other features: Link Soup is a topical collection of links to sites that are not in the guides, or have not yet been organized into a guide topic.

Help or FAQ: Yes.

Other Top Personal Finance Scout Sites

Invest-o-Rama!
www investorama.com
This is a directory of investing sites on the Web with more than 11,000 annotated descriptive links in 141 categories, as well as links to research on any stock and a corporations directory of more than 4,930 public companies with Web sites. This site is huge! It's maintained by Doug Gerlach, a writer and expert on Internet investing and investment clubs.

Realtylocator.com
www.realtylocator.com
This site offers over 100,000 real estate links nationwide, geographically arranged. For each location, links include agents, architects, apartments for rent, homes for sale, new homes and builders,

inspectors and appraisers, title and escrow, realtor associations, assisted living, and lenders and mortgage brokers. General categories include government information, movers, relocation, organizations and tools and services for real estate professionals. Information Resources include links to tools and calculators, neighborhood information, and school information for most of the school districts in the United States.

Search Engines

FinanceWise

www.financewise.com

FinanceWise searches a global directory sponsored by the U.K. *Financial Times*, by business sector, company name, or other keywords in sites selected for financial content. Free registration is required.

InvestorSeek

www.investorseek.com

InvestorSeek is a financial search engine that searches 1,000 sites that contain information about this topic.

SmartSearch

www.investorguide.com/SmartSearch.htm

SmartSearch engine from Investor-Guide uses HotBot technology to search only financial sites with a focus on business news, educational information, and articles about investing.

20

Ready Reference Resources on the Web

Have you ever had one of those "Of course!" moments where you hear a statement that confirms something you've always thought, but had never put into words? I had such a moment during one of those interminable discussions about the Internet and the World Wide Web and the impact it will have on the information world. After listening to panelist after panelist talking about Internet users and what they want, someone in the audience got up and said, "I wish we would stop talking about people on the Internet as users or readers, but think about them as learners." Of course!

While casual browsing is certainly going on online, for the most part, people heading to the Net are going there to learn about something. Thanks to the hard work of dedicated "cybrarians," there is a virtual library of ready reference material available on the Internet, organized and ready for your use when you need to know. The criticism that the Internet is like the world's largest library, but all the books are dumped on the floor and there is no catalog, is unfair when it comes to the area of resources to answer those daily Who, What, When, Where, Why questions we all deal with.

Many standard reference materials, dictionaries, gazetteers, atlases, thesauri, are available from their original publishers. Whether it is the Central Intelligence Agency's invaluable *World Factbook* (www.cia.gov/cia/publications/factbook/index.html), or the classic *Bartlett's Familiar Quotations* (www.columbia.edu/acis/bartleby/bartlett/) or *Roget's Thesaurus* (www. thesaurus.com), many of the reference books you would turn to in the past to check a fact or settle a bet are available for look-up on the World Wide Web. Sources of statistics, definitions, calculations, and citations can be found in abundance, and usually for free.

But, be sure to check the currency of the information because sometimes the particular source used is not as recent as you might think. The Project Bartleby Web site's version of *Bartlett's Familiar Quotations*, for example, is the 9th ed., 1901. You won't find quotes from Benjamin Spock, Dorothy Parker, or Winston Churchill there. And Project Gutenberg's electronic version of *Roget's Thesaurus* is from 1911, so don't look for current slang or contemporary usage there.

Another reason to look carefully and to check the Web site that is making the resource available is that some references are copied all over the Web. The CIA's *World Factbook* can be found at the Bell Lab's Research site (portal.research.bell-labs.com/cgi-wald/dbaccess/411) with a handy search template feature, but look carefully—it is the 1993 edition. If you want the most recent edition, go to the source, the CIA. With the changing borders and place names that have happened in the past decade, it is essential to verify the creation date of information in the source you are using as a reference. In fact, if you can't verify the source or the date of the information you are looking at, go find a site with a source that provides that essential information.

Take the time, too, to really compare these online resources. There are a number of online dictionaries, but it's helpful to determine which one has the best search, or extra features, or is usually easy to connect to. Finding those sites with reliable, easy-to-use, and available resources will make your hunting for that elusive quote or date or conversion as satisfying as walking into a well-organized library.

In no other area is the idea of evaluation of Internet materials as closely linked to the evaluation you would do of print-based materials. When using reference sources in print form there is a basic evaluation checklist: accuracy, authority, objectivity, currency, and coverage. This is the same checklist you should use before relying on resources you find on the Internet.

If this book had been written a few years ago, there would have to have been a note on what is missing. Some of the graphics intensive reference books, particularly atlases, would have been under-represented. That is no longer the case. The problem now is not that graphics-rich resources aren't available, the problem is the download time it takes to get them.

Some of the best reference books have not made it to the Web, since giving away their work does not fit into their marketing plan. But information about the book (or CD-ROM version) can be found on the Web. One example, the excellent explanatory book, *The Way Things Work*, is not available on the Web but you can order the book or CD.

It is no surprise that the best of the ready reference compilation sites are compiled by librarians. But some niche reference sites are interesting resources with both odd and esoteric resources co-mingled with standard works. Michael Moncur's Quotations Page (www.starlingtech.com/quotes/) includes links to standard quotation references as well as a searchable database of humorist Dave Barry's quotes. The ultimate collection of calculators (www-sci.lib.uci.edu/HSG/RefCalculators.html) has the predictable sorts of calculations available, but also links to calculators to figure out how much fragrant oil to add to a soap recipe and what kind of cigar to get based on certain criteria, such as length of smoke, wrapper color, and flavor.

One of the interesting developments on the Internet in the area of ready reference has been the ways that people have conceived of sites and services that help Internet "learners." We will look at the ready reference compilation sites of note, but there are also services, such as the Usenet FAQ Archive (www.faqs.org/faqs/), which indexes the Frequently Asked Questions lists found in numerous newsgroups and locates the one you need, and specific encyclopedic sites created from typical ready reference questions, such as the Hennepin County (Minnesota) Library's Fugitive Fact Finder (www.hennepin.lib.mn.us/catalog/fff_public.html). Research It! (www.itools.com/research-it/research-it.html) helps learners by providing search templates to more than thirty basic reference look-ups.

Since the Internet is a great way to link not just to documents and information, but also to people, some of the most innovative services in the area of ready reference are links to people. Services such as "Ask a Librarian" (www.iren.net/cfpl/forms/aal_form.html) from the Cedar Falls Public Library and "Ask Zach" (www2.gasou.edu/library/form.html) from the Zach S. Henderson Library of Georgia Southern University let you send e-mail forms with reference questions to librarians who will help you with an answer. So, if you have simple, quick, reference questions, the librarians on the Internet, both virtual and real, have made finding the answers much simpler and quicker.

Here are a few of the great Ready Reference sites on the Internet.

Ready Reference—Who

Biographical Dictionary
www.s9.com/biography/
Profiles of 25,000 notable men and women from ancient times to the present.

Biography.Com
www.biography.com/
Searchable online version of the Cambridge Biographical Encyclopedia.

Ready Reference—What (is the definition of . . .)

A Web of Online Dictionaries
www.facstaff.bucknell.edu/rbeard/diction.html
Links to more than 600 dictionaries in more than 150 different languages.

One Look Dictionaries
www.onelook.com/
A metasearch site of dictionaries, one search looks in 509 online dictionaries.

Ready Reference—What (is the top ranked . . .)

Price's List of Lists
gwis2.circ.gwu.edu/~gprice/listof.htm.
"The Internet contains numerous lists of information. Many of these lists present information in the form of rankings of different

people, organizations, companies, etc. This collection is designed to be a clearinghouse for these types of resources."

Ready Reference—When

The Calendar Zone
www.calendarzone.com
Nicely annotated links to hundreds of online calendars organized by such topics as Cultural, Event, Geographic, Historical, Holidays, Reference, Religious, Women.

Information Please Almanac
www.infoplease.com/
What happened (or will be happening) when—this standard reference book is chock full of fun facts and useful information.

Ready Reference—Where

U.S. Gazetteer
www.census.gov/cgi-bin/gazetteer
From the Census Bureau, look up place names or ZIP codes and get maps and census information.

The Getty Thesaurus of Geographic Names
www.ahip.getty.edu/vocabulary/tgn.html
Find out where in the world over 1,000,000 places are located. The source of the information is given—a nice feature.

Atlapedia Online
www.atlapedia.com/
Full color physical and political maps of all the countries of the world.

Ready Reference—Why

Encyclopaedia Britannica Online
www.eb.com

For all your "why" questions, there is an answer in the Britannica. This site has a subscription fee, but it's worth it—you can check it out for free for a week.

Encyclopedia.Com
www.encyclopedia.com/
Find out the why's on 17,000 topics from the Concise Columbia Electronic Encyclopedia. Brought to you by Electric Library, it's free and full of fast facts.

Ready Reference—How

How Stuff Works
www.howstuffworks.com/
Everything, from car engines to thermometers to helium balloons to Boolean logic, is explained in simple text and clear graphics.

Calculators Online Center
www-sci.lib.uci.edu/HSG/RefCalculators.html
Links to over 7,100 different calculators, from how many teaspoons in a liter to how much child support you would have to pay in different states.

The Salary Calculator
www2.homefair.com/calc/salcalc.html
How much would you have to make in your new job to be equivalent to what you are making now? Use this site to find out.

Great Scout Sites for Ready Reference Resources

Internet Public Library/Ready Reference Collection
www.ipl.org/ref/

Contact: University of Michigan
David Carter, Director
610 E. University, Room 4033 SEB
Ann Arbor, MI 48109-1259
ipl@ipl.org

Why we picked this site: We picked the site because it is a great example of all we have been looking for in all of the scout sites we've selected for the book. The links are well organized and logical, there are annotations about the sites, and notes about the currency of the information. As they say on the FAQ, "What we are trying to do is explore what the rich history and intellectual traditions of librarianship have to offer the dynamic but, let's admit it, chaotic world of the Internet. Librarians have tried for a few hundred years to make sense of the world of information and knowledge stored in physical media . . . . why not try to find out what we can do with digital media?" For the seeker of good sites in most areas, but particularly in the Ready Reference area, what the folks at the Internet Public Library have been trying to do has been very successful.

Created: In January 1995, a class in the School of Information and Library Studies at the University of Michigan began the project; the Internet Public Library was online seventy days later.

How many sites: There are over 20,000 in the whole Internet Public Library site, about 3,000 of them in the Ready Reference area.

Audience: The IPL is intended for the general Internet community and the Reference area is aimed at an adult audience. There are separate areas of the IPL for teens and kids.

How sites are selected: The affiliation with the University's library school has helped create an "army of students" taking one of the classes that IPL Director David Carter teaches. The students who help work on the IPL resources get "practical engagement" credits by answering reference questions online and scoping out good sites to add. Some sites are submitted by users but they, for the most part, don't make the cut for inclusion in the resource list. Just as in a good "physical" library, the librarians at this virtual library employ various review sources to help identify sites that should be reviewed and possibly added to the directory. Other sites make it in if they have been used in answering one of the reference questions that come to the "Ask a Question" desk.

How it's supported: Funding from the University of Michigan School of Library Science and various grants have kept the service going. Bell & Howell Information and Learning recently announced a 3-year sponsorship with substantial funding. Most of its $100,000 annual budget goes to the four staff members of the IPL.

Searching: Just like walking into a public library, it takes a few minutes to orient yourself at the Internet Public Library. The home page gives you links to a number of areas (online serials, newspapers, Internet resources for teens, and the Reference Center). Click on the Reference Center and you'll get a drawing of a cozy looking reading room with book shelves and a librarian at a desk. There are various subject areas indicated around the room: Science & Technology; Computers & Internet; Arts & Humanities; Health & Medical Science; Law, Government & Political Science; Business & Economics; Social Sciences; Entertainment & Leisure; and, the area we are focusing on in this chapter, Reference. Click on the Reference shelf and you get a listing of subcategories: Almanacs, Biographies, Census Data and Demographics, Dictionaries, Encyclopedias, Genealogy, Geography, News, Quotations, Telephone, each with a brief annotation of the content area.

Select one of the areas, Almanacs, for example, and you get the listing of selected reference works on the Internet. You'll find a search box in the areas' pages or a link to search from the Reference Center page (look for a link from "search the collection"). If you use the Search box, you can type words into the box, select whether you want the words to be ANDed or ORed together (i.e., if you want business census resources, type in "business census" and select "and"). The search will find any words in the title, address, keywords, subject headings, or descriptions of the site.

What you get: Each entry has a link to the site, detailed descriptions of site contents, an Author note (who put the site together along with the e-mail address), Subject headings (many of them with hyperlinks to a page of additional resources in that subject area), and Keywords. The subject headings are "controlled vocabulary" terms that are consistently used, the keywords are free-text terms the indexer decides might help someone looking for a particular type of source or subject.

Design: The Reference Desk page with the mapped drawing is an inviting entrance into the well-selected resources of the Internet Public Library.

Other features: Click on the Reference Desk and get a query form to "Ask a Question." This is a great example of tying the print resources and the human resources together into an all-around service for reference seekers. They get about forty to fifty questions a day, and accept about half of them.

Ready Reference Using the Internet
www.winsor.edu/library/rref.htm
Contact: Ellen Berne, Director of the Library
The Winsor School, Boston MA 02215
eberne@tiac.net

Why we picked this site: Ellen Berne, Director of the library at the Winsor School, took the metaphor of the vertical file (subject-organized folders with useful and esoteric information) to create this very intuitive and easy-to-use ready reference resource. You know how thrilling it is to open a folder and find just the piece of information, statistic, or contact name that you need readily inside—you get that same thrill with this simple, selective resource for fast facts. If you need information about gorillas, they link you to the Sea World Animal Resources handbook—you'll get all the fast facts you need. Sometimes the Web gives you too many choices; at this site, the librarians have done what librarians do best, selected some of the best information and made it easy for you to find and use it.

Created: Berne started it in 1995 as a print guide to gopher sites. "I found that I was using index cards to keep track of useful sites and that wasn't working, so I approached my dial-up Internet service and asked if they would be interested in putting a subject list on the service. When we made the transition to the Web, I made an arrangement with the University of Massachusetts to have the page there."

How many sites: 400–500 links, about 350 separate subject headings.

Audience: Designed for reference librarians to use for ready reference queries.

How sites are selected: Berne keeps a file of sites she wants to check out and, about every four months, reviews the sites for inclusion and checks all the links for dead links. She relies heavily on government sites for information, particularly for statistical references. The three main criteria she uses when selecting sites are the stability of the site, the authority, and the currency of information available. When she links to a non-government site, particularly information in an organization's site, she will make a note of any bias or agenda the organization might have. One of the big sources for new sites to add is the alert service Net Happenings.

How it's supported: No support; this is an individual effort but one with a long-term commitment.

Searching: This is a very simple listing of topics with the only browsing function a clickable alphabet that moves you to the beginning of the topics listed under that letter.

What you get: Under each topic, such as Asian Art, earthquakes, headaches, immigration, you get a brief annotation of the reason this site was selected, the content, and a direct link to the area of the site with the information.

Design: A very simple listing, in alphabetical order, of the topics with links to information about the topic. This is like looking through a file cabinet, simple and straightforward.

Other Good Scout Sites

Desk Top Reference Agent
www.ll.mit.edu/Deskref/
Provides table-based links to Almanacs, Quick References, and a Reference Center. Nicely organized by categories of questions.

Fulltext and Ready Reference Resources
www.clark.net/pub/lschank/web/mu-ref.html
Good annotations on the list of resources help make the selection of the right site easier.

Desk Ref: Quick Reference Links
ansernet.rcls.org/deskref/
The subject/resource-oriented grid lets you select a topic or type of resource and get a listing of good sites.

Ready Reference Resources on the Internet
www.mcls.org/homepages/ref/wwwref.htm
The annotations mostly describe the source or provide a brief review of the site.

Part III

Arts
&
Entertainment

21

Art & Architecture Resources on the Web

The words "art appreciation" may bring memories of sleepy darkened classrooms and slides projected on a screen pulled over the blackboard. Some folks may recall the visual (and physical) overload of rushed marches through must-see museums on a long-awaited trip to Europe.

Whether you're an artist yourself, or just know what you like, the Web can turn your computer screen into a virtual museum of art. Of course, the image on the screen cannot compare to the experience of viewing the canvas on which Van Gogh's brushstrokes depicted the *Starry Night*. But whether you're planning a museum trip, or studying an artist, or hoping to buy a poster, or just enjoying the view, you can visit art and architectural works around the world—or those created only in digital form by a whole new breed of artists—with just a click of your mouse.

There are thousands of art sites around the Web, but the specialized audience of art lovers and "starving artists" does not enjoy the same degree of commercial investment or grant support that backs extensive search sites and portals in business, government, science, and popular culture. Once you go beyond Yahoo! in your searching, most art-specific subject sites are labors of love, developed, maintained, and supported by the traditional Internet community of academia, librarians, and individual enthusiasts.

The Pioneer Sites

Tim Berners-Lee wasn't thinking about art when he created a language and networking protocol for hyper*text* that started the Web spinning. But when Nicolas Pioch, a student at École Polytechnique in Paris, opened the WebMuseum—then called WebLouvre—in March 1994, eyes around the world popped open with delight at this use of technology to promote art.

Pioch wrote: "The WebMuseum was not made as part of any official or supported project. There's not grant [sic] behind that, it is total pleasureware(tm). I decided to start working on this exhibit because I felt more artistic stuff was needed on the Internet, so the WebMuseum took over my free time (nights and weekends . . .) since mid-March 1994 . . . . No support, no funding, no manpower: the WebMuseum is a collaborative work of its visitors contributing to expand and improve the WebMuseum."—*From the last "What's New" announcement in June 1996.*

A pioneer on the Web frontier in its wild early days, Pioch's innovative site later faced the legal issues that ensued with the evolution of the Internet as a popular global medium of communication and commerce. Issues like the copyrights on art works and on the photographs of the art works and even the name of the site—a tribute to France's national museum—created problems for Pioch. The WebMuseum stopped adding to its exhibits in 1996, but can still be enjoyed at metalab.unc.edu/wm. And now, hundreds of museums and galleries, from the Museum of Modern Art in New York to the new Guggenheim Museum in Bilbao, Spain, are presenting exhibits on the Web; even artists without agents can display their works for comment, criticism, or sale.

Art librarian Mary Molinaro's ArtSource (www.uky.edu/Artsource) is another pioneer site; this one, however, continues to be updated and improved. About this annotated subject-specific listing of selected art sites, Molinaro wrote: "ArtSource is a project that started in the Spring of 1994 when the Web was relatively young. As a service to art librarians, I began putting together a page that listed art resources that were becoming available on the Web via Mosaic. At the time I thought it would be a comprehensive list. As usage of the Web exploded it soon became apparent that a comprehensive site would be highly impractical! I realized that a selective site would be much more helpful to users. The site has developed over time to be what it is today. Please realize that the BEST way to find information on art-related topics is to talk to an art librarian who can use both Internet resources AND a print collection."

> **CAUTION:** The subject-specific search sites for art and architecture are usually easy to view. But when visiting the graphics-rich art and architecture content sites you'll be pointed to, be prepared to wait! Graphical sites use a lot of bandwidth and those photographic reproductions may take some time to load. At modem speeds of 28.8, page viewing can seem unbearably slow. Some sites also require the installation of software plug-ins to view features created in video, Shockwave, 3-D, or Virtual Reality Modeling Language (VRML).

Art & Architecture Information on the Web

If you're looking for artists and their works, virtual tours of museums across the globe, news about auctions and sale prices, the name and credentials of an architectural firm, or an artist to paint your portrait, the Web offers a wide palette of art resources. Increasingly, as with other topics, sites may require a subscription, a membership, or a fee. But there are multitudes of sites to fill your art appetites with delight, free of charge and travel budgets.

Types of art and architecture information include:

> **Dictionaries:** ArtLex Dictionary of Visual Art, with more than 2,800 terms (www.artlex.com).

> **Exhibitions and galleries:** World Wide Arts Resources offers extensive searchable listings of commercial and non-commercial exhibits, self-submitted (www.wwar.com).

> **Image collections:** The Great Buildings Collection Online— Images of more than 750 great buildings from around the world and across history (www.greatbuildings.com/gbc/buildings.html).

Databases: Getty Museum and Institutes, including scholarly databases of art terms and artist names (www.getty.edu).

Museums: Guggenheim Bilbao Museum (www.bm30.es/guggenheim), Diego Rivera Museo Virtual (www.diegorivera.com, Estate of Keith Haring (www.haring.com/), Museum of Modern Art (www.moma.org).

Libraries: The Frick Collection—art reference library catalog FRESCO (www.frick.org/html/fresco.htm).

Art shopping: Electric Gallery, opened in 1994 (www.egallery.com), represents more than 200 artists online.

Art schools: Another searchable database from World Wide Arts Resources provides listings of art education programs (www.wwar.com).

Organizations: AIA Online Network—membership site for the American Institute of Architects (www.aiaonline.com).

Directories of architects online: Cyburbia Architecture Resource Directory (www.arch.buffalo.edu/pairc/architecture_resource_directory.html).

Stolen art: Art Loss Register—register but no searching (www.artloss.com).

Art news: ArtNet magazine—online publication with news, reviews and features (www.artnet.com).

What's missing: As with many subjects on the Web, there are gaps in information and sites from developing countries and other places without much technological infrastructure. Museums and contemporary artists in China, Central and South America, and Africa are poorly represented except when included in Western museums and exhibits. Basic art reference works, like encyclopedias, are not yet available and few art magazines and journals have established a presence on the Web.

Great Scout Sites for Art & Architecture

**Internet
ArtResources.**™

Internet ArtResources

www.artresources.com
Contacts: Bob Ferguson and Doug Taylor, Publishers
Sound Data, Incorporated
2601 Elliott Avenue, Suite 3148
Seattle, WA 98121
bobf@sounddata.com or dougt@sounddata.com

Why we picked this site: Internet ArtResources is a database of listings for art galleries, museums, artists, and exhibitions in the real world, with hyptertext links to sites on the Web. Publisher Doug Taylor wrote: "Each listing must have a physical location—not just a cyber presence. Our focus is to provide the art collector with a resource for finding galleries that show a particular artist, to find the galleries/museums in a particular city or region or to locate where a particular artist's works are on view (museum or gallery) . . . . The idea behind IAR was to include all visual arts locations, not just those with websites."

Attempting to compile thousands of art resources available on and off the Web is a daunting task that ArtResources accomplishes with much care. Although the sites here are mostly submitted for complimentary listing, the information is checked before going in. "We are in the midst of sending out verification letters to all listings (yes—nearly 5,000 galleries alone) to see if they still exist physically as well as whether the URL is still valid," Taylor wrote. The sub-categories of the site, including galleries, artists, schools, and events, makes it easier to pinpoint the type of resource you are seeking.

Created: January 1995.

How many sites: Over 1,500 links to Web sites.

Audience: The fine arts collector/enthusiast wanting to locate particular types of art or see when and where particular artists will be exhibiting.

How sites are selected: The directory listings are complimentary and self-submitted. Anyone wishing to be listed on the site must have a physical location or work that can be physically viewed in a studio, gallery, or other location—not included are cybergalleries or artists whose work is only visible on the Web. More thoroughly described are paying clients that have contracted to have a full Web site created with images, artist information, show information, and whatever else they want to add to educate the online visitor.

How it's supported: Web design services and arts business software sales.

Brought to you by: Sound Data, Inc. and Ferguson Taylor Group Inc.

Freshness: A date stamp on all entries show when they got into the database; most of the sections have weekly updates.

Topics covered: Database of directory listings includes galleries, museums, artists, art publications or booksellers, art shows, fairs, events or expositions, and art schools.

Contents: There are five directory areas in ArtResources:

- **Galleries:** Directory of spaces that have works of art for sale to the public and that have a location where people can go and look at the art for sale.

- **Artists:** Artists without representation are listed here with information on galleries where their work can be seen.

- **Museums:** Spaces with works available for viewing at certain days and times.

- **Expos/Fairs:** Listings for events where booths are set up with multiple vendors exhibiting and selling their art.

- **Schools:** Places where arts courses are taught.

Searching: You may search by gallery or artist name, location, type of medium, or any combination of these.

What you get: Listings of art spots in the real world with links to Web sites when available. There is also original content created for this site, including articles and reviews of exhibitions.

Advanced searching: Boolean searching (AND, OR) and truncation can be used.

Design: Graphically rich and well designed; may be slow loading at lower modem speeds.

Other features: News Briefs are brief news items and press releases from throughout the visual arts community. Listings designated by a camera icon are accompanied by images.

Help or FAQ: Help and hints for constructing good searches are provided.

Read about it: Reviewed by the Internet Scout, August 8, 1997 (scout.cs.wisc.edu/scout/report/archive/scout-970808.html#11).

The gateway to art, design, architecture & media information on the Internet

ADAM

adam.ac.uk/

Contact: Tony Gill, Project Leader

Surrey Institute of Art & Design

Falkner Road

Farnham, Surrey GU9 7DS U.K.

tony@adam.ac.uk

Why we picked this site: We chose ADAM as an excellent example of a structured, selective, and descriptive searchable online catalog created by professional librarians whose chief concern is quality of resources. The ADAM team finds resources according to a collections policy, evaluates their quality against selection guidelines, and uses the traditional tools and skills of librarianship (such as cataloguing rules for keyword indexing, classification, and controlled terminology) to create the catalog entries. ADAM project leader Tony Gill wrote: "Evaluation feedback consistently shows that our users really value the quality-filtering role that we provide, particularly now that our database is growing to a usable size. As technical and information standards continue to develop (e.g., metadata and technical interoperability standards), we will hopefully start to provide a more integrated way of finding high-quality information on the Web."

According to the documentation provided: "Quality of Resources is key to the success of ADAM. No matter how sophisticated the search engine may be, if the resources it identifies are of poor quality then the information is of little use." We heartily agree.

Created: December 1995.

How many sites: 1,400+.

Audience: ADAM is designed to serve the needs of the higher education art, design, architecture, and media communities in the United Kingdom, as well as the general public worldwide.

How sites are selected: The criteria for selection include information content (relevancy, comprehensiveness, authorship, and currency), accuracy, presentation (textually, i.e., writing style, or graphically, i.e., image clarity), authoritativeness, and structural design (physical appearance, logic, and navigability). User feedback is encouraged and a form for nominating sites is provided.

How it's supported: Funding from Joint Information Systems Committee of the U.K.'s Electronic Library Programme.

Brought to you by: ADAM is being jointly developed by nine consortium partner institutions, led by the Surrey Institute of Art and Design, Glasgow School of Art, and Web host, the University of Northumbria at Newcastle. A steering group meets three times a year to make strategic decisions about the development of the service.

Freshness: Additions were made on the day the site was viewed.

Topics covered: Fine Art, Design, Architecture, Applied Arts (including textiles, ceramics, glass, metals, jewelry, and furniture), Media (including film, television, broadcasting, photography, and animation), Theory, Museum Studies and Conservation, and Professional Practice related to any of the above. Prominence is given to collecting appropriate U.K. resources, although European and worldwide resources are selectively included.

Contents: A searchable catalog of descriptive entries, indexed by word and keywords, that link out to Web sites and mailing lists relating to the topics covered.

What you get: Search results are in the form of a catalog record including a paragraph-long description of the site and its resources, a link to the site and its address (or subscription instructions for mailing lists), and a display of the indexing keywords, including country and organization.

Advanced searching: ADAM's search engine offers Boolean searching (AND, OR), case-sensitive or truncated word searches, and title-only searching. ADAM's Tony Gill reports that the project is working on "a new database system that will provide much more sophisticated functionality, multiple search screens for more advanced features, an enhanced browse-by-category subject tree, etc."

Design: Simple clean fast interface, with search box prominently featured.

Other features: What's New (top twenty most recent additions).

Help or FAQ: Extensive documentation of the project's criteria, policies, and participants is offered, as well as search help and instructions and training for would-be contributors.

Architecture Virtual Library
www.clr.toronto.edu:1080/VIRTUALLIB/arch.html
Contact: Dr. Rodney Hoinkes, Head of Design Applications
Centre for Landscape Research
University of Toronto
230 College Street
Ontario, M5T 1R2 Canada
rodney@clr.toronto.edu

Why we picked this site: This site is an example of one of the many excellent subject-specific search sites that have been created and maintained over a period of years by individual Netizens. Part of the network of individual guides networked through the World Wide Web Virtual Library (vlib.org/Overview.html), the Architecture Virtual Library and its companion Landscape Architecture

Virtual Library (by the same author) are truly labors of love, subject expertise, and diligence. Not all the Web Virtual Library offerings are as complete or current as these two extensive guides.

Created: 1994.

How many sites: 2,500 links are listed.

Audience: The general Internet community with specific interest in architecture.

How sites are selected: Sites are selected by Hoinkes from user submissions, which can be made via a Web form. Hoinkes writes: "All submissions are checked for accuracy (in address, title, keywords, etc.), edited if needed (often to remove extra 'qualitative' descriptions), and then updated into the public database."

How it's supported: Hoinkes collects, catalogs, and posts the materials on this site on his personal time, from the Web community's submissions via e-mail. University of Toronto provides the hardware.

Freshness: The site owner runs a program that tests the links for validity. Twenty to fifty new links are added each week.

Topics covered: Architecture: the primary point of focus for this library is the collection of references to the electronic resources on the Internet. It is an attempt to be fairly definitive within that realm only—not a library covering all material about these subjects, only those that exist virtually and contributed by groups internationally.

Contents: Browsable or searchable database of annotated listings of Web sites relating to architecture, including history, construction, projects, models, publications, schools, government, organizations, research, firms, jobs, events, conferences, competitions, architecture news, and Internet community communications via mailing lists and WebBoards.

What you get: A search provides a brief listing and link to a site and annotation with indication of date site was last checked, size of page, and image on the page retrieved.

Advanced searching: The database search form allows you to search by title, organization, URL, keyword, and free text.

Design: Use the non-frames version, as the frame design does not fit easily into all browsers.

Other features: The Hot list shows which sites listed are currently most popular—the Vatican Museums were recent favorites.

Read about it:
Hoinkes, Rodney. "The Architecture and Landscape of the Learning Web," Computers and the History of Art, Teaching-Images-Internet Special Edition (rubens.anu.edu.au/chart/ or www.clr.utoronto.ca/PAPERS/CHArt95.html).

More Recommended Scout Sites for Art and Architecture

World Wide Web Virtual Library Museums Page
www.comlab.ox.ac.uk/archive/other/museums.html
Since 1994, Jonathan Bowen has been compiling the most extensive searchable list of links to museums on the Web. This is another excellent page connected to the World Wide Web Virtual Library.

AECInfocenter
www.aecinfo.com
AECInfoCenter is a commercial site specific to the architectural, engineering, construction, and home building industries. Information includes product technical specifications, product listings,

industry events, classified ads, original content, and interactive discussion forums. For architecture, AECInfocenter provides searchable and browsable subject-classified annotated listings of firms, schools, software, hardware, publications, associations, newsgroups, and other sites of interest on the Web.

Gateway to Art History

www.harbrace.com/art/gardner/

A companion to the Harcourt Brace college textbook, Gardner's Art Through the Ages, this is an innovative attempt by a mainstream publisher to provide Web context to the material in the printed version of a textbook. The site is the work of Christopher Witcombe, Professor of Art History at Sweet Briar College in Virginia. Witcombe also maintains the award-winning "Art History Resources on the Web" (witcombe.bcpw.sbc.edu/ARTHLinks.html).

World Wide Arts Resources

wwar.com

This is a huge site with large searchable databases of artists, museums, commercial resources, galleries and exhibitions, art education sites, and publications. Created by Markus Kruse, it also features classified ads, a chat forum, and listings for performing arts. Searches may bring up duplicate sites or sites that may be irrelevant to the subject matter—a liability of self-submission of sites without strong monitoring.

For More Information

Harmsen, Leif. "The Internet as a Research Medium for Art Historians." April 1996 (art-history.concordia.ca/AHRC/essay.htm).

Jones, Lois S. *Art Information and the Internet: How to Find It, How to Use It*. Phoenix, Arizona: Oryx Press, 1998.

22

Entertainment Resources on the Web

Lights, cameras, action. Raise the curtain. Groove with the music. Veg out in front of the tube. Get entertained!

According to the Consumer Expenditure survey of the Bureau of Labor Statistics, the average American spends an average of $1,700 a year entertaining him/herself. Movies, plays, dance, concerts, television—in all they are a considerable money expenditure and an even more considerable time expenditure. Think about investing three hours to see a play or go to a show or concert, and you'll want to make a wise investment. The World Wide Web can help.

Entertainment resources on the Web run the gamut of reviews to help you select what to see or do, calendars and guides to help you find out when and where things will be, and ticket sales services to get you in. Then, if you loved the show, there are fan sites where you can get every bit of information possible about that smoldering star or hot performer, and studio- or agency-sponsored sites where all the "official" information about a movie or star can be found.

Be careful when looking at entertainment sites. Bias and propaganda are rampant—from the bias of a gushing fan, to the propaganda of the hype in marketing a show or movie. Particularly in the area of reviews, be sure to determine who is writing the review and what that person's stake is in it. Look for reviews from mainstream publications that don't accept perks or deals and, in the best of all worlds, are not beholden to the production or person they are reviewing.

Use these Entertainment guides to help you find how and where to spend those entertainment dollars. Then, relax, sit back, and enjoy the show.

Great Scout Sites for Entertainment—Movies

The Internet Movie Database
www.imdb.com
Contact: help@imdb.com
84-88 Pinner Road
Harrow, Middlesex HA1 4LF U.K.

Why we picked this site: Do you want to know everything about a specific movie: past, present, or future? Go no further. This is the ultimate resource about movies. The Internet Movie Database's objective is "to provide useful and up-to-date movie information freely available on-line." It does this, and then some. According to the introduction, it currently covers over 170,479 titles with over 2,462,516 filmography entries and is expanding continuously. The metainformation about the site is excellent, giving you all the details and hints about how to use this extensive movie resource wisely and well.

Created: 1996.

How many sites: There are links to more than 30,000 external movie Web sites in addition to all the movie-related information within the IMDB. The database is updated weekly with new information.

Audience: Movie lovers everywhere.

How sites are selected: Information in the movie listings come from a variety of sources, including movie press kits and interviews with people involved in the movies. IMDB also relies on users' input to supplement the entries. The external links available for movies and TV programs in the IMDB send you to: information about when the show is on TV, cinema show times, official sites for the program from the production company or studio, miscellaneous sites (many of them fan sites), FAQ sites, photographs, sound clip(s), video clip(s).

How it's supported: This is a project of the highly success-ful online bookstore Amazon.com and is funded by advertising and sponsorships.

Searching: You can search by the title of a movie or by a name. With the title search, putting in any word in the title will give you a listing of movies with that word in the title. Click on the title you want to go to the full entry. With name searches, there are several ways to get at the name. You can put in the full name (i.e., Kevin Spacey), or just a partial name and the type of person you are looking for (actor/actress, costume designer, director . . .). There are two types of searches, a "sub-string" search where parts of the word you search for will be found (i.e., put in Annette and you'll get actress names with Jeannette, too), and a "fuzzy" search (i.e., put in Annette and you'll also get a listing for Babette and Julian Carette— very fuzzy). Click on "more search options" and you'll get search boxes for specific kinds of searches, Movie/TV title search (where you can specify movie only, TV only, or both), Cast/Crew Name Search (where you can specify actor or actress only or crew member only), Character Name Search, (where you can specify male or female), Word Search (to locate a particular word in quotes, taglines, trivia, and any one of ten other categories). IMDB has one of the more elaborate search function types of any Web site, but its use is very well explained.

What you get: Each of the entries about a movie contains any or all of the following:

Film Content: alternate versions, quotes, soundtracks, plot summaries, trailers; *People*:biographies; *Filming Business:* business information, filming locations, technical information, movies in production; *Awards and Reviews:* awards, ratings, recommendations; *Fun Stuff:* crazy credits, goofs, trivia. The key information about the movie is in the main part of the page; the left-hand margin lists all the other information. If there is information in that area available about the movie you're looking at, it will have a link.

Design: The design of this information-filled site is logical and well organized. The cues about where and what information is available are clear and easy to use. Overall, this is just an excellent resource.

Here are a few other movie sites:

Movie Clicks
www.movieclicks.com/
A listing of movies now playing and those on video with links to the "official Web sites" for that movie. Click on one of the links to the movie and a different browser opens up and takes you there. This is a great service if what you want is the studio's propaganda about the show.

MovieFone
www.moviefone.com
Figured out the show you want? Now go find out where to see it. MovieFone (formerly MovieLink) is a great service that provides one-site shopping for all your movie information. Plug in your ZIP code, select the movie you want to see and it will give you today's showtimes at area theaters. There are even links to a short synopsis of the movie, the official movie site, Internet Movie Database, a place where you can buy the soundtrack, and where to go to find news and gossip about the movie.

Great Scout Sites for Entertainment—Plays

Playbill Online
www.playbill.com
Contact: Playbill Inc.
52 Vanderbilt Ave., 11th Floor
New York, NY 10017
webmaster@playbill.com

Why we picked this site: What do you read when you're in the theatre before the lights go down and the curtain rises? Well, *Playbill*, of course. So it makes sense that that's where you should go when you have questions about the theater. Their Web site is a massive and authoritative collection of news, notices, and, in the Theatre Central section, links to "the largest compendium of theatre links on the Internet."

Created: Playbill Inc. bought the Theatre Central site and incorporated it into the Playbill site in 1996.

How many sites: Around 2,000 links.

Audience: Playgoers, playwrights, actors, and others interested in the theatre.

How sites are selected: Self-submission, but the links are checked for validity by the editors at Playbill.

How it's supported: Playbill Inc., which has been publishing programs for plays for 114 years, sponsors the site.

Topics covered: Celebrity sites, Cabarets, Classical Music, Dance (with breakdown of categories of dance), For the Playwright, London Theatre, Miscellaneous, Audition Notes, Musical Theatre Sites, Non-professional Companies, Theatre Listing Guides, Production Companies, Professional Theatre Companies, Publications and Discussions, Shakespeare, Show Sites, Specialty Professional Theatre Companies, Stagecraft, Theatre Books-Scripts-Music, Training and Education, Unions, Contracts, Directories and Associations, Stage and Technical Crew.

Searching: The listings can only be browsed by topic.

What you get: An alphabetical listing of links in that category with descriptions of the site submitted by the site creator.

Design: The home page is busy, with the layout of a pamphlet chock full of information, but the links listings are clean and simple.

Other features: Looking for what's playing on Broadway—or off-Broadway, or national tours, or the London theatre? You can check out the links to plays and the theatres they are playing in. Wanting to pick out great seats for that trip to the theatre? The Playbill site has seating charts. Also, the Connections feature is a directory of actors/actresses, directors, playwrights, and others connected with the theatre who might want to contact each other.

There are a number of other theatre links sites, but most are very specific, dealing with just musical theatre or staging design, for example, or they are regional like Culture-Net for Canadian culture links (www.culturenet.ucalgary.ca/index.html) and Gravel Walk to Theatre on the Net (www.ettnet.se/~pferm/gravel.htm), which focuses on European, especially Scandinavian, theatre and playwrights. One other link to general theatre sites is Theatre Link (www.theatre-link.com), which is nicely organized but not very selective.

Great Scout Sites for Entertainment—Concerts

The interesting thing about concerts is that now they come to you, you don't need to go to them. The Web's constantly improving audio download capacities and "real-time" audio streaming make musical events a part of your browsing experience. Look at the Yahoo! category Net Events: Arts and Entertainment: Music (events.yahoo.com/Net_Events/Arts_and_Entertainment/Music/) to get a listing of the live concerts available on the Net.

If you are interested in real rather than virtual concerts, there are regional concert listings all over the Net, including Real Concerts, a South African site with all the latest concert information (www.realsa.co.za/).

The Ultimate Band List
www.ubl.com/concert/
Contact: Artists Direct
17835 Ventura Blvd.
Encino, Ca 91316
ubl@ubl.com

Why we picked this site: The Ultimate Band List is the ultimate portal site for people interested in music. For the concert-goer, the Concert Listings area, linked to the home page, is a source for touring dates and venues for tours. There are music links, music news, and a "shopping cart" feature that lets you buy the latest recording from that band you just saw. Their links are well annotated and logically organized, which is music to the music information seeker's ears.

Created: 1997.

How many sites: Over 40,000 sites.

Audience: Music lovers and music sellers.

How sites are selected: Sites are self-submitted but checked by people at UBL to make sure they go into the right areas.

How it's supported: Advertising and online retail sales.

Searching: In the Concert Listing search you can type in an artist's name (get a listing of tour dates and places), a city you are interested in (get a listing of upcoming concerts for the next two months), or a venue (get a listing of concerts there for the next two months). The information in the concerts database comes from Pollstar.

There is also a search of the whole UBL site that gives you a comprehensive and well-organized listing of links about particular artists (get a listing of Web sites on the artist, bulletin board/newsgroup sites, archives of information about the artist, the artist's record label, tour information, links to where you can get the tablature for songs, and MIDI music sites), albums (get a listing of the tracks on the album with links to real audio cuts, reviews, credits, related albums). You can either type in a band's name or click on a letter of the alphabet and get to a listing of bands/artists, then click to get the links list. The listing of bands is somewhat difficult to read, as the two columns make alphabetical browsing somewhat confusing.

You can also browse by categories in the "Links by Type" area (see subjects below). Find the search functions by scrolling down the home page and look in the left-hand column.

Subjects Covered: For each of the artists/bands listings, links are organized by Archive, Audio-Video, FAQs, Lyrics, Mailing Lists, MIDI-Files, Misc., News, See Also, Tablature, Tour Dates, Genre.

What you get: See above.

Design: There is so much going on with this site—you can buy music, find out about artists, chat with others interested in music—it's no wonder it's a busy-looking design. Once you've read through the options and features of the UBL, the navigation will make sense. Locating the search functions is a challenge, but worth it.

Other features: Music news, upcoming releases of albums, links to radio stations around the world, online music events, recaps of all the music charts and rankings on the Net.

Great Scout Sites for Entertainment—Television

Ultimate TV

www.ultimatetv.com

Contact: 15821 Ventura Blvd., Suite 410

Encino, CA 91436

feedback@ultimatetv.com

Why we picked this site: Just as a site called the Ultimate Band List was the ultimate for concert goers, the Ultimate TV site just has to be the ultimate for television watchers. This site has it all, the latest TV news, complete TV listings, you can even create your own personalized TV listing of your favorite channels and what they offer.

Created: 1997.

How many sites: 10,639 links for 1,418 shows, including more than 1,200 Web pages.

Audience: Couch potatoes and TV aficionados around the world.

How sites are selected: Sites about TV programs are submitted to the UTV staff, which checks the links and puts them in the proper categories. Adding and modifying site listings, which used to be done by individuals, are now done only by the UTV staff.

How it's supported: Advertising and online retail sales.

Searching: There are a variety of searches possible when looking for information about a television program. *Current TV Season*

Shows: There is a select box for 1998–99 TV Season Shows; just pull down the box and select one of the shows. *Search a specific show:* Put words into the search box and locate information about a specific show. *Browse shows alphabetically:* Just click on a letter and a list of programs starting with that letter is retrieved. Select one of the programs for the listing of links about that program. *Browse by Category:* click on one of the following genres and get a listing of programs that fall into that area: Action, Adventure, Animated, Children's TV, Comedy, Countries, Documentary, Dramas, Education, Game Shows, Miniseries, Music, News, Political, Public Access, Science Fiction, Soap Operas, Specials, Sports, Talk Shows. *Browse by type of resource:* click on one of the following resource types and get links to shows: E-mail address, Episode Guides, FAQs, Forums, Mailing Lists, News Groups, Other Web Sites, Web Pages.

What you get: When searching for a current TV program, you get a page with photos of the stars, information about the production, a brief history of the show, and links to such topics as books, forums, chats, episode guide, fan sites, mailing lists, FAQs, newsgroups, and other links. In addition, links to the official site/studio and an e-mail address to reach the show's producers are given. If you look for a past TV program, you get all the same links without the page of information about the show (so no picture and history/production information package).

Design: Another busy site with lots of features, but once you get to the show listings, the display is clean and easy to use.

Other features: Links to television station Web sites around the world.

For More Information

Waugh, Ian. *Music on the Internet (And Where to Find It)*. Carle Place, NY: Cimino Publishing, 1998.

23

Hobbies and Crafts Guides on the Web

Do you spend your spare time crocheting, building miniatures, doing stained-glass lampshades, building birdhouses, designing mosaics, or decoupaging furniture? Do you collect stamps or Beanie Babies, go bird-watching, gather rocks, garden, or home-brew beer? If you have time to do those things, you're probably not spending nearly enough time on the Web! Actually, if you do enjoy those crafts and hobbies, then taking a bit of time away from your favorite pastime to go online will be well worth it because the Web abounds with resources, hints and tips, suppliers, and other aficionados of every type of hobby and craft.

I love to do mosaics and have a hard time finding supplies—tiles in the right colors, grout dyes, tile saw blades. I can now find all those on the Web. I can even do a virtual tile design at the Tile Design Workshop (www. ipns.com/lajoie/minitiles/tilegrid.htm). Many of the hobbies and craft sites are commercial sites; they want to sell you the items you need to satisfy your obsession. But others are good resources for ideas and techniques.

One of the hot areas on the Internet is for collectors. The number of Internet auction houses that are trading in stamps, coins, and sports memorabilia is growing. One of the biggest, Collectors Universe (www. collectors.com/), brings together hundreds of Internet auction sites. So, gentlemen, start your bidding, but be careful. Internet auctions are increasingly an area where you should be very cautious, and check the credentials of the site and the validity of the deal. According to Internet Fraud Watch, frauds related to Internet auctions moved from not even being in the top ten in 1996 to being the third-most common Internet scam in 1997.[1] By 1998, fraud on Internet auctions was the number one complaint with over 25 percent of complaints being related to auctions.[2] So, if your hobby is collecting, do check out the opportunities of the Internet auction blocks, but keep your eyes open!

Here are a few of the best techniques for finding hobby and craft sites. Only one is fully profiled, because it has the most qualifications for our selection of a Great Scout, but the other two are great resources—they just don't fit the profile of a "Great Scout." See, too, the list at the end of some other good Craft and Hobby resources, but not necessarily ones that provide a listing of links to other Web sites.

The Top Scout Site for Hobbies and Crafts

About.com
home.about.com/hobbies/
Contact: About.com
220 East 42nd Street
New York, NY 10017
reachus@miningco.com

Why we picked this site: We love About.com. It epitomizes the spirit of the Great Scout by using hundreds of great scouts to create great guides to resources. We wanted to profile this particular About.com guide compilation because of the thoroughness of the hobby and craft topics covered and to point out the work that About.com does for so many subject areas.

Created: 1997. Originally called The Mining Co.

How many sites: 500 topic guides in the whole site, 58 of them in the hobbies/games area.

Audience: Barbie Doll collectors, genealogists, jewelry makers, trivia game players, and all manner of other hobbyists, gamers, and crafters.

How sites are selected: About.com's guides develop the individual topic guides, following a basic template. The guides scout out sites; there are no submissions although each guide does have an area where people can suggest a site.

How it's supported: Advertising and online commerce transactions fund About.com.

Topics covered: There are three categories in the Hobbies Guides area: Arts/Crafts, Collecting, Pastimes. Under each of these categories there are subcategories, like Basketry, Bead-work, Knitting, Needlepoint, Quilting, and Weaving in the Arts/Crafts area; Action Figures, Barbie Dolls, Books, Cookie Jars, Minerals, Miniature Cottages, Pins, Sports Trading Cards, Stamps in the Collecting area; and Aviation, Beekeeping, Casino Gambling, Crossword Puzzles, Genealogy, Magic and Illusion, Model Railroading, and Treasure Hunting can be found in the Pastimes area.

Searching: There is a search box to locate particular guides in the About.com site, or you can use the pull-down box to select an area of About.com. Once you get to an area, however, you just select the guide you want (Basketry, for example) and click to the guide.

What you get: Each of the subject guides provides specific features including Net Links (a categorized listing of links on the topic), In the Spotlight (articles about the topic), Forums (where you can post a message), Chat (for real-time conversation), Events (monthly calendars of events), Newsletter (to get an e-mail newsletter on the subject of the guide), and Guide Bio (with information about the credentials of the person who is creating and maintaining the subject guide). Down the left-hand side of the Guide home page are the categories for the list of links. The links are highly selective and usually well annotated. Clicking on one of the links takes you to the linked site.

Design: The About.com Guides are well designed with lots of white space and no clutter. The predictability from Guide to Guide with regards to the features they offer make using Guides across different subject areas a pleasure.

Another Great Scout Guide to Finding Hobby and Craft Sites

Britannica: Encyclopaedia Britannica's
Internet Guide
www.britannica.com
Click on their "Arts & Entertainment" link. Select "Leisure," then "Hobbies." Here you will get a selection of link subjects: Antiques and Collecting, Crafts, Home and Garden, Magic, Models and Model Making, Photography, Stargazing (Astronomy), Toys and Dolls, Other Hobbies. Select one of those to get some further subject breakdown (e.g., select Crafts and get thirty-two sub-categories including Basketry, Beading, Calligraphy, Candle Making, Flower Arrangement, Knotting, Origami, Quilting, Woodworking). Select one of the sub-categories and a short list of well-annotated and carefully rated sites will be displayed. You know with the Britannica listings that sites that are linked to at least got a "Noteworthy" rating (the next best being Recommended, then Excellent, Superior, and Best of the Web).

Another Technique for Finding Hobby and Craft Sites

Perhaps no other area than hobbies and crafts is as appropriate for using the new idea of WebRings. WebRings, an informal and voluntary linking among Web sites with related topics, have become a great way to browse through Web sites. Go to WebRings (www.webring.org), enter the topic you are interested in into the search box (we put in "crafts"), and you'll get a list of WebRings with that topic in the description of the WebRing. The keywords related to the WebRing, a description, then the number of Web sites linked in the ring are given. When searching for "craft" WebRings, I got 185 different WebRings, from Medieval Archery and Craft WebRing, Native American Crafts, Craft and Hobby WebRing (with 560 sites), Christmas Cooking & Crafts, and Gaia's Circle for Pagan Crafters. Click on one of the WebRings and you'll get the options of going to a random site in the ring, browsing a list of the sites on the ring, or going to the sponsoring page for the ring. Go to one of the largest of the Craft WebRings, the Craft and Hobby WebRing (www.zianet.com/mmlhess/craft.htm), for example, and read their explanation of the purpose of the WebRing. "The Crafts and Hobby WebRing is a Webring that aims to bring all craftsmen-related Web pages under one roof. A WebRing is a continuous loop of Websites with Next and Previous buttons that take you from one site on the ring to the next. The Craft and Hobby WebRing is a linked neighborhood of Websites devoted to the arts."

Other Crafts Sites

FamilyFun Magazine's Crafts Index
www.familyfun.com/filters/mainindex/crafts.html
This site, from Disney's Family.com, has hundreds of craft projects for kids and grown-ups to do together. Each project links to a page with complete instructions and other ideas for projects.

Free Craft Offers
www.ppi-free.com/freestf2.htm
Just what it says, free stuff. Click on the category you are interested

in, say, Crochet, and find information about where you can send in for free patterns, materials, and other craft supplies.

CraftSearch, HobbySearch, SewingSearch, QuiltSearch

www.craftsearch.com/

CraftSearch, and the other searches available at this site, allow you to search by ZIP code or by store name to locate craft and hobby stores and suppliers. The ZIP code search, however, has you enter only the first three digits of the zip code, but then retrieves craft stores in areas where the three numbers you entered are any part of the ZIP code (even the end of the ZIP code), so it is not a very specific search technique. It is a nice spin-off of the national telephone directory services, though, in its focus on hobby and craft stores.

Endnotes

1. Murphy, Kathleen. "Fraud Follows Buyers Onto Web." *InternetWorld*, Oct. 20, 1997 (www.internetworld.com/print/1997/10/20/markcomm/ 19971020-fraud.html).

2. McWilliams, Brian. "Hustlers Working Online Auctions." PC World News Radio, March 6, 1998 (www.idg.net/idg_frames/english/content. cgi?vc=docid_0-78005.html).

24

Literature, Language, and Libraries on the Web

Words, words, words.

The most essential skill for navigating the Web is literacy. Notwithstanding the growing cacophony of multimedia bells and whistles on the information highway, the Web is for readers, writers, and people who revel in text.

For those of us bookworms who stayed up late at night reading with a flashlight under the bedcovers, or whose vacation dreams include a good novel and a hammock, or who visit bookstores and libraries for fun, the Internet has become a primary destination. And for those whose dreams extend to being published as writers, the Internet is a wide open market for our work. Anyone can be a publisher and anything can be published, if you learn a little HTML and get your own bits and bytes of space on a Web server.

Although reading *War and Peace* screen by screen may not be appealing, there's sheer pleasure in the idea that works of great (and not so great) literature can be found and called up for perusal with the click of a mouse, even if the public library and the bookstore are closed for the night. And, the digitization of text allows you to search with ease through the pages for the word or quote you are seeking.

The cyberspace library is still tiny compared to the pages on the shelves of a local library, but it's growing daily and there are many ongoing projects that seek to fill the infinite storage space that the Internet offers with texts and manuscripts. Just as the characters in Ray Bradbury's *Fahrenheit 451* committed great books to memory, there is a community on the Web dedicated to preserving literature in digital format for readers today and in the future. So, from the Bible to the works of Shakespeare to the poetry of Pablo Neruda, the number of texts available increases as fast as they can be typed (!) in or scanned and digitized.

The Web's global reach is reflected in the virtual Babel of languages it has grown to encompass. Technology has made it possible to view the original text versions of works in Chinese ideographs or Cyrillic alphabets as well as English translations. For language learners, there are dictionaries, online language courses, and audio aids. Even newly created languages like Star Trek's Klingon are represented.

Publishers and booksellers are now aware of the vast audience for their wares among the book lovers on the Web. Thousands of sites promote publishers' booklists or offer books for sale. You can buy books on the Web at either a megastore like Amazon.com or from one of the scores of dealers in rare and out-of-print books in specialized subject areas.

When Amazon.com came online, a book purchase was my first electronic commerce transaction; even though I was wary about sending credit card information across the Web, the products offered were simply too enticing to pass up. The small world of antiquarian book hunting has been turned completely upside down by the Web; small work-from-home dealers now post their catalogs and take orders around the world, night and day.

Literary works created specifically for and on the Web comprise a growing trend. Whether self-published or selected for digital publication in a number of e-zines (electronic magazines), fiction, prose, and poetry made for the Web are gaining greater attention, critical recognition, and a lot of new fans. Science fiction is a popular genre for this type of publication.

The Internet is also a library of real libraries, where the books are cataloged and arranged in order on the shelves. In the early 1970s, I got a job typing catalog cards of the New York Public Library's Research collection onto magnetic tape for one of the earliest online catalog projects. The digitizing of text was promoted by the library community; librarians have pioneered the use of computers to find and preserve books and the information about them. But even those pioneers had no idea about how their electronic catalogs would be used today. The Web opens the catalogs of many of the world's greatest libraries for your perusal. You can search the holdings of the Library of Congress or the New York Public Library from your home in St. Petersburg, Florida, or St. Petersburg, Russia. At many university sites you can even find out which books are out to a borrower.

Finding out where the books are online is made easier by using these scout sites created by book lovers, librarians, and wise entrepreneurs who realize that the book business has the potential for big business on the Web. Our selection is based on the comprehensiveness, reliability, and authoritativeness of the sites, and their unique features. Most allow you to search by author, title, type of literature, and subject area.

Happy reading!

What's missing: The issue of copyright is *the* biggest issue in the area of literature on the Web. Most of the literature presented on Web sites is out of copyright protection, which means it's at least fifty years old. Frequently, older editions of current works may be posted, but they will not contain updates or new material. Copyright owners justifiably keep their attorneys' attention trained on any uncompensated publication of their works. Pirated versions of literary works do turn up, as do fans' selective presentation of favorite poems or lyrics; note that these efforts are not authoritative and may contain errors.

Types of Literary Materials on the Web

Authors' "Fan" pages: There are many Web sites created by literary Netizens for their favorite authors and works. A list of these by author, genre, or period appears at Literature Resources for the High School and College Student, by Michael Lee Groves, a teacher at West Linn-Wilsonville School District-Oregon (www. teleport.com/~mgroves/names.htm). Beat Generation: Ginsberg, Kerouac, Ferlinghetti, Burroughs, and others, are highlighted at Literary Kicks (www.charm.net/~brooklyn/LitKicks.html).

Bestseller lists: *Publisher's Weekly* Bestsellers lists in Hardcover Fiction and Nonfiction, Children's, Religion, Computer, Mass

Market Paperback, Trade Paperback, Audio Fiction, and Audio Nonfiction (www.bookwire.com/pw/bsl/bestseller-index.html).

Bookstores and book dealers: Amazon.com, the online megastore (www.amazon.com); City Lights Publishers and Booksellers (www.citylights.com); Alibris for a searchable database of out-of-print bookdealers' catalogs (www.alibris.com).

Book reviews: *The New York Times* book reviews since 1980 are available at the newspaper's site (www.nytimes.com); you can contribute your own review at Amazon.com.

Dictionaries: Merriam Webster Online offers WWWebster Dictionary and WWWebster Thesaurus, Word of the Day, and more (www.m-w.com) The Symbolism Dictionary is for those who need an explanation of symbolist terms (www.umich.edu/~umfandsf/symbolismproject/symbolism.html).

New books: The text of first chapters of new and current books is a tantalizing offer at *The Washington Post* (www.washington post.com).

Poetry: One of several literary collections at Carnegie Mellon University's English Server is a collection of poetry texts (english-server.hss.cmu.edu/poetry).

Publishers: Book catalogs from the biggest publishers to the smallest specialized presses and university publishing operations are available in the widest variety. Random House offers books@Random with news, features, puzzles, and special treats for kids (www.randomhouse.com/); Columbia University Press offers new and recent books (www.cc.columbia.edu/cu/cup/); Cadmus Editions sells signed limited editions of John Hopkins' *The Tangier Diaries* (www.cadmus-editions.com).

Science fiction: The Internet Speculative Fiction Database is an effort to catalog works of science fiction, fantasy, and horror. It links together bibliographic data, like author and publication bibliographies, award listings, and magazine and anthology content listings (www.sfsite.com/isfdb/).

Women writers: A Celebration of Women Writers is a collection of texts, bibliographies, and links by and about women writers throughout history. You can get involved by joining a collaborative effort to type in texts (www.cs.cmu.edu/afs/cs.cmu.edu/user/mmbt/www/women/writers.html).

Great Scout Sites for Literature

The On-Line Books Page

The On-Line Books Page
www.cs.cmu.edu/books.html
Contact: John Mark Ockerbloom, Editor
The On-Line Books Page
School of Computer Science
Carnegie Mellon University
Pittsburgh, PA 15213
spok+books@cs.cmu.edu

Why we picked this site: This is the place to look for digital versions of written works, wherever they are located on the Web. This site collects online texts in English from a variety of projects, including the Carnegie Mellon University English Server, the Internet Wiretap collection, Columbia University's Project Bartleby, and the electronic texts collection at the University of Virginia, as well as many individual contributions to the online virtual library. The listing includes all subject areas, including psychology, history, science and social sciences, as well as literature.

One week in September 1998, 39 new books were added, including *Lost Illusions* by Honoré de Balzac, *Walden* by Henry David Thoreau, *Mrs. Warren's Profession* by George Bernard Shaw, and *The Decay of Lying* by Oscar Wilde. Be aware that not all online texts are in HTML format and you may be viewing older text files from Gopher or FTP directories, or many other document formats.

Created: 1993.

How many sites: 9,000 English text sources around the Web.

Audience: Book lovers!

How sites are selected: The books must be legitimately available free in full text—no copyright violations or pay-per-view. The books must be in English and listed as a book in the online catalog of a major library; there are a few exceptions for significant electronic-only books. The text must be stable and well formatted.

How it's supported: Carnegie Mellon University provides the space for this volunteer site, a labor of love by John Mark Ockerbloom.

Topics covered: Books, serials, links to archives of text collections.

Contents: Browse by author, title, or subject (arranged by Library of Congress subject classification). Search by author or title.

What you get: List of titles, with author, format, location, and link to the text.

Advanced searching: No.

Design: Plain text.

Other features: Banned Books Online, Celebration of Women Writers, archives of major freely accessible magazines, journals, and newspapers.

Help or FAQ: The Inside Story tells you how online books and this site are produced. You can also learn how to participate in building the global online library of the future and see a list of books that are currently being worked on by volunteers.

Read about it:

"Movable Type: Electronic Books and Online Libraries, for Free or for a Fee, Are Changing the Face of Reading." *Fortune, Technology Buyer's Guide Special Issue,* November 16, 1998: 270.

The Human Languages Page
www.june29.com/HLP
Contact: Tyler Chambers
tchamber@lynx.dac.neu.edu

Why we picked this site: This site is a comprehensive catalog and searchable database of language-related Internet resources. It's been a longtime reliable favorite for its links to over 100 languages from Afrikaans to Yiddish—including Klingon, the language created for the Star Trek movies. Here's where to find online language lessons in Hawaiian, Welsh, and Bengali, as well as French, Spanish, and Japanese. There are no ratings on the value of the sites or lessons listed, but the variety and comprehensiveness of the resources on this site make it a winner. There are over 100 software sites listed here for language programs, fonts, and computer-based tutorials. Here's where we found our handy program to view Web pages in Chinese, Japanese, and Korean.

Created: June 1994.

How many sites: 1,900+ covering more than 160 languages.

Audience: Language learners and the general public interested in languages, linguistics, native language literature, translation, and computer tools for language.

How sites are selected: From site owner Tyler Chambers: "I don't publish a set of criteria, and I have the ultimate control over what gets added. At the most basic level, the site has to be useful to someone learning a language—it can't just be IN a foreign language. The different sections have their own criteria—the Languages and Literature section uses mainly the one I mentioned; the Products and Services section has to be language-related somehow (and for sale); Schools and Universities have to be either language schools or the language departments of universities, etc."

How it's supported: Advertisements.

Topics covered: Languages and literature (from A to Z), language schools and institutions, linguistics resources, products and services, organizations, jobs, dictionaries, language lessons.

Contents: Browse categorized list or search by keyword in title or description. Resources include directories, dictionaries, translation services, multi-lingual sources, texts, and archives, as well as products relating to language use and study.

What you get: Hit list of sites and brief descriptions with links out to sites.

Advanced searching: No.

Design: No-frame, text-based design, and clearly labeled navigation buttons make this site fast and easy to view.

Other features: You can browse the directory in German, Spanish, French, Italian, or Portuguese. There is also a new online Bookstore feature for purchasing language books in partnership with Amazon.com.

Help or FAQ: Explanation of simple search and use of page is provided in "About" section.

Read about it:

Vallone, Julie. "Computers Made Plain." *Investor's Business Daily*, October 23, 1998: A5.

Libweb: Library Servers via WWW
sunsite.berkeley.edu/Libweb
Contact: Thomas Dowling
OhioLINK-Ohio Library and Information Network
2455 North Star Rd., Suite 300
Columbus, OH 43221
tdowling@ohiolink.edu

Why we picked this site: This is just a simple list of libraries on the Web, but what a list! And, it's updated daily. If you love to go to the library, now you can visit them around the world twenty-four hours a day, although some library catalogs inexplicably close down online service on nights and weekends. The greatest reward for scholars, researchers, and students is the ability to search the catalogs of remote libraries. Sometimes you can even get into special collections online. Be aware that many library catalogs still require use of the older telnet protocol rather than a browser interface and you'll have to have telnet available on your computer to get in.

Created: May 1994.

How many sites: Over 3,000 home pages from libraries in over 90 countries.

Audience: Librarians and library users.

How sites are selected: Sites are approved for inclusion only if submitted by representatives of the institution to be listed as a library. A submission form is available.

How it's supported: The site is supported as part of the Digital Libraries SunSITE (sunsite.berkeley.edu) from University of California at Berkeley and Sun Microsystems.

Topics covered: Academic, public, national, state, and special libraries and their online catalogs in the United States, Africa and the Middle East, Asia, Australia and New Zealand, Canada, Europe, Mexico, the Caribbean, Central America, and South America.

Contents: Browse by location and institution or keyword search for location, library type, name, or other information.

What you get: A relevancy ranked list of hits, with metainformation from the database and a link to the site.

Advanced searching: Field searching is available in the WAIS database. Fields available for searching are site (the name of the institution), location (physical location including city, state, and country), type (library type: academic, public, special, school, national, state), and affiliation of library (consortial affiliation).

Design: Text-only, no frames, fast and easy.

Other features: Library-Related Companies links are an additional feature.

Help or FAQ: No.

Read about it:
Balas, Janet. "Library Consortia in the Brave New Online World." *Computers in Libraries*, April 1998, 18: 42.

Other Top Literary Sites
A Literary Index
www.vanderbilt.edu/AnS/english/flackcj/LitIndex.html
This is a Swiss Army knife of scout pages. It's a descriptive and

evaluative guide to Internet literary resources, significant collections of links indexes crammed into one great page. Contents include Literature Indices, Doing Literary Research, English Departments and Literary Institutes, Archives of Electronic Texts, Books and Presses, Composition, Rhetoric and Writing, and the Teaching of Literature. Small enough to carry in your pocket! Chris Flack is the guide.

Wisdom Literary Search
www.thinkers.net
Wisdom is a Yahoo!-inspired directory and search engine related to books, creativity, literature, authors, thoughts, publishing, and words. There are more than thirty main categories, including Authors, Book Trade, Literary Styles, Literary Genres, and Online Literature, with sub-topics under each. Wisdom offers a focused guide to the literary world as a quick finder of anything related to literature, writers, researchers, and readers. It's new, so the number of sites is growing. Sites may be submitted; all are reviewed before acceptance into the searchable database by the Prav Kaps of Cerritos, California, who created this site. You can also build your own free literary Web page here.

For More Information
Williams, Margot. "Web Pages That Are Far From Being Word Perfect." *The Washington Post*, July 21, 1997: F19.

25

Sports on the Web

Take me out to the virtual ballgame! Sports sites are probably, after pornography, the most prolific spectator sites on the Web. Although you won't get much exercise except in your clicking finger and wrist, you will find information on every sport imaginable on the Web, from Archery to Yachting.

I have to admit, this is a hard chapter for me to write. I'm not a sports nut. The highs and lows in my life do not revolve around this week's performance of a favorite team. But I have a brother who is still loyal to the old home football team, the Miami Dolphins, even three years after leaving Miami for Phoenix, Arizona. Here's what he says about the wonders of Web-accessible sports: "I miss the Dolphins, who never get shown on TV here. So I've been coming to the office on Sundays and using the National Football Leagues' (www.nfl.com) "Game Day Live" applet. It's almost like watching the game. Even better, I also use RealAudio to listen to WQAM Sports Radio (www. wqam.com/), the station that broadcasts Dolphin games. (OK, I admit it's a guy thing.)" So, if you're like my brother and you need your sports fix, look to the Web for everything you need in sports.

Sports sites on the Web provide official game information, rules, and strategies. During the Olympics, the USA Olympics Web site provided detailed information in the Sports A to Z section (www.olympic-usa.org/sports/) about the rules by which the judges graded performances. Over in

Pro sports, if you are confused by the refs' calls in that Sunday afternoon football game, or Monday night basketball game, you would think the official rule book would be the place to go on the Web. But finding them is no easy task. I looked and looked and found the NBA's official rules on their Web site (www.nba.com/basics/rules/) and the NFL's rules on their site (www.nfl.com/randf/rulesdigest.html). A Web site for referees and umpires had a great list of links to other sports' rules:

Baseball: www.majorleaguebaseball.com/library/rules.sml

Soccer: www.fifa.com/fifa/handbook/laws/index.laws.html

Hockey: www.cs.rpi.edu/~kennyz/Hockey/rulebook/rulebook.html/

If pro sports is your particular addiction, it doesn't matter which of the alphabet soup of leagues you are interested in (NFL, NHL, NBA, ABL . . .), there is an abundance of sites to help you follow the teams. Yahoo!'s Sports pages provide a constantly updated source of both the latest news and the essential links for following pro sports play, no matter if it's hockey, golf, football, baseball, or basketball. Go to Yahoo! Sports (sports.yahoo.com/) for a page with current game scores, player news, and links to key sites.

NCAA college sports coverage is just as prolific as the pro teams with sports information available on all the regular big sports coverage sites: ESPN (espn.go.com), Allsports (www.allsports.com), CNN/Sports Illustrated (www.cnnsi.com), The Sporting News (www.sportingnews.com).

And if "real" sports aren't your bag, you can check out the fantasy teams. A great scout site for fantasy league information links can be found at the Fantasy League Report (www.tflreport.com/links_index.html).

Even Little League sports bases are covered on the Web. Go to the Little League Web site (www.littleleague.org/) for all kinds of information.

The biggest concern in using sports sites is that there is so much information, so many Web sites on any particular sport, that sorting through which one will give you what you need can be difficult. If all you want is news and gossip, there are any number of places to go, including all the news Web sites (if you want to see local coverage of a game played elsewhere, find the newspaper or TV station Web site for the area at www.mediainfo.com). But overall compilations of statistics of sports or, as we saw, finding the official rules, can be a game of fits and starts, clicking around the Web.

The bottom line with sports sites, as with all information found on the Internet, is determining the source, and the agenda, of the information. A fan site won't be a reliable place to go for an unbiased opinion about how a team is doing, nor will the official team site. You may want to go to the reliable sports reporting venues to get that.

Great Scout Sites for Sports

Sport Quest
www.sportquest.com/
Contact: Sport Information Resource Centre
1600 James Naismith Drive, Suite 107
Gloucester, Ontario K1B 5N4 Canada
webmaster@sportquest.com

Why we picked this site: The sponsor of this site, SIRC (The Sports Information Resource Centre), has been around for more than twenty-five years, serving the sports research needs of information seekers. Their online database, SportsDiscus, distributed through the Dialog service, "collects, organizes, and distributes sport-related practical and research information found in magazines and periodicals, books, theses and dissertations, conference papers and related research reports." The Web version picks up that mission and provides well-organized links to selected and submitted sites.

Created: December 1995.

How many sites: About 13,000 sites. That number stays fairly steady due to the disappearance of some sites and the addition of others. There is a clean-out check every three months to discard sites that are no longer operational.

Audience: Sports fans, coaches, and players and students or researchers working on sports topics.

How sites are selected: Sites in the directory are both self-submitted and located through browsing by SIRC staff. Initially, all the sites in the directory came through the searching of SIRC staff, but they have started to allow sites to suggest themselves for submission. Any submitted sites are checked by the SIRC staff. They look for sites that promote sports and active participation, and will not include sites that bash an individual player or that have no significant content.

How it's supported: Advertising and the selling of the other SIRC sports databases and products.

Topics covered: Eighty-two different sports are listed in the directory, including such unusual ones as Unicycle Hockey, Broomball, Ultimate Frisbee, and Sumo Wrestling.

Searching: You can browse through the sports and sports categories and sub-categories or use the search engine. Browsing is facilitated by the careful categorization of the sports topics, an outgrowth of the thesaurus of terms used in their bibliographic databases. Look at "Cycling," for example, and find sub-categories for Mountain Biking, Road Racing, and Track Racing. Click on one of those sub-categories, Mountain Biking, and there is a further breakdown to Associations, Clothing, Countries, Equipment, Events, Resorts, Clubs and Teams, FAQs (a very useful sub-category, it gets you to the Frequently Asked Questions lists that can answer most of the basics about the sport), Magazines and E-zines, Videos.

The search function is very simple with just two text boxes. Enter one word in one box and click on "search" or put a word in each box and select a connector for the words (and, or).

What you get: A listing of the relevant sites, in alphabetical order, with links and some with annotations submitted by the person suggesting the site to the directory.

Design: This site is very simple and clean and easy to figure out.

SearchSport: The Sport Directory
www.oldsport.com
Contact: Will Barnes
SearchSport
will@oldsport.com

Why we picked this site: "No more endless searching for sports sites." This is an ambitious motto, and one very much appreciated by those sports fans wandering the Web. Although there doesn't appear to be much in the way of evaluating the submitted sites in this directory, the careful organization, the good search capability, and the useful information about the site (when it was added to the directory and how many people have linked to it), make this a notable sports links scout site.

Created: November 1996.

How many sites: 2,200 with the addition of another 60–70 a week. The links are checked monthly and cleaned out if no longer working.

Audience: Sports fans of every persuasion, from archery to wrestling.

How sites are selected: Sites are self-submitted. They are checked for accuracy and relevant subject categorization. Sometimes sites submit their addresses a number of times to help ensure they come up in a search. If this happens, the editors at SearchSport delete the site from the database.

How it's supported: Advertising.

Topics covered: There are fifty-two sports categories, with the usual suspects as well as the more unusual ones, such as Fencing, KorfBall (a Dutch game), Orienteering (using a map to get through a wilderness area), Skateboarding and Snowboarding, Sky Diving, Sled Dog Racing, Squash, and Surfing.

Searching: You can browse by sport by clicking on one of the sports categories or use the search function. To search, plug in the term(s) you want to search on, click on "keyword" or "phrase" (if there is more than one term) or you have the choice of doing an "AND" or an "OR" search to designate different relationships between the multiple terms you enter.

What you get: The retrieved sites are organized by sports topic with links to the site and the submitted description for each site. The date the site was added to the directory is included as is the number of hits there have been on the site from the SearchSport site.

Design: The cluttered look and dark sidebars of the home page are off-putting, but the retrieved links frame is clean and easy to read. However, I wish you didn't have to scroll so far down the page to get the links.

Other features: If you love sports, all sports, you don't care which sport, then you'll enjoy the "Random Links" feature. Click on it and you'll go to a sports site of the system's choosing.

Another Sports Directory Site

SportSearch.com

www.sportsearch.com

SportSearch has a mission we can certainly cheer for. "As the all-encompassing search engines/directories continue to become more and more irrelevant, with fruitless searches and directories littered with dead links, we will constantly strive to keep our network clean, with active and relevant sites." They do a nice job of that, along with very good, clear annotations of each site in the links directory. Another great feature is the specialty links lists that are in pull-down boxes on the home page: Scores (links you to a variety of current score sites), Local Sport Pages (takes you to the sports pages of dozens of newspapers sites), Online Sports Networks (connects you to seven different sports networks online), and Fantasy Resources (the place to go when you want to make up your ideal team).

For More Information

Leebow, Ken, et al. *300 Incredible Things for Sports Fans on the Internet.* Fayetteville, AR: VIP Publishing, 1998.

Edelman, Rob. *Baseball on the Web.* Indianapolis, IN: IDG Books Worldwide, 1998.

Wolff, Michael. *Net Sports: Your Guide to Sports Mania on the Information Highway.* New York: Dell Books, 1997.

Part IV

Science & Technology

26

Computing and Internet Information on the Web

If you're new to computing, if you're a newbie on the Internet, or both, technology anxiety may be affecting you right now. It seems unfair that we need to know more about the workings of our computers than we do about our cars, refrigerators, or televisions. We have to choose which one to buy, get a good price, make sure we have all the compatible components, cables, and software and then we have to bring it home and set it up. And that's just for openers.

Before even getting onto the Web, we need to pick a service provider, set up an account, figure out how to configure the modem and make the connection and maybe download and install a browser. Each step of the way, we're confronted with new technical jargon, challenges to our motor skills, poorly written instructions, and terrifying error messages. And we've all heard about viruses that eat your hard drive and hackers who steal your bank account numbers. Help!

Don't worry. Help is out there on the Web if you know where to find it. From the tech support pages at Internet providers, computer and modem manufacturers, software companies, and Netscape's and Microsoft's megasites to computer forum discussions, user groups, individual hobbyist Web pages, and help files from university computer science departments and technical publications, helpful people and their sometimes contradictory advice are tucked away in many corners of the Web.

First of all, the FAQ—Frequently Asked Questions document—is the Internet community's name for topical and instructional guides written by Netizens and site owners. If your question is about anything related to computing or the Internet, a FAQ will probably be available. If the answer isn't there—be sure to read the FAQ first—you can post a question to one of the many Web forums, newsgroups, and discussion groups that exist around specific computer platforms, programs, and products.

What's the "Black Screen of Death"? For those mysterious acronyms and words in computerese, there are updated online dictionaries and jargon guides. Is there really a virus in your e-mail? Virus prevention, virus cures, and virus hoaxes are explained and debunked in detail on many useful sites, including the home pages of your virus protection software company, where virus updates can be downloaded.

If you're shopping for a new computer, more software, or peripherals, the Web offers a full range of services from reviews and product descriptions to comparison shopping and your purchase via cyber-transaction. Do you want to read the manual? It's probably online. Do you need Internet training? A variety of tutorials can be found. Do you want to make your own Web page? Web design guides, free graphics, helpers, programs, and advice are abundantly available. For anything about the Internet, the Internet is the place to go. From lessons for beginners to discussions among expert programmers, every level of computer skills is represented. And if you're looking for freeware, shareware, or software for sale, the Web is the place to read about it, find it, download it for free, or buy it.

If you've caught technology fever, follow the news about the latest company deals, product releases, "bug" reports, job prospects, and market activities. Computer magazines, technology newsletters, tipsheets, and wire services cover every aspect of this growth industry, including government regulations, privacy, security and Year 2000 issues, mergers and acquisitions, marketing, international cyberlaw, and innumerable predictions about the future. Technology's past is also represented, with well-documented histories of computing and the Internet in exhibits, museums, timelines, and archives online.

For anything cyber or tech, the Web is the place to find the most current information and the liveliest discussions with more detailed news than newspapers, magazines, or television can make room for. Things change so fast in the technology area that it's difficult to keep up. But there are great scouts who are keeping up for you. When you visit the scout sites below, be sure to check "What's New" because there will always be something brand new.

> **CAUTION:** Take it from us, it's very difficult to search for information about computers and the Internet by using Web search engines. Just try putting any combination of computer or Internet-related keywords in the search box—you'll get millions of hits! That's why we count on the scout sites to point us in the right direction to get what we're looking for.

Computing and Internet Materials on the Web

Dictionaries: The Jargon File (www.elsewhere.org/jargon_search), BABEL: A Glossary of Computer Oriented Abbreviations and Acronyms (www.access.digex.net/~ikind/babel.html), Free On-line Dictionary of Computing (wombat.doc.ic.ac.uk/foldoc/index.html).

Encyclopedia: Tech Encyclopedia with more than 11,000 definitions of computer terms and concepts from the *Computer Desktop Encyclopedia* (www.techweb.com/encyclopedia).

Internet: The List (of Internet Service Providers) (thelist. internet.com), Geography of Cyberspace (www.cybergeography. org/geography_of_cyberspace.html), John December's summary of Internet tools (www.december.com/net/tools).

Megasites: Commercial technology sites that combine content, shopping, news, links, and discussions include the major portals at C|Net (www.cnet.com) and ZDNet (www.zdnet.com).

Museums and archives: Virtual Museum of Computing (www. museums.reading.ac.uk/vmoc), Museum of Soviet Calculators (members.xoom.com/_XOOM/adavie/soviet/html), the Internet Archive project (www.archive.org).

Organizations, associations, and user groups: ACM Association for Computing Machinery (www.acm.org), Electronic Privacy Information Center (www.epic.org).

Technology news: Articles and updates from major print computer publications including *Information Today* (www.infotoday. com), *PC Week* (www.zdnet.com/pcweek), *InternetWeek* (www. internetwk.com), Wired (www.wired.com/wired) and Internet-only news services and e-zines like *Netsurfer Digest* (www.netsurf. com/nsd/index.html) and C|Net News (www.news.com).

Great Scout Sites for Computing and Internet Information

Computer and Communication Page
cmpcmm.com/cc
Contact: James E. (Jed) Donnelley
Webstart Communications
2835 Benvenue Avenue
Berkeley, California 94705
contact@webstart.com

Why we picked this site: This site provides a huge list of sites relating to computers and the Internet, comprehensively listing computer- and communication-related companies and organizations. It provides several points of access, including browsing, searching, cross references, keywords and geographic codes. Although the entries are limited to one line, they are packed with standard keywords and extensively cross-referenced. The list of computer-related newsgroups with links to each group's FAQ is great. The links to other computer link lists and compendium of general computer and communications pages make this a dedicated one-stop shopping site for this important topic and a great scout.

Created: December 1993.

How many sites: 10,000.

Audience: Computer professionals and the general public.

How sites are selected: "During the last couple of years I have had to limit registrations to quality links," wrote Jed Donnelley. "Most of the registered entries are 'companies'—which we have various limitations on. Most of the entries in the other categories (e.g., Standards, the compendium, the various cross-reference sections, media, etc.) I seek out myself."

How it's supported: Banner advertising.

Topics covered: Computer and Communication Companies, Media (magazines and newsletters with substantial free online content), Organizations, Programs and Projects, Usenet groups and FAQs, Standards, and links to other indexes on computers.

Contents: Lists of Web links related to computers and the Internet organized by topic and cross-referenced by geography and keyword. Browse by company name, by keyword, by geography or search. This guide is particularly rich in company listings, with succinct keyword annotations for product, service, and location. There are also direct links to resources by computer platforms and protocols.

What you get: You get a one-line annotation—a list of meaningful standardized key words—for each listing you retrieve or find while browsing. Listings are also annotated for "New" and "Extensive"!

Advanced searching: You can choose to search with Boolean expressions (AND, OR). You may also search from a page of standard search terms or search by geographic areas from the geographic areas page.

Design: As the site claims, "no fancy graphics or other distractions to get in the way."

Other features: The most recent 200 listings are browsable and highlighted. There is also a link to the searchable Internet Conference Calendar (conferences.calendar.com) from Automatrix.

Help or FAQ: Yes.

Virtual Computer Library

www.utexas.edu/computer/vcl
Contact: Christine M. Henke
Academic Computing and Instructional Technology Services (ACITS)
University of Texas, Austin
vclib@www.utexas.edu

Why we picked this site: This site provides easy access to a selective list of computer and Internet-related sites for college students that new users will also find helpful. There is a particular emphasis on places to go for help—instructional manuals, online books, user groups, and other academic computing centers where help files are available. Its focus is on using computers and the Internet for learning.

Created: April 1994.

How many sites: 1,500+.

Audience: University students and the general public.

How sites are selected: Sites are selected based on computer-related content by Christine Henke of the Academic Computing and Instructional Technology Services at University of Texas, Austin.

How it's supported: University of Texas.

Topics covered: Academic Computing Centers, Book Reviews, Computer Technology, Conferences, Documentation, FAQs, Internet Information, Journals/Magazines, News/Press Releases, Nonprofit/Government Organizations, Online Books/Dictionaries, Publishers, User Groups/Associations, Vendors Index, WWW Information

Contents: Selective lists of academically oriented links are browsable by topic and sub-topic. The Internet Information section, for example, includes sub-topics for Annotated Bibliographies, Directories, General, Guides, Indexes, Magazines & News, and Products & Services.

What you get: There is no search feature, but pages are clearly arranged by topic. At the top of each page is a hyperlinked display of the sub-topics; below are all the individual listings under the sub-topics. There are no annotations.

Advanced searching: No.

Design: Plain text, easy navigation from each page.

Other features: Links to computer book reviews, links to university computer centers and computer user groups across the United States.

Help or FAQ: No.

Other Top Computer and Internet Scout Sites

What Is

www.whatis.com

This is a great informational site about computers, technology, and the Internet with a very creative arrangement. It's a searchable encyclopedia and dictionary with over 1,500 definitions and topical entries containing over 5,000 hyperlinked cross-references and over 3,000 links to others sites for further information. Each entry is an article with definition, description, context, and links to further information. There's also a tutorial on how the Internet works, a useful table on Internet speed, a "word of the day," a "top 20 list," and a list of handy tools like calculators, country codes and "all the file formats in the world." The down side is the framed display.

Nerd's Heaven: The Software Directory Directory

boole.stanford.edu/nerdsheaven.html

This is a scout site for software that points you to every major software directory on the Web, including shareware, freeware, public domain, vendors, and more. The topics include General Software, Internet Software, Operating Systems, Scientific Software, Windows Software, Macintosh Software, Other Platforms, User Groups, Commercial Vendors and Nerdly Interest.

The Information Economy: The Economics of the Internet, Information Goods, Intellectual Property, and Related Issues

www.sims.berkeley.edu/resources/infoecon

Site by Hal R. Varian, the Dean of the School of Information Management and Systems at the University of California at Berkeley. The professor's annotated links to reports, documents, and information about the economics of the Information Age and the Internet are searchable and browsable for these topics: Accounting & Measuring Traffic; Announcements; Background and Reference; Electronic Commerce (especially rich in this area); Electronic

Publishing; Government Resources; Intellectual Property; International; Intranets; Miscellaneous Resources; Network Economics; Policy and Law; Pricing; and Security, Privacy, and Encryption. He'll also send you e-mail whenever each section is updated!

27

Environmental Information on the Web

On the land, on the sea, in the air—these are the areas students, activists, journalists, and researchers interested in the environment are exploring. And the World Wide Web is a great place to find all the information you need about the land, water, and air that makes up this big wide world, whether you want information about its make-up, its health, or its inhabitants.

Environmental information Web sites are sprouting from every kind of group—straight research outlets as well as fervent advocacy groups. This makes environmental research an area where careful investigation of the purposes of the Web site's creation, the agenda of the group sponsoring it, and the funding of the research or information gathering is especially critical. Read a press release about drilling in the North Sea on the Greenpeace site (www.greenpeace.org) and read about the same issue on the Shell Oil site (www.shell.com), and you will get different views. For people seeking balance and a perspective on the Earth's health, the resources on the World Wide Web are as welcome as the first robin of spring. But finding the right resources can be difficult.

A speech by U.S. Vice President Al Gore in 1996 sums this up well: "We now hold around the world an incredible wealth of information about the Earth and its inhabitants. That information could have a profound impact on our ability to protect our environment, manage natural resources, prevent and respond to disasters, and ensure sustainable development. Unfortunately, many potential users either do not know that it exists or do not know how to access it."

The health of this planet and the role that information about it plays are viewed with such importance that Environment and Natural Resources Management has become the first initiative for the Global Information Locator Service (GILS) project. The impetus behind the project is stated this way: "Every year, the Federal Government spends billions of dollars collecting and processing information (e.g., economic data, environmental data, and technical information). Unfortunately, while much of this information is very valuable, many potential users either do not know that it exists or do not know how to access it. We are committed to using new computer and networking technology to make this information more accessible to the taxpayers who paid for it." GILS is attempting to establish a standard for the labeling of information stashed in research centers and servers around the world, creating a sort of universal cataloging standard that will fulfill the goal of making it "easy for people to find information of all kinds, in all media, in all languages, and over time." Information about this ambitious project can be found at www.gils.net/index.html. A pilot of the Environmental and Natural Resources Management project, Eco Companion Australasia, can be found at www.indexgeo.com.au/ec/.

While projects to create a consistent and comprehensive cataloging scheme develop, the environmental resources from advocacy groups, government agencies, environmental assessment (and solutions) companies, hobbyists, reporting services, and publications proliferate. The need for careful compilers to sort through and classify relevant sites and the need for education about interpreting environmental information grow.

There are a number of sites where information about how to understand environmental issues is available. Facsnet, a service from the Foundation for American Communications, provides backgrounders and fact sheets on environmental issues (go to www.facsnet.org and search for "environment"). The United States Environmental Protection Agency has done an excellent job of organizing its tipsheets, backgrounders, data, and regulations in helpful groupings for particular users: kids, students and teachers, concerned citizens, researchers and scientists, business and industry, and state-local and tribal resources (www.epa.gov).

Great Scout Sites for Environment Resources

Amazing Environmental Organization WebDirectory
www.webdirectory.com/

Contact: info@coastline.com

Why we picked this site: It is no coincidence that this perhaps immodestly named Web site has the look of an environmental Yahoo! Started in 1994 by John Dickson, around the time that Yang and Filo began tracking Web sites for Yahoo!, this comprehensive subject site has put organized categorization on environmental information. Dickson found the niche of environment to be of particular interest and decided to make his mark on the World Wide Web by tracking the resources available about the big wide world. Its popularity and visibility was greatly enhanced when it attracted the attention of Netscape and became the top choice on the browser's "search" listing for three years. It is the largest exclusively environmental organization directory on the Web and includes sites from over 100 countries. A staff of twenty-three helps ensure that submitted sites are checked, that the annotations are useful, and that the links stay fresh.

Created: Started in May 1994.

How many sites: Between 75,000–80,000 with a dozen or so added each day.

Audience: Researchers, advocates, activists, and students—anyone with an interest in the environment.

How sites are selected: Sites are self-submitted, but every submitted site is looked at. About 50 percent of the submitted sites are not added to the directory because they do not fall into the category of environmental information or resources. Indexers at the directory add the subject categories and check the submitted site descriptions for spelling and edit for clarity or length. They run a software link-checking program once a month to locate broken or missing links in the directory.

How it's supported: An initial plan for funding through banner ads has been dropped and the site is now sponsored by and funded through profits in Dickson's Web hosting company, Coastline Communications Corporation.

Topics covered: The main categories are: Agriculture, Animals, Arts, Business, Databases, Design, Disasters, Education, Employment, Energy, Forestry, General Environmental Interest, Government, Health, Land Conservation, News and Events, Parks and Recreation, Pollution, Products and Services, Publications, Recycling, Science, Social Science, Sustainable Development, Transportation, Usenet, Newsgroups, Vegetarianism, Water Resources, Weather, Wildlife.

Searching: Just like Yahoo!, the Amazing Environmental Organization WebDirectory can be searched two ways. Browse through the subject categories and sub-categories by clicking on one of the areas. For example, click on Energy and get a listing of relevant sites for that broad category as well as more sub-headings: Alternative Energy, Conservation, Energy Efficient Systems, Fossil Fuels, etc. Some of the sub-headings have further subject breakdown, for example, Alternative Energy breaks down into Biomass, Geothermal, Hydroelectric, Solar, Wind, and Wood.

The other search uses the custom-built search engine, which retrieves items with the entered search words in the title or description of listed sites. The search function is simple and effective, but it can be confusing. The search box on the home page of the

WebDirectory is simply a fill-in box. You are not instructed that if multiple words are entered, it is assuming an "and" search (put in "lakes rivers pollution" and you will get only listings with all of those words). However, if you pull up the search box by clicking on the "Search" button on one of the other pages, you'll get a different search function, one that has the search box and a pull-down box letting you select the search to be for "all" the words (the "and" search) or "any" of the words (the "or" search).

What you get: A listing, organized by subject categories, of the sites with the words. Each item on the results list has the link to the site and a brief description of the contents of the site.

Design: This has a very simple design; the home page is just the search box, the listing of subject categories, a link to the Environmental Bulletin Board and to the feature.

Other features: There is an Environmental Bulletin Board for messages and questions about the environment. They have an occasional feature on an environmental adventure, such as Douglas Quin's Antarctic Journal.

Help or FAQ: There is not much information available about the search features to be found.

EnviroLink
www.envirolink.org/search/
Contact: The EnviroLink Network
5808 Forbes Ave., 2nd Fl.
Pittsburgh, PA 15217
support@envirolink.org

Why we picked this site: The mailing list exchange of information between twenty student activists in 1991, started by Josh Knauer while he was a freshman at Carnegie Mellon University, has grown into a huge resource site for environmental concerns. It became a Gopher site and then one of the first fifty publicly available sites on the World Wide Web. From there, it has grown into a full-service site for environmental non-profits, in addition to its mission to continue the exchange of information started so long ago. The mission statement on the information page describes well the reason for creating the site and the purpose they hope to serve: "At EnviroLink we're committed to promoting a sustainable society by connecting individuals and organizations through new communications technologies. We recognize that our technologies are just tools, and that the solutions to our ecological challenges lie within our communities and their connection to the Earth itself. Our organization does not take any positions on any environmental issues, it exists solely to act as a clearinghouse on the Internet for the environmental community, which is incredibly diverse in its views."

Created: Started in 1991 as a mailing list exchange between twenty student activists.

How many sites: Between 30,000–40,000, adding about 20 to 100 sites a day.

Audience: This site is designed for the non-profit environmental community worldwide and to provide easy access to mainstream folks who might not consider themselves activists.

How sites are selected: Sites are self-submitted but each submission is checked by one of the administrators. Content must be from a non-profit or governmental Web site (or from select, high-quality commercial sites, such as environmental magazines). The content on the Web site must be original so personal pages with links to favorite Web sites will not be included, nor will other environmental search engines. The main criterion is whether or not the information on the site contains valuable environmental information. About 50 out of 100 submitted sites are selected.

How it's supported: Using the public radio or television funding model, the site is funded by appropriate corporate underwriters and grants from some software developers. In addition, a new online environmental marketplace, GreenMarketplace (www.greenmarketplace.com), provides some funds through part of the proceeds of sales on the site.

Searching: From the home page, click on EnviroLink Library to get to the directory of environmental sites. There you have several options for locating resources:

- Browse by one of the 180 or so subject headings (everything from acid rain to biodiversity to deforestation to ecofeminism);
- Browse by one of the categories of: Actions You Can Take, Education, Events, General Info, Government, News, Organizations, Publications;
- Click on one of the icons for Air, Water, Fire, Earth, Flora & Fauna;
- Search using the "Quick Library Search" box or the Advanced Search.

With Quick Library Search, you enter search words and the search engine looks for listings with those words in the title, keywords (selected by administrators), or the short summary of Web site contents. Advanced Search provides more options, including searching for "all the words," "any of the words," or "exact phrase." Also, you can search within a listing, finding words only in the title, or keywords of the listing. You can also specify the Category areas (see above) and the display of the results found (title only or long description).

What you get: The results of your browsing by category or search are displayed in categorized groupings. For example, click on "Fire" and the resulting page displays links to the "Fire" sub-categories (alternative energy sources, energy conservation, energy sciences, fossil fuels, nuclear energy, pollution from energy), then the group-ings of "Fire" sites organized by Educational Resources, General Resources, Government Resources, Organizational Resources, Publication Resources, News Resources. Each of the resources listed under those areas has two links—one directly to the cited Web site, the other to a "summary" page about the site. Clicking on the Web link brings up the Web site within the Envirolink page frame (so if you want to see the actual address of the site you have gone to, click the right mouse button and select "View Frame Info"). If you click on the "summary" link, you'll get to one of the best features of this guide, a page with contact information about the site, the site's Web address, summary information, and a long description of the site's contents. There is even a handy little "Send to a Friend" fea-ture that e-mails the site's address. If the referenced item is a news story, clicking on the "summary" link pulls up the full text of the news item.

Design: The heavy use of frames on this site does make the response time somewhat slower, but the design and navigation of the site are clear and easy to use.

Other features: Free Web hosting to over 400 non-profit organi-zations, a bulletin board for environmental messaging, real-time chat, an Environmental Art Gallery, and other features make this a site well worth visiting.

Other Environment Directories
EcoNet
www.igc.org/igc/econet/
One of the Institute for Global Communications' issues-oriented Web sites (others include LaborNet, PeaceNet, WomensNet, ConflictNet), EcoNet is a news and current awareness service as well as a finding tool for relevant related Web sites. Use the "Issues

Directory" pull-down menu on the home page and select an area of interest (Atmosphere & Climate, Environmental Law, Energy, Forests, Greens Movement, etc.) and you'll get a resource page with highly selective links to and abstracts about environmental sites. Each of the resources pages is organized differently. The Environmental Law page, for example, is organized first geographically, and then by non-profit institutes, law firms serving industries/corporations, publishers, government, etc. Some of the resource pages have a search function, but most are just listings of the relevant resources. This is a great site for finding activist-related information.

State Environmental Web Sites Directory
www.rgf.com/EnvironLinks.html
Click on the table and you'll link to each state's environmental Web site.

Good Sites

Environmental Protection Agency
www.epa.gov/enviro/zipcode_js.html
Want to see how your particular area is doing, environmental health-wise? Check it out by ZIP code, pollution, hazardous waste, watershed conditions, and trends at the EPA's site.

Environmental News Network
www.enn.com
Read the latest news and views about environmental concerns on the Environmental News Network, voted one of the top fifty news sources on the Internet by the *American Journalism Review*.

Sierra Club
www.sierraclub.org
Some great environmental organizations have great Web sites with information and resources about their activities: Greenpeace and the Sierra Club are good examples.

Environmental Defense Fund's Chemical Scorecard
www.scorecard.org/env-releases/
Want to find a cause? How about checking on polluters in your neighborhood? Find the businesses that are causing pollution in your area at the Environmental Defense Fund's Chemical Scorecard site.

Best Environmental Directories
www.ulb.ac.be/ceese/meta/cds.html
The "Best Environmental Directories" site, an alphabetical list of environmental resources, is available in English, French, Italian, Dutch, and German.

About.com
environment.about.com
Check out a history of multimedia environmental information on the Web and get links to great environmental resources in About.com's excellent resource guide.

28

Science on the Web

Scientists were on the Internet way before it was cool. The early years of global computer networking—originally on the Department of Defense Advanced Research Project Agency's 1970s ARPANET and then on the National Science Foundation's 1980s NSFNET—centered around use of the network for research and education by academic and scientific researchers.

Scientists used the pre-Web Internet—e-mail, telnet (dial-up access to remote computers), file transfers, and newsgroups—to communicate and share research findings among the world-wide scientific community. I hadn't even heard of the Internet until my distinguished biologist cousin gave me his university e-mail address in 1991.

Scientists were first on the World Wide Web, too. In fact, the Web was invented for research scientists at the Center for Particle Physics (CERN) in Switzerland by Tim Berners-Lee. In 1989, Berners-Lee proposed a project to share and distribute information among researchers in remote locations and across hardware and software platforms based on the use of hypertext links and browsers. You can read his original proposal on his home page ("Information Management: A Proposal," 1989, www.w3.org/History/1989/proposal.html).

Even a visionary like Berners-Lee could not predict the enormous growth of the Web, its popularity, and the commercial potential that his invention unleashed. As the Web expands and reaches out to consumers, business people, and kids, the topic of science continues to grow and mature. Science's roots are deep on the Internet; where newcomer and more popular subjects may not yet have built up a significant body of literature in the Web's brief lifespan, the tools and texts of scientific research in various forms have resided on computers linked to the network for many years.

Today a wide variety of materials related to physical science, life science, computer science, and their practical applications are available on the Web for all knowledge levels. Science is still frequently first in the development and use of new Web applications and technology as well. Many of the innovations that have propelled the Web into prominence were created by researchers supported by scientific institutions and research grants. For example, the Visible Human project at NIH, which is creating anatomically detailed, three-dimensional representations of the male and female human bodies, and the supporting projects, like Syracuse University's viewer projects to make these data "visible" with the use of Java and VRML (virtual reality modeling language) programming. The wealth of information and remarkable images from our nation's space program provided through NASA and its centers are of significant interest.

The whole range of popular science magazines and scientific journals have moved onto the Web with comprehensive educational sites. From *Scientific American* and *Discover* to *Nature, New Scientist*, and the *Astrophysical Journal*, the Web versions of the print publications offer selected articles from current issues, text archives, science news updates, special features, and Web resource recommendations from the editors. However, magazines usually do not publish the full text of all articles on their Web sites—to keep print subscribers paying for their snail mail versions—and scientific journals are frequently offered as Web subscriptions with pay-per-view article archives. Often, as with Cell magazine, you can search the archives and retrieve citations, but you have to be a subscriber to read the articles.

Television's science programs and specialty cable channels, like the Public Broadcasting Service's Nova and the Discovery Channel, are also well represented with innovative sites that supplement and complement the educational content of their shows with multimedia in-depth features, updates, and fun stuff for kids. Science museums, like San Francisco's Exploratorium and New

York's American Museum of Natural History, have made their presence known around the globe with Web versions of exhibits and other materials from their collections.

If you're looking for a particular scientist, an expert in a scientific field, or faculty members and programs at universities or research centers, you can look in the many directories and catalogs available from institutions, academic societies, membership organizations, and cyberspace-based groups and discussions. You can even "ask a scientist" at many sites where experts will take your e-mail questions and answer them on the Web. Before you ask, check the archives to see if the question has been asked and answered previously. Don't do this the day before the homework is due; it may take some time before the expert gets to your question in the long queue.

Answers to science questions from kindergarten through high school to college, graduate school, and beyond can be found in many places and in many forms on the Web today. An interactive Periodic Table of the Elements provides clear descriptions of each element as well as references to sources of detailed information on more advanced levels. Glossaries, dictionaries, texts, and encyclopedias are there for your reference needs.

Interesting and comprehensive sites have been created for people and discoveries in the history of science ranging from MendelWeb (detailing the life and work of the father of genetics) to many Albert Einstein sites and the Nobel Prize winners and their achievements. For more advanced levels of science and mathematics and their applications in engineering, aerospace, computer programming, and other disciplines and professions, the Web is a major venue for communication and information sharing. Science news—including daily updates and announcements of results of current research and new discoveries—is distributed over the Web with the urgency of sports news and stock price changes. Job postings, grant announcements and other professional opportunities, as well as proceedings of conferences and publication of research findings, are resources that make the Web an indispensable tool for researchers, teachers, and science professionals working in industry and government.

Great scouts in science on the Web are available for each specific scientific discipline as well as the general guides that we've picked as our top choices. Use the general guides to get to the specific and you'll be sure to find exactly what you're looking for—or the person or place that can point you to it.

CAUTION: For those unfamiliar with the protocols of science research: Be aware that you may find research findings and papers posted on the Web that have not gone through the peer review processes that are followed by scientific journals and academic societies before publication. Anyone can be a publisher on the Web and you must check for the authority and credibility of the source. Ask a scientist!

Science Materials on the Web

Ask a Scientist: *How Things Work: The Physics of Everyday Life* is the title of a book by University of Virginia physics professor Louis A. Bloomfield and a Web site where questions and answers can be posted and found. Questions include "Would it be possible to put a thermometer inside a microwave oven?" and "If one metric ton of antimatter comes into contact with one metric ton of matter, how much energy would be released?" at (landau1.phys.virginia. edu/Education/Teaching/HowThingsWork/home.html). At the MAD Scientist Network (www.madsci.org), experts answer questions for all grade levels in twenty-six areas of science; recently Jen, grade 7–9 asked, "What exactly is air?" and was answered by an MIT graduate student. Mad Science also offers many links to other Ask a Scientist pages in its categorized Web directory, for example "Ask an Astronaut" at the National Space Society (www.nss.org /askastro/home.html).

History of Science: MendelWeb (www.netspace.org/MendelWeb) constructed around the text of Gregor Mendel's 1865 paper, "Experiments in Plant Hybridization" (in German and English), A. Einstein Image and Impact (www.aip.org/history/einstein), an exhibit from the Center for History of Physics at the American Institute of Physics, Nobel Prize winners at the Nobel Channel (www.nobelchannel.com), the Nobel Prize Internet Archive (www. nobelprizes.com), or the official Web site of the Nobel Foundation (www.nobel.se).

Magazines and journals: Read them online—*Scientific American* (www.scientificamerican.com), *Discover* (www.discover.com), *Cell* (www.cell.com), *Nature* (www.nature.com), *New Scientist* (www. newscientist.com), and the *Astrophysical Journal* (www.journals. uchicago.edu/ApJ/journal).

Museums: Visit San Francisco's Exploratorium (www. exploratorium.edu), New York's American Museum of Natural History (www.amnh.org) and its Research Department Web (research.amnh.org), or London's Natural History Museum and its dinosaur data files (www.nhm.ac.uk).

National Aeronautics and Space Administration: Just start here and keep on exploring through time and space at one of the most popular sites on the Web (www.nasa.gov).

Periodic Table of the Elements at Los Alamos National Laboratory (pearl1.lanl.gov/periodic).

Television programs: Schedules, events, background, and special features from PBS's Nova (www.pbs.org/wgbh/nova) and the Discovery Channel Online (www.discovery.com).

Visible Human: Visible Human data at the National Library of Medicine (www.nlm.nih.gov/research/visible/visible_human.html); Visible Human viewers at Syracuse University (www.npac.syr.edu/ projects/vishuman/VisibleHuman.html).

Great Scout Sites for Science

Physical Sciences, Engineering,
Computing and Math INFOMINE
lib-www.ucr.edu/pslsearch.html
Contact: Fred Yuengling
Science Reference Librarian
Science Library
University of California
Santa Cruz, CA 95064
yuengli@scilibx.ucsc.edu

Why we picked this site: One of the first of the academic virtual libraries, located physically at the University of California at Riverside, INFOMINE is unique for its comprehensive and well-organized annotated listings selected by academic librarians at nine University of California campuses and Stanford University. The annotations are great! There are many access points provided—a whole range of browsing and searching functions and a highly developed indexing system—offering a range of choices for different levels and interests. The database is updated frequently with new links highlighted in the "What's New" section. The physical sciences, engineering, computing, and mathematics are covered in depth in this area of the larger INFOMINE library, which includes equally impressive separate subject files for biological, agricultural, and medical resources and for government information. The entire INFOMINE virtual library comprises over 17,000 resources and received over 6 million accesses in 1998, according to Steve Mitchell of the University of California at Riverside Science Library. "It is important for the university community to retain an objective, non-commercial, finding tool dedicated to preserving open access to what we see as the 'information commons' of the Internet. As the information and educational activities of the academic community become ever more inseparable from activities that occur on or over the Internet, think of the costs to academia of NOT having INFOMINE and other similar tools," Mitchell wrote. Note that there are many resources listed and described that are available only to students of the Riverside campus or participating university library users.

Created: January 1994.

How many sites: 1,700+.

Audience: University of California students and scholars and the general public at university level.

How sites are selected: University of California librarians and bibliographers select sites that are useful as scholarly information resources in research or educational activities at the university level.

How it's supported: University of California libraries and grant funding from the U.S. Department of Education and the Librarians Association of the University of California.

Topics covered: Astronomy, chemistry, computer science, earth sciences, engineering, environmental sciences, geology, mathematics, physics, programming languages, systems, and weather. Types of information include pre-print bulletin boards, databases, electronic journals, subject guides, software repositories and others.

Contents: Annotated, indexed links to resources in topical areas. You can browse for information by title, table of contents, subject, keyword, and What's New. You can also search by title, subject, and keyword. Library of Congress subject terms and other standardized lists are used for indexing.

What you get: The search result list presents records with concise descriptive annotation, URL, and link to the resource. Each result record displays viewable and hyperlinked standardized indexing terms that allow further broadening or narrowing of the search.

Advanced searching: Complex searching, including Boolean operators, truncation, field limiting, and useful functional subject terms like *virtual library, comprehensive, databases, e-journals, reference resources,* and *subject guides,* can be added to produce more precise results.

Design: No graphics, quick and simple, but alphabetical browsing lists are so large that they are unwieldy; use the search interface.

Other features: Collections of links to reference tools and educational resources for these subject areas add additional value.

Help or FAQ: The "help searching INFOMINE" guide is recommended reading.

Read about it:
Mitchell, Steve, and Margaret Mooney. "INFOMINE: A Model Web-based Academic Virtual Library." *Information Technology and Libraries,* March 1996, v.15 (1), (infomine.ucr.edu/pubs/italmine. html).

SciCentral
www.scicentral.com
Contact: Guy Orgambide, Ph.D.
SciLink, Inc.
1125 North Utah Street
Arlington, VA 22201
scicentral@scicentral.com

Why we picked this site: SciCentral is a top scout site for science because it is a true "guide to guides" for over 120 specialty science topics. You won't stay at this site too long, but it is a great first stop on a search for topical resources. Although the listings are not annotated, the high degree of selectivity we see at this site makes us comfortable with the choices offered. SciCentral is low tech but rates high in usefulness. Its added features give the site a boost in content.

Created: June 1997.

How many sites: 50,000.

Audience: Professional scientists and science enthusiasts.

How sites are selected: Staff of professional scientists selects sites for inclusion. According to Orgambide, the main criteria are thoroughness and scientific accuracy of the information; ability of the site to facilitate the retrieval of specific information for professionals and enthusiasts; uniqueness of the information and dynamics of the site, including rate of updates, interactivity, and sense of community. For the K–12 Science area, the criteria are educational merit, ease of use, and overall appeal to a younger audience.

How it's supported: Currently supported by sponsors; dedicated advertising space is separated from resource listings.

Topics covered: Main index pages for Biological Sciences, Health Sciences, Physical Sciences, Engineering, and Earth & Space Sciences (and subsections for more than 100 specialties within these areas), as well as pages devoted to resources for Women & Minorities in Science, U.S. Government Agencies, and Institutional Directories.

Contents: Top level pages include a gateway to specialty discipline pages, career resources, companies and products, conferences and events, databases, funding resources, guides to topical journals online, news sources, and discussion groups. Specialty discipline pages list resource links by type: comprehensive directories, specialized resources, databases, software, and selected articles. Most of the directory listings are "guides to guides." High quality individual subject sites are sparingly awarded the "specialized resources" category. Selected articles are recent items and stories available freely on the Web.

What you get: A simple keyword or Boolean search form brings you to the full page of listings with site names and links. There are no annotations. The site index displays all main pages and specialty sections in a browsable form.

Advanced searching: No.

Design: Easy to navigate, frame-free, fast loading pages, attractive layout.

Other features: A search of the science news wires—EurekAlert, Newswise, Science Daily, UniSci—is provided for recent research and current awareness. The site also offers a special section of educational science resources for kids in grades K–12.

Help or FAQ: No.

Other Top Science Sites

Scout Report for Science and Engineering
wwwscout.cs.wisc.edu/scout/report/sci-engr/index.html
Subscribe to this free bi-weekly publication of reviews of recommended Web sites and documents for research, learning resources, data, and current awareness, or read and search it from the Internet Scout home page at the University of Wisconsin. We believe that reading this publication is the best way to keep up with new Web sites and documents in this subject area.

Mad Scientist Network

www.madsci.org

This lively, kid-friendly site from Washington University School of Medicine in St. Louis works both as an interactive Ask-An-Expert educational resource and as a scout for the best subject specific guides in twenty-four science areas. The searchable link directory also includes pointers to information on science careers, ideas for science fair projects, related scientific newsgroups, and suppliers of science experiment products.

The Tree of Life

phylogeny.arizona.edu/tree/phylogeny.html

This is a collection of about 1400 Web pages with information about the diversity of life, arranged in a taxonomic tree of organisms with one page for each group, including photos, descriptions, references, and links to Web resources. The signed pages are written by biologists around the world and coordinated by David Maddison at the Department of Entomology of the University of Arizona. Pages on the tree vary in completeness from skeletal pages that are merely links between complete pages, to complete pages that have been peer-reviewed. It's a work in progress. The tree is browsable and searchable but somewhat difficult to navigate because its arrangement is complicated to those unfamiliar with phylogeny and taxonomy. Much valuable information resides here, so it's worth the trouble.

New Scientist Keysites

www.keysites.com

From the editors of this British weekly science and technology magazine, this site includes Planet Science Hot Spots—a browsable but not searchable directory of recommended and annotated science-related sites in seventeen topical areas. Additional features include Site of the Day and the Netropolitan A-Z archive of the publication's weekly Internet column's links.

For More Information

Thomas, Brian J. *The Internet for Scientists and Engineers 1997–1998: Online Tools and Resources*. Piscataway, NJ: IEEE (Institute of Electrical and Electronics Engineers), 1997.

Index

About the authors

Nora Paul is Library Director and faculty member at the Poynter Institute for Media Studies in St. Petersburg, Florida, responsible for holding seminars on news research and news library management, computer-assisted reporting, and leadership in new media newsrooms. Previously, she spent 12 years at *The Miami Herald*, where she was the Library Director, and later the Editor of Information Services.

Nora has been a consultant on research services and information management for the Associated Press, the *San Antonio Express-News*, the Time Warner Research Department, and the *San Jose Mercury News*.

A frequent speaker at journalism conferences, Nora has held Internet training courses in Russia, South Africa, the Netherlands, Denmark, and England. She writes a monthly column in *Uplink*, the newsletter of the National Institute for Computer Assisted Reporting, and is a frequent contributor to *Searcher* magazine. She is the author of *Computer-Assisted Research: A Guide to Tapping Online Information* (now in its 4th edition from Bonus Books).

Margot Williams is the Research Editor and Internet Trainer in the newsroom of *The Washington Post*. She was a member of the investigative reporting team that won the 1999 Pulitzer Prize for Public Service. Previously, she worked as a research librarian at Time Warner, *The Poughkeepsie Journal*, and *The Washington Post*, and wrote a monthly column about using the Internet for *The Post's* "Consumer Tech" section.

In 1996 and 1998, as the recipient of the Special Libraries Association/ Freedom Forum fellowship, Margot traveled to Hong Kong and Manila to train journalists in the use of the Internet. In 1997, she was an adjunct professor at the George Washington University School of Media and Public Affairs, teaching investigative reporting with the Internet.

Margot is a frequent speaker on research and Internet topics at news industry associations, including Investigative Reporters and Editors, the Poynter Institute, the American Press Institute, the Asian-American Journalists Association, the Freedom Forum, Computers in Libraries, Internet Librarian, and the Special Libraries Association/News Division.

More CyberAge Books
from Information Today, Inc.

The Extreme Searcher's Guide to Web Search Engines
A Handbook for the Serious Searcher
By Randolph E. Hock

"Extreme searcher" Randolph (Ran) Hock—internationally respected Internet trainer and authority on Web search engines—offers straightforward advice designed to help you get immediate results. Ran not only shows you what's "under the hood" of the major search engines, but explains their relative strengths and weaknesses, reveals their many (and often overlooked) special features, and offers tips and techniques for searching the Web more efficiently and effectively than ever. Updates and links are provided at the author's Web site.

Softbound • ISBN 0-910965-26-9 • $24.95
Hardbound • ISBN 0-910965-38-2 • $34.95

Super Searchers Do Business
The Online Secrets of Top Business Researchers
By Mary Ellen Bates • Edited by Reva Basch

Super Searchers Do Business probes the minds of 11 leading researchers who use the Internet and online services to find critical business information. Through her in-depth interviews, Mary Ellen Bates—a business super searcher herself—gets the pros to reveal how they choose online sources, evaluate search results, and tackle the most challenging business research projects. Loaded with expert tips, techniques, and strategies, this is the first title in the exciting new "Super Searchers" series, edited by Reva Basch. If you do business research online, or plan to, let the super searchers be your guides.

Softbound • ISBN 0-910965-33-1 • $24.95

net.people
The Personalities and Passions Behind the Web Sites
By Thomas E. Bleier and Eric C. Steinert

With the explosive growth of the Internet, people from all walks of life are bringing their dreams and schemes to life as Web sites. In *net.people*, authors Bleier and Steinert take you up close and personal with the creators of 35 of the world's most intriguing online ventures. For the first time, these entrepreneurs and visionaries share their personal stories and hard-won secrets of Webmastering. You'll learn how each of them launched a home page, increased site traffic, geared up for e-commerce, found financing, dealt with failure and success, built new relationships—and discovered that a Web site had changed their lives forever.

Available: Dec. 1999 • Softbound • ISBN 0-910965-37-4 • $19.95

Ask for CyberAge Books at your local bookstore.
For a complete catalog, contact:

Information Today, Inc.

143 Old Marlton Pike, Medford, NJ 08055 • 609/654-6266
email: custserv@infotoday.com • Web site: www.infotoday.com